Systematics

F. Leroy Forlines

D1570118

A

Study

of the

Christian System

of

Life and Thought

Randall House Publications
114 Bush Road—P. O. Box 17306
Nashville, Tennessee 37217
1975

©1975
Randall House Publications
Nashville, Tennessee

Printed in the United States of America

INTRODUCTION

Whenever a person picks up a book on a subject of this nature, one of the first questions that arises in his mind is, "What qualifies the author to write on this topic?" The answer, as far as this work is concerned, is apparent to those who know F. Leroy Forlines. To begin with, Professor Forlines has studied approximately a decade in institutions of higher learning in America. He is a graduate of Free Will Baptist Bible College, holds the M. A. from Winona Lake School of Theology, and was graduated from Northern Baptist Theological Seminary with the B. D. His most recent degree, the Th. M., was awarded by Chicago Graduate School of Theology. The years Professor Forlines spent in these institutions enabled him to be tutored by some of the best evangelical minds from both England and the United States of America.

Additionally, Professor Forlines has spent over fifteen years teaching at his alma mater. For many of these years, he has been both Professor of Systematic Theology and Dean of Men. Recently, he assumed the position of Dean of Students. In the dual role of professor and counselor, he has been vividly impressed with the importance of interpreting theology in such a manner that it influences one's total life, not just the Christian's thinking. This book is by no means his first attempt to show the relationship of a person's theology to his overall life. Previous ventures in this realm include his booklet, *Morals and Orthodoxy*, which discusses the relationship of orthodoxy to orthopraxy, and his full-length book entitled *Biblical Ethics*.

With this rich and varied background, Professor Forlines has approached this work. Thus, the reader may expect to profit from his attempt to logically build a systematic view of Christian truth. His arguments are cogent, his style informal, and his passion for both truth and virtue are manifested throughout the work. Hopefully, the people for whom this volume was written will match the zeal he has had in pursuing the truth of God so that they may apply it to the people of God.

Douglas J. Simpson

PREFACE

My experience in Christian service has, for the most part, been that of a college teacher and a student dean. Being a teacher has caused me to be deeply interested in truth from an academic viewpoint. Being a student dean, along with an interest in my own personal needs, has caused me to have a deep interest in the fact that truth is for life. This book is an outgrowth of these two areas of experience and concern. It has been my desire to speak to the total personality.

Truth is unchanging, but the scene to which truth addresses itself, while having the common ingredient of sin and need of redemption, undergoes change. While presenting timeless truth, I have tried to be aware of and address the current scene. I have been more concerned about the current scene as influenced by secularism than the current scene of conflict and controversy in the theological world, though the theological scene has not been totally neglected.

This book has been written for a broad reading audience. For that reason I have tried to be as simple as the subject matter could allow. At the same time, I have touched on several areas and have presented somewhat different approaches on subjects which I trust will be of interest to those who are well read in these areas.

I have a high respect for the opinion of those who are devout scholars of the Bible, but I have not hesitated to be critical of their views when they appear to me to be in error. I expect my own ideas to be so criticized by others.

The reader will observe that there is not complete uniformity in the credit lines. This was made necessary in order to comply with various requests made by publishers who have granted permission for use of material under their copyright. I would like to express my appreciation to these publishers for allowing me to use their material.

It is my prayer that this book will be an instrument in the hands of God to bring glory to the name of Jesus Christ.

F. Leroy Forlines

CONTENTS

1

Introduction

Within a generation of time, the increase of people's knowledge of the physical universe has been astounding. This includes making knowledge available to the masses that was once known only by a few, and many discoveries of which most had never dreamed. It is common knowledge now that the nearest star other than the sun is said to be four and one-half light years away with a light year being the distance light travels in a year at the rate of 186,000 miles per second. We are also told that some stars are millions of light years away. The last generation has introduced the splitting of the atom, the harnessing of atomic energy, television as a means of mass media, space travel, heart transplants, etc.

At the same time that people's knowledge of the physical universe has been increasing, the certainty that many had with respect to answers to the inescapable questions of life has been eaten away by the cancer of naturalism in its various forms. Naturalism seeks to explain everything in terms of natural causes and effects. It either fails to believe in a god, or, if it does, it does not clearly attribute to this god any specific supernatural acts in the physical, moral, and spiritual realms.

It is impossible for us to escape asking such questions as: Is there a God? If so, what is He like? How can I know Him? Who am I? Where am I? How can I tell right from wrong? Is there life after death? What should I and what can I do about guilt? If we are going to have peace and satisfaction, we must have answers to these questions that our total being will accept. We cannot permanently suppress these questions. We cannot, on a permanent basis, accept just any answer.

The person who has, on the one hand, learned of the vastness of the universe and the potential that lies within it, while on the other hand, has found himself with no sure and satisfactory answers to the inescapable questions of life is in deep trouble. He is capable of experiencing a feeling of lostness that few people could have experienced before this present time. He is overwhelmed by the vastness of the universe. He is overwhelmed by the secrets that have been unlocked that have made so many inventions and discoveries possible. He is frustrated by the fact that men have been able to navigate the universe and send space ships to the moon and planets, but have given him no acceptable answers to questions that he cannot avoid asking. He cannot find purpose and meaning in life. He does not know how to deal with guilt, loneliness, depression, and despair. Out of his despair he cries out, "Who am I?" "Where am I?" "What direction should I take?" With his ear turned toward naturalism, he hears no voice that bears truth that will set him free. From the agony of unquenchable thirst, more and more are turning to illegal drugs, alcohol, and promiscuous sex. These may bring temporary thrills, but in the long run they become a part of the problem. The odor of unbelief, uncertainty, fear, loneliness, boredom, depression, despair, and pessimism permeate the atmosphere.

Not everyone has drunk the full cup of naturalism. Some have maintained an unshaken faith in Jesus Christ and the Bible as God's revelation to man. Others, while they have not reached the point of complete rejection of the Christian faith, have had their faith seriously shaken by the inescapable encounter with the forces of naturalism, particularly in high schools and places of higher education. With many, the kind and extent of damage may be hard to assess, but they have not been able to breathe the atmosphere of unbelief, uncertainty, fear, loneliness, boredom, depression, despair, and pessimism and still remain unharmed.

We live in the midst of hungry, confused, and frustrated people. It is my conviction that the words of Jesus, when He said, "And ye shall know the truth, and the truth shall make you free" (John 8:32), are true for people with the problems prevalent in our society.

I. THE PURPOSE OF THIS STUDY

This study is designed to present the basic truths of the Christian faith. It is written out of a heart of redemptive concern. There is evangelistic concern for the person who is not a Christian that he may come to know Jesus Christ, whom to know is eternal life (John 6:68). There is concern for the person who is already saved that he may grow in the likeness of Christ (Romans 8:29), and that he may be able to appropriate the all sufficient grace of God in the midst of the complexities of life (2 Corinthians 12:9). This redemptive concern has a twofold motivation: (1) That people may

2

be delivered from the misery and distress that go with the power of darkness both in this life and the life to come, and be translated into the kingdom of God's dear Son and experience that joy, peace, and satisfaction that belong to that kingdom both in this life and the life to come (Colossians 1:13). (2) That God may be given His rightful place of honor and glory in our hearts and minds that belong to Him as our Sovereign Lord and Redeemer (Philippians 2:9-11).

II. THE APPROACH OF THIS STUDY

A. Life Oriented

Traditionally, the tendency has been to make a sharp distinction between the academic, which deals with the content of truth, and the practical, which deals with the application of truth. In studying the content of truth, the ideal was to be objective. It was felt that to combine the study of content with the application of truth was to contaminate objectivity with subjectivity. To be objective was to seek to be detached from the subject under study. A person was to study as if it made no difference what conclusions he reached.

In my opinion, honesty, not objectivity, is the ideal for a Christian in his pursuit of truth. Objectivity seeks to make a person a neutral investigator of truth. Why is a person supposed to be more capable of discovering truth if he is a neutral investigator rather than one who is deeply involved in what he is doing and feels strongly about it? Who learns the most about art—a person who is neutral about art or a person who loves art? Who learns more about baseball—one who studies with a feeling of detachment or one who is deeply involved? It may take a strong commitment to honesty to be honest when a person is deeply involved in a matter. Yet, this is what must take place. Honesty and deep involvement must be found in the same person in order to reach the highest degree of proficiency in discovering the truth.

It is particularly important that we study theological truth as interested and involved persons because theological truth is for life. It must not be a mere mental exercise. It must be experience oriented. It is for the total personality.

Many times authors have chosen to write in the third person as a means of maintaining a higher degree of objectivity. This caused the author to write as a detached person. It, to a large extent, removed his writings from life. There was a missing dimension that kept many outstanding works on theology from speaking to the heart. They were not designed to speak to the heart. That was left for devotional studies.

It is not my aim in this study to be objective. I am writing as a deeply involved and deeply concerned person. I want the reader to feel that I care and that what I say is real to me. Therefore, I will write in the first person. I will endeavor to be honest. Since I am subject to human frailties, I may not always achieve this; nevertheless, it will be my guiding ideal.

I think there has been an increasing awareness that pure objectivity is neither possible, nor desirable. In the Introduction to his book, *Theories of Revelation, An Historical Study 1860-1960,* Dr. H. D. McDonald, after pointing out that he will endeavor as much as possible to let writers speak for themselves in their own words, explains:

> But we have not hesitated at various places to give our own criticisms; as we have also sought to give, as far as we conceive it, a positive statement.
>
> In taking such an attitude we have not been unmindful of the subtitle which announces our investigation of 'an historical study.' We would, however, plead that it is quite impossible to approach a subject without any presuppositions. This is specially so in theology where a man's convictions should be deep and meaningful.
>
> The truth is that the man who says he is altogether objective in this study knows not of what he speaks. Even in the realm of science it is no longer a tenable view to conceive of the scientist as, so to speak, one who stands over against his data having no postulates. Indeed, the whole scientific endeavor would be a fruitless proceeding if this were so.1

To combine the academic and the practical does not mean that in this study the full implications of the practical will be developed as might be in a book more completely devoted to the practical. I believe truth is practical. Truth is for life (John 8:32). Any presentation of truth that does not appeal to life has a missing element. We may not be able to show a life application from every sentence or paragraph, or even every page, but the process of discovering truth should also be a process of learning more about how to live in a complex world.

B. Systematically Oriented

When the term "doctrine" is applied to a study of the Christian system of truth, it refers to a topical study of basic Christian truths. As a rule, such a study is designed to set forth the Biblical teachings on these subjects. Little or no attention is given to gaining a rational understanding of one's faith and to showing the interrelatedness of doctrines one to another. Also, limited attention is given to differing views of interpretation.

4

Systematic theology covers essentially the same areas that a more or less complete work on doctrine covers. It attempts to help a person get a rational understanding of his faith. In its attempt to be systematic it seeks to lay a foundation and build a structure of thought on that foundation. Attention is given to how the structure grows logically out of the foundation and how the doctrines relate one to another to produce harmony in the system. As a rule, a systematic theology is more thorough than a doctrinal treatment. It gives more documentation for what is set forth and gives more attention to different views. Most of my experience has been in teaching systematic theology rather than doctrine. This study will take on the tone of a systematic theology, but will, as a rule, be less thorough than works that are usually accorded the title "Systematic Theology."

III. THE PRESUPPOSITIONS

By presuppositions, I mean the basic beliefs that are essential for a particular type study to be conducted. At this point, I am not raising the question how or whether these presuppositions can be proved. That will be discussed when these presuppositions come up for elaboration in the study. I am saying that at all times these presuppositions will be treated as true and that they are necessary for the study as a whole. There is no neutral platform from which to start. We cannot start "nowhere." We must start somewhere. Honesty requires us to make this admission.

A. That God Exists As The Triune God And His Self-revelation Is Seen In:

1. Jesus Christ
2. The Bible
3. In nature and the experience of men

B. That God's Revelation Is For Man And Can Be Known By Him

Man is created in God's image for a relationship with God. The truth that the Maker reveals is designed to meet the needs of the one He has made in the condition his experiences have put him. It is the very purpose of God's truth to set us free (John 8:32). Truth must always be studied with that in mind.

The design of our being created in the image of God, along with the divine aid that is provided for us, creates the possibility for us to understand the truth. Apart from this confidence there would be no theology.

5

C. That Truth Is An Integrated And Harmonious Whole

We will not propose to treat all truth. However, we affirm that all truth is an integrated and harmonious whole. For those who wish to see all truth in this way, a study of theology is foundational. It puts all truth in proper perspective. To deprive one's knowledge of theology is to deprive it of the perspective that is necessary to meet the needs of the total personality.

D. That All of Life's Experiences Operate Within The Framework Of The Four Basic Relationships And Involve The Four Basic Values

The four basic relationships are: (1) Man's relationship with God. (2) Man's relationship with other people. (3) Man's relationship with the created order. (4) Man's relationship with himself. Man is a relationship creature. All of our experiences in one way or another involve one or more of the four basic relationships. This involves both our actions and our thoughts.

The four basic values are holiness, love, wisdom, and ideals. Man is a value oriented person. He is so constructed that he cannot erase the categories right and wrong, good and bad, from his being. One or more values are involved in all of life's experience including both actions and thoughts. The four basic values furnish the guiding principles for the proper functioning of the four basic relationships.

It is the function of theology to identify God, man, and the created order and to show the system of truth that is derived from the application of the four basic values to the four basic relationships. This system of truth becomes the foundation for the application of the four basic values to its four basic relationships in actual life.

IV. THE AIM

It will be the aim of this study to present a system of doctrinal truth that is: (1) Christ centered. (2) Bible based. (3) Life oriented.

CHAPTER ONE
NOTES

1. H. D. McDonald, *Theories of Revelation*, London: George Allen & Unwin LTD, c. 1963, p. 9.

Revelation

When presenting a system of thought, there is the question of where to start. In a system, ideas are interwoven. No part of the system stands alone without involving other parts. God is completely separate from the Bible, man, and the rest of creation. However, He cannot be described fully without using the Bible and without mentioning man and the rest of creation. The Bible is so integrally related to God, man, and creation, that it cannot be fully described without mentioning these. Dr. J. Oliver Buswell, Jr. stated the case well when he said:

> ...Our system of doctrine is an integrated whole; each part dependent on and contributory to every other part, so that wherever one begins, he will be obliged naively to assume the rest, until the whole field is surveyed.1

A good case could be made for using another starting point, but since only one can be chosen I will choose to start with revelation and inspiration, or the Bible. My reason for this is the fact that whatever place we start, our chief source for data will be the Bible. Since that is true, it is logical to first talk about that primary source of data. There may be some temptation to think of the Bible as standing outside the system furnishing material with which to build the system. This is not the case. It is so integrally related that no such separation can be made. It is an authority within the system.

There seems to be the feeling on the part of some that somewhere in the universe of thought there is a neutral platform from which all people should start, and that there is some standard of truth that exists outside a system of thought by which it can be tested. It is my viewpoint that such a neutral platform and such a

8

detached standard for testing truth do not exist. Systems of thought must be examined from within.

So far as rational tests are concerned, a system that proposes to explain the whole of reality must prove to be satisfactory to our total personality as thinking, feeling, acting beings. Logic cannot divorce itself from life and become an accurate judge of a system. I believe the following tests are a step in the right direction to establishing criteria that will protect the interest of the total personality: (1) Is there internal consistency, i.e., is the structure logically related to the foundation? Do all the parts fit consistently together? (2) Is there internal sufficiency, i.e., are the causes adequate to produce the effects attributed to them? (3) Does it conform to that which is undeniably true? (4) Does it answer the inescapable question of life? Regardless of how well a system passes the first three tests, if it cannot pass the fourth test, it is not an adequate system and must be rejected.

It would be an unbearable universe if man were so constructed that he could not escape asking certain questions, and yet there were no answers that could be found. I am not saying that all imaginable questions must have answers, but I am saying that questions that are written indelibly in the constitution of man must be answered.

I. THE CURRENT SCENE

There is no problem in life so important as finding answers to the inescapable questions that arise from within us. The questions: Is there a God? and if so, how can I know Him and what is He like? stand at the top of the list of these questions because the answer to these determines the way the other questions will be answered.

The modern search for knowledge has created a painful predicament for those who have come under its sway. With many the scientific approach to knowledge is either altogether, or for all practical purposes, the sole source of knowledge. In science the only data that is admissible is sense data (that which is known through the five senses assisted by instruments of precision). If sense data is the only admissible data for rational reflection, it is obvious that there can be no place for God. Either He does not exist, or He cannot be known.

The heavy reliance upon science, on the part of many, has left little or no place for religious knowledge and experience. Science is viewed as resting solidly on sound research, but religion is viewed as having no sound basis for its existence. This is true since religion depends for its existence on knowledge that exists outside sense data. This attitude has brought about a cleavage between science and religion. In speaking of the pathos of perpetuating this cleavage, Dr. Carl F. H. Henry comments:

9

The integrity of human experience is also threatened. The modern man is torn psychologically by irresolvable tensions and inner frustrations. He finds himself irremediably religious by nature, yet he is unable to correlate the scientific claim and the spiritual-moral claim. The resulting scientific—religious conflict, productive of a divided self, has impaired the intellectual and practical vigor of multitudes. An unintegrated personality is forerunner to a disintegrated personality.[2]

What happens to a person who is convinced that rational knowledge can be gained only from reflection upon sense data? What does he do with these inescapable questions? He may try to avoid them by diverting his attention to other things such as quick thrills and excitement through drugs, alcohol, sex, and rock music, or he may take the nobler route of humanitarianism. The problem is that the longer he tries these routes the more he will discover that the inescapable questions have arisen out of inextinguishable longings.

A person may be naive and not really be aware of the conflict. He may, in his academic pursuits, follow the method of study that assumes that knowledge is restricted to scientific knowledge. Having been reared in Western culture and under a Christian influence, he may hold to the values of that culture without any real reason for doing so other than he finds them emotionally satisfying. This describes many people in our society. Their foundation has been cut away, but it has not dawned on them. A value system cannot go on indefinitely suspended in the air. Either it must rest upon a foundation or it will be eventually rejected.

There are many who see clearly that a conflict is created by restricting knowledge to scientific knowledge and at the same time trying to cope with the inescapable questions of life. They realize that the game of diverting their attention away from the problem through thrills, excitement, and humanitarianism will not work. There are basically four approaches that are followed in trying to cope with the problem.

The first approach is to stick with the idea that the only knowledge is scientific knowledge and conclude that there are no answers to these questions that voice themselves from within. Such an approach concludes that there is no meaning and purpose to life. The only thing for a person to do is to cast off restraints, indulge in whatever brings temporary relief, and do his own thing. Many from the counterculture would fall into this category.

A second approach is to cling tenaciously to the idea that the only rational knowledge is scientific knowledge and out of desperation seek relief from a leap into the realm of the irrational. In Dr. Francis Schaeffer's book *Escape From Reason*, he speaks about a lower story and an upper story. Scientific knowledge would fit in the lower story and the things related to the inescapable questions of life would fit into the upper story. Concerning those who seek refuge within the irrational, he explains:

> ... In the lower story, on the basis of all reason, man as man is dead. You have simply mathematics, particulars, mechanics. Man has no meaning, no purpose, no significance. There is only pessimism concerning man as man. But up above, on the basis of a non-rational, non-reasonable leap, there is a non-reasonable faith which gives optimism. This is modern man's total dichotomy.3

He further explains:

> Because the rational and logical are totally separated from the non-rational and the non-logical, the leap is total. Faith, whether expressed in secular or religious terms, becomes a leap without any verification because it is totally separated from the logical and the reasonable. We can now see, on this basis, how the new theologians can say that though the Bible, in the area of nature and history, is full of mistakes, this does not matter.4

Out of desperation a person reaches out and believes in something that he hopes will bring satisfaction though by his own standard of knowledge what he does is contrary to his rationality. This is the approach in neo-orthodoxy and existentialism. For a being as deeply rational as man, such an approach cannot bring lasting satisfaction.

A third approach to dealing with the problem tries as much as possible to be on good terms with those who restrict knowledge to scientific knowledge. They try to accept everything possible in the package of naturalism, but they break camp enough to bring religion into the picture. When the compromise with naturalism is over, they have risen little higher than humanitarianism with a religious flavor. This system fails to recognize the seriousness of human conflicts and the depth of guilt that man is experiencing. It is too much like treating cancer as if it were no more serious than a common cold. This is the approach of theological liberalism. As the people in this group see that such an approach is untenable, they tend to move toward the first two approaches.

The fourth approach is to reject the idea that all rational knowledge is restricted to scientific knowledge. God is viewed not as an impersonal object to be found, but as a Person who speaks. God created man in His own image (Genesis 1:26). The inescapable questions are the logical outcome of the design of God's creation of man. They contribute to the possibility of God's speaking to us and receiving a response from us. It is my conviction that this is the only approach that can satisfy the deepest longing of man. This view makes possible a unified knowledge of, to use Shaeffer's words, "The lower and upper stories"—or the whole of reality.

II. GOD'S SELF-REVELATION THE ONLY ANSWER

God is not perceivable to the five senses, nor to any instruments that man has at his disposal. This makes revelation necessary if we are to know Him. The fact that He cannot be known through the senses is not the only reason that He can be known only through revelation. The fact that He is personal makes revelation necessary for our knowledge of Him.

Though we can see human bodies, we get acquainted with human personalities only as they are revealed through expressions, acts, and words. The difference between the revelation of Divine personality and human personality is this. Human personality is revealed to us through bodily expressions, actions, and words which are perceivable through the five senses. This means that while a person cannot be well-known unless he chooses to make himself known, he may reveal some things about himself without intending to do so. Since God is not visible and does not speak in a voice audible to us, unless by a special move He chooses to make, He can be known only if He deliberately chooses to make Himself known.

If God be viewed as impersonal, He is an object that cannot be perceived through the senses. If He be impersonal, He cannot speak. Therefore, He cannot be known. In such a case, a person can only speculate about a god which he is not sure is there. Paul says, " . . . the world by wisdom knew not God . . . " (1 Corinthians 1:21). Paul probably has reference to the fact that the finest striving of the human mind as illustrated by the Greek philosophers Socrates, Plato, and Aristotle had failed to find or know God. The same verdict would be pronounced upon the strivings of philosophers since that time. Pantheism, deism, agnosticism, and atheism all show the futility of man's attempts to locate the ultimate. The very idea that God must be found implies the idea of an impersonal god. If God be personal and has not spoken to the human race, the words of Elijah to the prophets of Baal would be in order, "Cry aloud: for he is a god; either he is talking [to someone other than the human race], or he is pursuing, or he is in a journey, or peradventure he sleepeth, and must be awaked" (1 Kings 18:27).

If God is personal, He can speak. As Christians, it is our conviction that He has spoken. The Christian God is not one to be found by us, but one who has spoken to us. God has revealed Himself to us. Concerning this revelation, Dr. Bernard Ramm says: "*Revelation is the autobiography of God*, i.e., it is the story which God narrates about himself. It is that knowledge *about* God which is *from* God." [5]

III. GENERAL REVELATION

General revelation refers to the revelation of God in the created order and the basic nature of man. Sometimes general revelation is referred to as natural revelation. A distinction is made between natural and supernatural revelation. The term "general" is better than "natural" since natural revelation, when distinguished from supernatural revelation, gives a possible inference that natural revelation is not supernatural. All revelation of God is supernatural. Berkhof observes: "The distinction between natural and supernatural revelation was found to be rather ambiguous, since all revelation is supernatural in origin and, as a revelation of God, also in content."6

There is some difficulty in knowing exactly what can be known of God in general revelation. David tells us, "The heavens declare the glory of God; and the firmament sheweth his handiwork" (Psalm 19:1). According to Paul, the eternal power and Divine attributes of God are clearly seen in the created order (Romans 1:20). (Commentators are, for the most part, agreed that the Greek word which, in the King James Version, is translated "godhead" means divinity or divine nature and embraces the attributes of God.) Paul indicates that this revelation of the eternal power and Divine attributes of God leaves man with no defense for his sinning (Romans 1:20).

Whatever may or may not be said about what may be known from general revelation, two things stand out as being unquestionably clear. (1) Man, as a sinner, has not properly read what may be known of God through general revelation. A look at non-Christian religions and the conclusions of philosophers substantiate this claim. (2) The story of redemption is not written in general revelation. Redemption revelation must be special revelation.

IV. SPECIAL REVELATION

In special revelation God actively communicates knowledge of Himself and His plan to a particular person or group. It is often said that had man not fallen, there would have been no need of special revelation. The total need of special revelation is attributed to sin. While it is granted that unfallen man could certainly read the general revelation of God better than fallen man, it does not follow that unfallen man had no need of special revelation as distinguished from general revelation.

The way we learn about persons would have required that God reveal Himself to man beyond that which was written in the created order and man's inner make-up. Unfallen man could not read the plan of God for him without a move on God's part to reveal such. There is no reason for believing that unfallen man could have picked out the tree of the knowledge of good and evil from the other trees, and could have known the consequences of eating its fruit apart from the special speaking of God. Neither is there evidence that it would have had such consequences apart from God's speaking. Dr. Kenneth Kantzer stated the case well when he said:

> Special revelation was no afterthought introduced to circumvent the fall of man, but was a part of the original divine economy. Only as a result of the curse and expulsion from the garden did such immediate converse between men and God become 'special' (Genesis 3:24).7

Sin did open a new chapter in the history of God's self-revelation. Man changed from a willing recipient of God's revelation to one who suppresses God's revelation (see *The Amplified Bible*, Romans 1:18). God's revelation is no longer addressed to one who is holy, but to one who has sinned.

In accord with God's holy nature and the previous warning given in Genesis 2:17, after the fall God's special revelation, of necessity, became a message of judgment. It was necessary that the special revelation of God to sinners involve a message of judgment. It was not necessary that this special revelation of God to sinners involve a message of redemption. The fact that it does set forth a message of redemption for sinners is grounded in the free and unparalleled love of God (Romans 5:6-8).

According to Paul in Romans 1:18-32, fallen man does read from general revelation the fact that, as a result of God's judgment, he is worthy of death (verse 32), but he tries to deny this by suppressing this knowledge. Paul does not speak of those who had only general revelation as those who "could" know the judgment of God if they would. Rather, he speaks of them as "Who knowing the judgment of God, that they which commit such things are worthy of death" (verse 32). The only way to understand verse 32 seems to be to understand Paul to say that deep down all people know this fact. Many would deny that they believe or know this about the judgment of God. They are suppressing into their subconcious mind a fact which they are denying with their conscious mind. Yet, what exists in their subconscious mind is knowledge.

The message of judgment in special revelation does not address itself to a person who is totally void of such knowledge. This message of sin and judgment is not strange language to the hearer. The moral knowledge of general revelation forms the basis of a point of contact for the message of judgment in special revelation. Special revelation seeks to awaken and clarify this knowledge of sin and judgment as a means of opening the way for the reception of the redemptive revelation.

Redemptive revelation is neither written in nature nor man's moral constitutions. Paul emphatically denies that anyone has read the redemptive message of God from general revelation. He says, "But as it is written, Eye hath not seen, nor ear heard, neither have entered into the heart of man, the things which God hath prepared for them that love him" (1 Corinthians 2:9). In modern language, Paul is saying that man by scientific research and philosophical speculation has not laid hold on redemptive knowledge. He not only has not, he cannot.

Just as emphatically as Paul denies that man reads redemptive revelation from general revelation, he positively asserts that God came to us with a redemptive message. He says, "But God hath revealed them unto us by his Spirit . . . " (1 Corinthians 2:10).

Special revelation to a fallen race has as its basic theme the message of redemption. It is centered in Jesus Christ. The initiative on God's part in providing redemption is rooted solely in His grace. With the first sin of Adam and Eve, God could have revealed Himself in judgment and closed the books on the human race so far as any positive relationship is concerned. God has never spoken to fallen angels with a message of redemption. God's holiness demands that sin be punished, but there is nothing in God's nature that demands that He offer redemption. It is the free act of His love.

The communication and reception of redemptive revelation is fraught with difficulty. The fact that man is made in the image of God has not been changed, but the image has been impaired. Men have resisted the revelation of God's righteousness (John 3:19). They have not welcomed with outstretched arms the Redeemer and His message (John 1:11). The damage suffered by the fall creates a problem in man's grasp of revelation, but it does not destroy the possibility of a grasp. Dr. Henry explains: "The divine image in man did not, in the fall, suffer to such an extent that man's *ratio* is now unable on the basis of general and special revelation to receive conceptual knowledge of the supernatural spiritual world . . . ."8

General revelation sets the stage for special revelation. The stage is set for man to receive a clearer message of sin and judgment. A feeling of need is present that can be clarified by special revelation to be the need of redemption. A longing is present that can be clarified to be a longing for redemption.

While standing firm upon our insistance that general revelation does not and cannot speak the message of redemption, we must keep in mind the words of Dr. G. C. Berkouwer when he says: "We must insist that 'general' revelation does not and cannot mean an attack upon the special revelation in Jesus Christ."9

It is extremely doubtful that a person who had never had any thoughts about sin or God, right or wrong, confused or unconfused, could be expected to take seriously a redemptive message. It is to the troubled heart that redemption makes an appeal.

As Dr. B. B. Warfield observes:

> ...It is important that the two species or stages of
> revelation should not be set in opposition to one another,
> or the closeness of their mutual relations or the constancy
> of the interaction be obscured. They constitute a unitary
> whole, and each is incomplete without the other.10

V. THE OVER-ALL FORM OF REVELATION

God did not choose to give us His revelation in the form of a
systematic theology. Romans gives us a logical treatment of doctrine,
but it would not be considered a systematic theology. On first
thought it may appear that we would have been better off if God had
chosen to give us a systematic presentation of doctrines. This would
likely have eliminated most of the controversy between Calvinism
and Arminianism. Any number of theological controversies would
have either never occurred, or they would have only had small areas
of difficulty.

While a systematic theology might have had some advantages in
clarifying some ideas, the way God has given His revelation to us
addresses life better. God's revelation is presented, for the most part,
as a record of God's speaking, acting, and dealing with people,
basically with Israel and the church, and their experiences with God.
We see truth demonstrated in terms of relationships. We see God's
faithfulness to His promises. We see judgment fall upon sin. We see
the sorrows and agony brought by sin. We see the joy brought by
righteous living and submission to God. We see people living in the
midst of a real world and hear them say:

> We are troubled on every side, yet not distressed; we are
> perplexed, but not in despair;
> Persecuted, but not forsaken; cast down, but not destroyed
> (2 Corinthians 4:8, 9).

The fact that God did not choose to give His revelation in the
form of a systematic treatment of doctrines is not to cast reflection
upon such an undertaking on our part. To take such an attitude
would be to fail to appreciate the type reasoning demonstrated in the
Book of Romans. However, when it comes to addressing life and
preparing to live, we gain far more from seeing the truth as it is
demonstrated in God's experiences with men and men's experiences
with God.

When we think about special revelation, we are thinking about
the Bible. It is the Bible that has preserved for us the redemptive
revelation of God. The study of revelation is complete only when we
have studied the inspiration and authority of the Bible.

16

CHAPTER TWO
NOTES

1. James Oliver Buswell, Jr., *A Systematic Theology of the Christian Religion*, Vol. 1, 2 Vols., Grand Rapids: Zondervan Publishing House, c. 1962, p. 6.

2. Carl F. H. Henry, "Science and Religion," in *Contemporary Evangelical Thought*, ed. by Carl F. H. Henry, New York: A Channel Press Book, Harper & Brothers, c. 1957, p. 249.

3. Francis A. Schaeffer, *Escape From Reason*, Downers Grove, Illinois: Inter-Varsity Press, c. 1968 by Inter-Varsity Fellowship, London, England, pp. 46, 47. Used by permission.

4. *Ibid.*, pp. 51, 52.

5. Bernard Ramm, *Special Revelation And The Word of God*, Grand Rapids: William B. Eerdmans Publishing Company, c. 1961, p. 17.

6. L. Berkhof, *Systematic Theology*, Third revised and enlarged edition, Grand Rapids: William B. Eerdmans Publishing Company, c. 1941, pp. 36, 37.

7. Kenneth S. Kantzer, "The Communication of Revelation" in *The Bible—The Living Word of Revelation* ed. by Merrill C. Tenney, Grand Rapids: Zondervan Publishing House, c. 1968, p. 69.

8. Carl F. H. Henry, "Divine Revelation And the Bible," in *Inspiration And Interpretation*, ed. by John F. Walvoord, Grand Rapids: William B. Eerdmans Publishing Company, c. 1957, p. 262.

9. G. C. Berkouwer, "General and Special Revelation," in *Revelation And the Bible*, ed. by Carl F. H. Henry, Grand Rapids: Baker Book House, c. 1958, p. 15.

10. Benjamin Brekinridge Warfield, *The Inspiration And Authority of The Bible*, ed. by Samuel Craig, Philadelphia: The Presbyterian and Reformed Publishing Company, c. 1948, pp. 74, 75.

Inspiration
and Authority

A study of revelation is not complete unless it involves a study of the inspiration and authority of the Bible. Special revelation has come to us in the Bible. We are intensely interested in this Book. We want to know what it claims for itself. We want to know if it answers for us the inescapable questions of life. We want to know if we can depend upon it. If we believe that we already know the answers to these questions, we want a rational comprehension of our faith. We want to add assurance to assurance. We are rational beings. We cannot escape this fact. At the same time, we cannot separate our reason from the rest of our personality. We want something that speaks to our total personality and helps us face the total responsibilities of life in the midst of the complexities of life as we face it.

I. THE ORIGIN OF SCRIPTURE

A. The Divine Authorship

Second Timothy 3:16 speaks of the Divine origin of Scripture. The Greek word which is translated in the King James Version as "given by inspiration of God" is *theopneustos*. This word means God-breathed. The Scriptures are a product of the breath of God. They are of Divine origin. In commenting on this passage, Warfield observes:

No term could have been chosen . . . which would have more emphatically asserted the Divine production of Scripture than that which is here employed. The 'breath of God' is in Scripture just the symbol of His almighty power, the bearer of His creative word. 'By the word of Jehovah,' we read in the significant parallel Ps. xxxiii.6, 'were the heavens made; and all the host of them by the breath of his mouth.' And it is particularly where the operations of God are energetic that this term . . . is employed to designate them—God's breath is the irresistible outflow of His power. When Paul declares, then, that 'every scripture,' 'is God-breathed,' he asserts with as much energy as he could employ that Scripture is the product of a Divine operation.1

The word *theopneustos* occurs nowhere else in Scripture. However, it is clear that Paul was using this strong term to ascribe to Scripture what it had already ascribed to itself. It has been said that such expressions as, "Thus saith the LORD," "The LORD saith," and "The word of the LORD came to such and such a person" or the equivalent are found more than 3,800 times in the Old Testament. Jesus referred to the Old Testament as being invested with that type of authority that no one but God could give (Matthew 4:4, 7, 10; 5:17, 18; Luke 24:44, 45; John 5:39; 10:34, 35; and many others). Second Peter 1:21 gives evidence of the fact that the message of the prophets was God's Word.

It is clear that when Paul said in 2 Timothy 3:16, "All scripture is God-breathed," he meant to include the whole Old Testament. The problem is: Did he also embrace the New Testament? I believe he did.

In 2 Peter 3:2, Peter puts the writings of the apostles on the level with that of the prophets when he admonished his readers: "That ye may be mindful of the words which were spoken before by the holy prophets, and of the commandment of us the apostles of the Lord and Savior." In 2 Peter 3:16 after referring to Paul's epistles, Peter refers to "other scriptures." To speak of "other" Scriptures means that Peter was considering Paul's writings as Scripture.

Paul, apparently, referred to Luke's writings as Scripture when he said in 1 Timothy 5:18, "For the scripture saith, 'Thou shalt not muzzle the ox that treadeth out the corn. And, the labourer is worthy of his reward.'" The first part of the verse is taken from Deuteronomy 25:4. The last part is taken from Luke 10:7. If Paul intends for "the scripture saith" to refer to the entire verse, he is considering Luke's Gospel to be Scripture.

Paul considered his own writings to be of Divine origin when he said: "If any man think himself to be a prophet, or spiritual, let him acknowledge that the things that I write unto you are the commandments of the Lord" (1 Corinthians 14:37).

The evidence given above supports the inclusion of the part of the New Testament that had been written up to that time in Paul's reference to "all scripture" in 2 Timothy 3:16. What about that part of the Bible that was written after 2 Timothy 3:16? I believe a case can be built for including that too as being God-breathed as Paul said all Scripture was.

If we ask a contractor what kind of brick he is using in a building, and he names a particular kind of brick we expect that he is not only telling us the kind he has been using, but also the kind he plans to use in the remainder of the building. When Paul said, "All scripture is God-breathed," he was telling us a characteristic of all writings that were appropriately called Scripture as he was using the term. The term would be equally applied to any later writing if it could be appropriately called Scripture. As Warfield explains:

> What must be understood in estimating the testimony of the New Testament writers to the inspiration of Scripture is that 'Scripture' stood in their minds as the title of a unitary body of books, throughout the gift of God through His Spirit to His people, but that this body of writings was at the same time understood to be a growing aggregate, so that what is said of it applies to the new books which were being added to it as the Spirit gave them, as fully as to the old books which had come down to them from their hoary past . . . . Whatever can lay claim by just right to the appellations of 'Scripture,' as employed in its eminent sense by those writers, can by the same just right lay claim to the 'inspiration' which they ascribe to this 'Scripture.' [2]

B. The Human Authorship

There are several factors which indicate that there is a human authorship of the Bible. The most obvious one is the fact that in many books the writer identifies himself (Isaiah 1:1; Jeremiah 1:1; Amos 1:1; Romans 1:1; 1 Corinthians 1:1; 2 Corinthians 1:1; Galatians 1:1-3; and others). Also, others refer to the writings of a particular author as being his writings (Romans 9:27, 29; 2 Peter 3:15, 16; and others).

That the Bible was written by human beings is too obvious to be debated. The question is: Were they amanuenses (secretaries) or were they in a real sense authors? Did the writers merely receive dictation or did their personalities as thinking, feeling, acting beings enter into their writings?

There is an abundance of evidence that the writers were more than secretaries. If Romans had been dictated by God, it is not likely that God would have dictated it to Paul, and Paul in turn would have dictated it to Tertius (Romans 16:22). If dictation had been the method, one would have expected it to have been given directly to Tertius.

Throughout the Bible one can detect the traces of the personalities of the writers. Their own style and vocabularies show in their writings. The personality of the writer does not manifest itself as strongly in some writings as in others. Books such as Kings and Chronicles, which depended to a great extent upon written records, would not reflect as much of the human author as the Book of Romans where Paul's thinking entered strongly into the book. However, the same is true in these types of writings even when Divine authorship is not involved. The total personality of the author is naturally less involved in some types of writings than others.

I am not denying that there is any dictation involved in Scripture at any time. The Ten Commandments would have been copied into the Book of Exodus from stones upon which God had written (Exodus 32:15-19; 34:1-4). In principle, this would be the same as dictation. At times, the prophets seemed to have been bearers of messages that would not have differed drastically from dictation (Jeremiah 34:1-7). Whatever may be said concerning the possible use of dictation, it was not the usual method used by God in the employment of human authors to give us the Bible.

C. The Nature of the Divine Influence Upon the Human Authors

The nature of the Divine influence upon the human authors is not fully explained to us. That there was such a relationship and that it guaranteed that what they said was the Word of God is made clear by Peter when he said: "For the prophecy came not in old time by the will of man: but holy men of God spake as they were moved by the Holy Ghost" (2 Peter 1:21).

The word which is translated "move" is the Greek word *phero* . It means to bear, carry, or bring. Concerning this word, Warfield explains:

> The term here used is a very specific one. It is not to be confounded with guiding, or directing, or controlling, or even leading in the full sense of that word. It goes beyond all such terms, in assigning the effect produced specifically to the active agent. What is 'borne' is taken up by the 'bearer,' and conveyed by the 'bearer's' goal, not its own. The men who spoke from God are here declared, therefore, to have been taken up by the Holy Spirit and brought by His power to the goal of His choosing.[3]

There have been several attempts to explain the nature of this Divine influence which is referred to by the term inspiration. Some have used the term illumination to describe this influence. It is said that the natural perceptions of the writer were elevated and intensified by the Holy Spirit. Illumination is experienced by all believers. The difference between Bible writers and other believers would be only a matter of degree.

To describe inspiration as illumination fails to do justice to 2 Timothy 3:16 and 2 Peter 1:21. Illumination is not an adequate explanation of how the Bible writers were borne along by the Holy Spirit to produce a product that can rightly be ascribed to God. It is obvious that illumination would not produce a product that could rightly be called God-breathed.

Another word that is frequently used to describe this Divine influence is the word dynamic. Usually the view is explained more in terms of the type product produced than in the nature of the influence, though the word itself speaks of the influence. It is used to refer to a much stronger influence than illumination. There is a particular interest that the writers be authors, not just penmen. The result produced is an infallible guide in matters of faith and practice, but not inerrant in matters not pertaining to faith and practice. As a rule, those who hold this view would speak of concept inspiration rather than verbal inspiration. A discussion of the weaknesses of this view will be given later when we look at the extent of the Divine influence in inspiration and the authority of Scripture. At this time let us pass by raising the question: Does this view do justice to 2 Timothy 3:16 and 2 Peter 1:21?

Plenary verbal is the name given to the view according to which the Holy Spirit used the writers to produce an infallible and inerrant Bible. However, these words do not describe the nature of the Divine influence. Rather, they speak of the nature of the product. There is no commonly used and accepted term that describes this influence.

In the last quotation from Warfield above, he pointed out that the Divine influence as spoken of in 2 Peter 1:21" . . . is not to be confounded with guiding, or directing, or controlling, or even leading in the full sense of that word." We have no word which will adequately describe it. This probably accounts for the fact that more attention has been given to the extent of inspiration and Biblical authority than the nature of the Divine influence.

The difficulty of describing the Divine influence on the human authors of the Bible arises out of the fact that we are dealing with a relationship between persons. The Holy Spirit is a person. The writers were persons. Mechanical relationships are more easily described and measured. Language tends to give us the choice between viewing a relationship as either active or passive. Where personal relationships and personal responses are involved, they do not submit to the simple analysis of active or passive.

We are not to think of the human authors as being passive only. In 2 Peter 1:21, we see both the active and the passive voice used with respect to the authors. They "spoke" (active) as they were "borne" (passive) by the Holy Spirit. The Holy Spirit acted upon one who was actively involved.

Though we cannot fully describe the relationship between the human authors and the Divine author, we can make certain definite conclusions:

(1) The Divine authorship is of such a nature that the Scriptures are God-breathed. They are of Divine origin. (2) The Divine relationship to the human author guaranteed that what the authors wrote was the Word of God. (3) The human authors were authors in the true sense of the word. Their personalities were actively involved in preparations to write and in their writing.

II. THE EXTENT OF THE DIVINE INFLUENCE IN SCRIPTURE

A. The Teaching of Scripture

Our approach throughout this chapter is to find out: (1) What the Bible specifically says about itself. (2) What can be inferred and what can be logically deduced about the Bible from its own statements. It is of vital interest what a book that claims to be a Divine revelation says about itself. We would expect a book that is a Divine revelation to make such a claim. We are concerned about anything it says about its basic nature. We do not accept every book that proposes to be a Divine revelation. But to reject all of them leaves us on the sea of life without a compass and without a North Star. We cannot chart the ocean of reality. To find a book that we truly believe to be a Divine revelation gives us answers to the inescapable questions of life. We come to know who we are, where we are, and where we are going. It takes away our lostness. It gives us purpose and meaning in life. Our beings cry out for this. We dare not separate our rational mind from the rest of our personality and let it cause us to reject the revelation God gives. I will reserve for a later chapter a discussion of why we believe the Bible. It will be treated along with why we believe in God. At present, let us return to our examination of what the Bible says about itself.

By the extent of the Divine influence we have two areas of concern: (1) Does it extend to all portions of Scripture? (2) Does it extend to the Words of Scripture?

It has been pointed out above that both Old and New Testaments are God-breathed (2 Timothy 3:16). There is a difference of opinion concerning whether the Greek should be rendered "all" or "every." *All* would refer to the entire body of Scripture as a whole. *Every* would embrace the whole, but would give stress to the parts that make up the whole. Concerning the significance of which is used, all or every, Warfield observes:

> In both cases these Sacred Scriptures are declared to owe their value to their Divine origin; and in both cases

this their Divine origin is energetically asserted of the entire fabric.4

The term plenary is used to embrace the idea that the Bible is inspired both in the whole and in every part. Warfield describes plenary inspiration as:

> ... the doctrine that the Bible is not *in part* but *fully*, in all its elements alike,—things discoverable by reason as well as mysteries, matters of history and science as well as of faith and practice, words as well as thoughts. 5

The word "verbal" is frequently added to plenary to make clear that the inspiration extended to the words used. The claim of verbal inspiration is clearly made in 1 Corinthians 2:13. Paul denied that redemptive truth can be discovered by human investigation in 2:9. In 2:10, he affirms that God has revealed redemptive truth by the Holy Spirit. In 2:13 concerning the truth received by revelation, he says, "Which things also we speak, not in the words which man's wisdom teacheth, but which the Holy Ghost teacheth."

The very fact that the Scriptures are spoken of as God-breathed (2 Timothy 3:16) means that the inspiration extended to the words used. It is the product that is said to be God-breathed. If the product itself is appropriately spoken of as God-breathed, it was necessary for God to bear a relationship to every part for it to be so described. Also, for the writers to be so borne along by the Holy Spirit that they spoke the message of God (2 Peter 1:21) necessarily infers that the inspiration extended to the words.

The words of Jesus, "For verily I say unto you, Till heaven and earth pass, one jot or one tittle shall in no wise pass from the law, till all be fulfilled" (Matthew 5:18), cannot be understood apart from verbal inspiration. The same can be said for Jesus' statement in John 10:35: " . . . The scripture cannot be broken."

B. The Relationship Between Concepts and Words

Some have spoken of thought or concept inspiration rather than verbal inspiration. It is held that God gave the writers the thoughts and they expressed these thoughts in their own words. In reality, this view is a view of revelation without inspiration. Revelation has to do with the giving of truth on the part of God. Inspiration is the Divine work of God in which the writers were borne along in the process of communicating that truth which they received by revelation.

If we truly speak of "thought inspiration," it cannot be separated from verbal inspiration. To speak of thought inspiration is to mean that God so moved upon the Bible writers that they communicated God's thoughts. The Bible has come to us in the

24

words of human language. If God inspired the writers to write in such a way that it guaranteed the communication of God's thoughts, it would of necessity mean that inspiration guaranteed the use of words that would convey these thoughts. If this be not the case, there is no inspiration, or it did not extend to the thoughts.

We cannot divorce the process of inspiration from words. As Dr. Clark Pinnock remarks: "Just because inspiration concerns the written text of Scripture it has to do with human words and language. Truth that is communicated must be related in language."6

Though we cannot divorce inspiration from words, it is not necessary to conclude that in no instance could any other word have been used by the writer. What we must insist upon is that in every case *appropriate words* were chosen that would convey God's thoughts. In cases where only one word would convey God's thought, we can rest assured that that particular word was used. This allows room for the particular writer to enter into his writing, but at the same time guarantees the communication of God's message. A comparison of different speeches by Jesus in the gospels seems to support this conclusion. We have the same message, but some variation in words.

While it was of utmost importance that appropriate words be used, we must keep in mind that the ultimate focus of God centered on the message. Appropriate words are important because they serve as a necessary means in the communication of God's message to us. Words are the means. The message (concepts or thoughts) is the end. There are benefits to be derived from observing that the ultimate focus of God centered on the thoughts or message rather than the words.7

If words, in which no other word could have been acceptable in any case, had been the main aim of God in giving us the Bible, the translation of the Bible would have been ruled out. Priority is given to the texts in the original language because in these we have the Word of God in words inspired of God. However, in so far as the message is properly translated from the Hebrew and Greek texts we have God's Word in our own language. We have the message of God, but not in the words in which it was originally given. We need not hesitate in calling a good translation the inspired Word of God. We do not claim verbal inspiration for translations because translators are not inspired in their work. This statement is true regardless of how accurate the translation may be. We do have God's message, and it is an inspired message.

Since the message is the end and words are the means, it follows that the Bible must be interpreted. Scripture memorization is good, but we must go beyond quoting the Bible. We must interpret its message and apply it to life.

The labor of textual critics is important in assuring us as much as possible that we have the same words that were used in the

25

original texts. However, when we realize that concepts are the main concern of God in giving us the Bible, we will see that in the unsettled points there is no real reason for alarm. Very seldom is the concept significantly altered in the variant readings no matter which is chosen. No Biblical doctrine is at stake because of variant readings.

C. The Question of Plenary Verbal Inspiration and Dictation

The critics of plenary verbal inspiration have constantly accused the advocates of plenary verbal inspiration of believing that the Bible was given from God by dictation. Plenary verbal speaks of the product, not of how it was produced. It would be possible for a person to believe in a plenary verbally inspired Bible and believe that it did come by dictation. However, works in which this is done are extremely few. It is very unlikely that most who accuse those who believe in plenary verbal inspiration of believing in dictation could name one advocate of dictation and then support the charge.

I know of no false charge of any kind that is more inexcusable than the blanket charge that accuses across the board the advocates of the plenary verbal view with believing in dictation. I attended a Bible college for four years. I have spent more than four years in seminary. I attended several summers at a seminary which for many years gathered some of the leading conservative scholars from America and from other countries. I have heard many people preach, both educated and uneducated. In all of my experience I have never heard one person advocate the dictation theory.

Dr. Laird Harris comments:

> No creed of any consequence in the Christian Church has taught the dictation theory, though, as we shall see, the creeds are full of assertions that there are no contradictions in Scripture, that all of it is to be believed, that God is the author of the whole, etc. And there are few if any theological authors of importance who have held to the dictation theory, even though the usual view through the history of the Christian Church has been that the Scriptures are true to the smallest detail.[8]

Dr. H. D. McDonald, in his book, *Theories of Revelation*, An Historical Study 1860-1960 says, "Prior to the year 1860, the idea of an infallibly inerrant Scripture was the prevalent view."[9]

Concerning the period that began with 1860, Dr. McDonald explains:

> The whole period following the general repudiation of inerrancy and the introduction of higher criticism has been marked by an attack on the 'mechanical' theory of

inspiration. It is just, however, to point out that this was a view of inspiration credited to the traditionalists generally rather than actually taught by them. 10

Later in the same chapter, Dr. McDonald explains that there were three important volumes in the period 1860-1960 that might so state the traditionalists' point of view in such a way that some might understand them to be advocating the mechanical view. These are: C. Wordsworth, *The Inspiration of the Bible*, 1861, p. 5; L. Gaussen, *Theopneustia: The Plenary Inspiration of the Holy Scriptures* (trans. David Scott, 1863), p. 24; cf. p. 281 J. W. Bargon, *Inspiration and Interpretation* reprint, 1905, p. 86. The latter refers to a sermon preached by J. W. Burgon at Oxford, 1860. Dr. McDonald explains that upon examination these men are not properly understood as supporting a mechanical view to the exclusion of human authorship.11

It should be quite obvious that there is absolutely no justification for the general charge that accuses the advocates of verbal inspiration of believing in the dictation view of inspiration. Such charges either represent poor scholarship on the part of people because they have not examined the writings of those who believe in verbal inspiration, or it represents dishonesty on their part. If they want to say that verbal inspiration logically requires dictation, they would have a right to make the statement though it would be an error in judgment. To make a blanket statement that those who believe in verbal inspiration believe in dictation is either scholastic irresponsibility or dishonesty.

III. THE INTERPRETATION OF SCRIPTURE

Before dealing with the subject of Biblical authority, I would like to give brief attention to Biblical interpretation. This will contribute to a proper context in which to discuss Biblical authority.

The Bible has come to us in human language. It used language in the same sense that it was used in ordinary speech and writing. That means that the Bible is to be interpreted by the normal laws of language. In the Bible, a noun is a noun. An adjective is an adjective. A verb is a verb. An adverb is an adverb, etc.

The approach to Biblical hermeneutics that studies the Bible in the light of the ordinary laws of language is called grammatico-historical interpretation. Terry explains, "The grammatico-historical sense of a writer is such an interpretation of his language as is required by the laws of grammar and the facts of history."12

This type of interpretation is referred to most frequently as literal interpretation. Terry says, "Sometimes we speak of the literal sense, by which we mean the most simple, direct, and ordinary meaning of phrases and sentences."13

While I accept what is referred to as literal interpretation, I go along with E. R. Cravens in preferring to use the word normal instead of literal. He comments:

Normal is used instead of *literal* (the term generally employed in this connection) as more expressive of the correct idea. No terms could have been chosen more unfit to designate the two great schools of prophetical exegetes than *literal* and *spiritual*. These terms are not antithetical, nor are they in any proper sense significant of the pecularities of the respective systems they are employed to characterize. They are positively misleading and confusing. *Literal* is opposed not to *spiritual* but *figurative: spiritual* is in antithesis on the one hand to *material*, on the other to *carnal* (in a bad sense). The *Literalist* (so called) is not one who denied that *figurative* language, that *symbols*, are used in prophecy, nor does he deny that great *spiritual* truths are set forth therein: his position is, simply, that the prophecies are to be *normally* interpreted (i.e. according to the received laws of language) as any other utterances are interpreted—that which is manifestly literal is regarded as literal, that which is manifestly figurative is so regarded. [14]

The diagram below will show the problem that arises from speaking of literal interpretation.

Literal Interpretation of Language

Literal | Language   Figurative | Language

Though such a conclusion is not intended, it looks as if figurative language is to be interpreted literally. Literal interpretation seems to be far more appropriate for literal language than for figurative language.

The diagram below will show the advisability of speaking of normal interpretation.

Normal Interpretation of Language

Literal | Language   Figurative | Language

In normal interpretation, we treat literal language as literal and figurative as figurative. This is the way we do it in life. It is the way we should do it in Bible study.

Normal interpretation or as it is more commonly called, literal interpretation, is the same approach as the grammatico-historical method of interpretation. Normal stresses the fact that the same basic principles are involved in Biblical interpretation that are involved in other uses of language. Grammatico-historical interpretation is descriptive of what normal interpretation is. It interprets in keeping with the laws of grammar and the historical context.

IV. THE AUTHORITY OF SCRIPTURE

In speaking of full authority for Scripture, the words "infallible" and "inerrant" are used. Concerning these words, Pinnock defines infallible as "incapable of teaching deception" and inerrant as "not liable to prove false or mistaken." [15]

A. Complete Infallibility and Inerrancy

Does the Bible teach its own inerrancy? Some, who may not deny inerrancy, say it does not. Dr. Everett F. Harrison says:

> Unquestionably the Bible teaches its own inspiration. It is a Book of God. It does not require us to hold to inerrancy, though this is a natural corollary of full inspiration. The phenomena which present difficulties are not to be dismissed or underrated. They have driven many sincere believers in the trustworthiness of the Bible as a spiritual guide to hold a modified position on the non-revelation material. Every man must be persuaded in his own mind.[16]

Many disagree with Dr. Harrison. They believe that the Bible does teach its inerrancy. I take my stand with those who believe the Bible does require us to believe in its inerrancy.

As we read the Bible we are met with a compelling impression that its contents are without error. The Bible gives not the slightest hint that error is found anywhere in its pages. Jesus and the writers of the New Testament use the Old Testament in such a way that we feel compelled to believe that they understood it to be without error. Dr. Roger Nicole says:

> From beginning to end, the New Testament authors ascribe unqualified authority to Old Testament Scripture. Whenever advanced, a quotation is viewed as normative. Nowhere do we find a tendency to question, argue, or repudiate the truth of any Scripture utterance.[17]

We do not draw our conclusions from a general impression alone. Jesus' statement, "Till heaven and earth pass, one jot or one tittle shall in no wise pass from the law, till all be fulfilled" (Matthew 5:18), requires us to believe that He thought the Old Testament was true in its smallest detail.

Jesus' statement, "The Scripture cannot be broken" (John 10:35), is synonymous with the statement, "The Scripture cannot be in error."

In the light of Matthew 5:17, 18 and John 10:35, it seems strange that anyone should say that the Bible does not require us to believe in its inerrancy.

Added to the above is the fact that the Bible teaches two inescapable conclusions which require us to believe a third inescapable conclusion. The first is that God cannot lie (Numbers 23:19; Titus 1:2; along with all the Biblical teachings on God's holiness and righteousness). The second is the Bible is God's Word (2 Timothy 3:16 along with numerous references where the Bible writers claim to be speaking the message of God). For the Scriptures to be God-breathed gives a Divine stamp on Scripture that makes it impossible for us to disassociate God from its every statement. These observations can be stated as follows:

Major Premise: God cannot lie.

Minor Premise: The Bible is God's Word. Therefore, the Bible cannot lie.

To say that the Bible cannot lie is to say that it cannot be in error.

B. The Limited Infallibility View

This view is commonly called the dynamic theory of inspiration. It takes the position that the Bible is an infallible authority in matters of doctrine and practice, but it may be in error at times on matters of history, geography, etc. These matters are frequently referred to as the phenomena of Scripture. It is felt that the Bible is generally reliable in these areas but not inerrant.

Among the advocates of this view belong A. H. Strong in *Systematic Theology*, Three Volumes in One, Philadelphia: The Judson Press, c. 1907, pp. 211-222; A. M. Hills, in *Fundamental Christian Theology*, Pasadena: Published by C. J. Kinne, Pasadena College, c. 1931, I, pp. 127-135; and W. W. Stevens in *Doctrines of the Christian Religion*, Grand Rapids: William B. Eerdmans Publishing Company, c. 1967, pp. 32, 33.

In addition to the support given above which speaks against this view, the following objections are raised against this view.

(1) There is such an intermingling of the historical, geographical, etc. with the doctrinal and practical that it would be absurd to argue for the possibility of the truth of one when admitting the possibility of error in the other. If such a view were true, it would be impossible to uproot the tares without damaging the wheat.

(2) Most of the adherence of partial infallibility would want to say the Bible is the Word of God rather than it contains the Word of God. If the Bible is the Word of God, He is its author and must accept responsibility for its contents. To admit error in a book reveals something about its author. Either he is ignorant or he is dishonest. Neither of these can be attributed to God. It is inconceivable that any Book that is rightfully called the Word of God can contain errors about anything. Those who advocate partial infallibility would be on safer ground logically if they said the Bible contains the Word of God instead of is the Word of God.

(3) If the Bible did not speak truth in the realm of facts knowable through our means of learning, it would fail to convince people about the way of salvation which can be known only through revelation. Jesus' statement involves this principle when He said to Nicodemus, "If I have told you earthly things, and ye believe not, how shall ye believe, if I tell you of heavenly things?" (John 3:12).

When the thought of a Divine revelation enters our minds, it seems that rooted deep and inescapably into our beings is the expectation of inerrancy. The concept of inerrancy has constantly entered the discussions of both friend and foe of the Bible. Friends have defended inerrancy. Foes have rejected inerrancy and have considered it grounds for rejecting the Bible as a Divine revelation. They have assumed it to be a self-evident truth that a Divine revelation would be inerrant.

We must not isolate our rational minds away from the rest of our personality. I am not suggesting that we not be rational. I am saying that we must function as a unitary whole. If we live in a universe with purpose and meaning, truth will speak to our total personality. We may be able to force our minds to believe in a Bible that is infallible in matters of faith and practice; or as Dewey M. Beegle has done in his book, *The Inspiration of Scripture*, Philadelphia: The Westminster Press, c. 1963, we may be able to grant the possibility of error in doctrinal matters. The question to be asked is: If we do, will we not be doing violence to our total personality?

Is the expectation of inerrancy for Divine revelation a part of the fall of man? Is it a trick of Satan? Or, is it written indelibly in the nature of things as a self-evident truth? To me the only satisfying answer is that it is a self-evident truth inherent in the very nature of things and implanted into my being by God in such a way that to try to suppress it or reject it is to do violence to my being.

It seems to be built into the very nature of things that in the long run to maintain the rest of the doctrines of orthodox Christianity requires belief in the inerrancy of Scripture. It is easy to describe a way that it can be done, but the direction of human personality is not that easily controlled. As Dr. Henry comments:

How much was at stake in a weakening of trust in the

historical reliability of Scripture was not at first obvious to those who placed emphasis on reliability of the Bible in matters of faith and practice. For no distinction between historical and doctrinal matters is set up by the New Testament view of inspiration. No doubt this is due to the fact that the Old Testament is viewed as the unfolding of God's saving revelation; the historical elements are a central aspect of the revelation. *It was soon apparent that scholars who abandoned the trustworthiness of Biblical history had furnished an entering wedge for the abandonment of doctrinal elements. Theoretically such an outcome might perhaps have been avoided by an act of will, but in practice it was not.* [Italics are mine] 18

C. Clarification of the Meaning of Inerrancy

By inerrancy, we mean that what the Bible says is true. The interpretation arrived at through the proper application of the laws of language is true. We should not call anything in the Bible an error unless we would by the standard of truth applied to the ordinary use of language.

Truth and absolute precision are not synonymous. In answer to a question concerning how many people were present on an occasion, all of the following answers could be true: 297, 300, 325 or some other figure in this general range. Only one of these could be precise. As a precise answer, 297 could be true. As an answer spoken of in round numbers, 300 could be true even if spoken by one who knew the answer was 297 if he did not claim it to be exact. The number 325 could be true as an estimate. Truthfulness is equated with precision only when precision is claimed.

A summary of a speech, if properly prepared, is true. Yet, a degree of precision may of necessity be lost in condensing the speech.

Two partial reports may appear to be in contradiction. Yet, a complete report may show the partial reports to be true and reconcilable.

In commenting on Biblical inerrancy, Dr. Harris explains:

This doctrine does not say that every sentence is spoken with a precision sometimes not possible for our ideas, to say nothing of our words. God's purpose was evidently to convey ideas within acceptable limits of accuracy. At one place He might date an event after six days, at another He says it was about eight days later .... Precision and accuracy are not terms exactly equivalent to truth. 19

The doctrine of inerrancy applies to the original manuscripts.

We believe in the basic reliability of the Greek and Hebrew texts. We do not claim that copyists made no mistakes in copying over the years. Textual critics assure us that we have a basically reliable text. When we make the distinction between words and ideas, even when we are not sure of the exact word, the truthfulness of the idea may not be at stake. Copyists' mistakes, whether in matters of faith and practice or the phenomena of Scripture, are not to be equated with errors in the ideas in Scripture. I am not denying that a copyist's mistake could not include a technical error, but it does not of necessity. Most seeming contradictions in the Bible as we have it can be explained without resorting to the conclusion that they were copyists' errors. Most are not errors at all.

It is only natural that a person would be concerned about what is referred to as errors in the Bible. As a rule, when a person examines these he finds answers to most without much difficulty. Soon he becomes so sure that answers could be found for the others if all the information were available that he abandons the search and spends his energies on other things. We can be sure that some of the greatest minds in the history of the human race have been fully informed on what were considered to be errors in the Bible, and at the same time have maintained their faith. The same is true today.

I am sure that some are ready to make light of the approach I have described above. I ask the question: Do not all of us use it in some area of thought? Do we abandon all certainty every time we face a difficulty? When a scientist does not get the effect that he thought the cause should produce, does he abandon his belief in the uniformity of nature?

The vastness of space and the endlessness of time are such that we cannot afford to be lost. To me the Bible as God's revelation gives a chart and compass that keeps me from being lost on the sea of life. I know who I am. I know where I am. I know where I am going. 20

CHAPTER THREE
NOTES

1. Benjamin Breckinridge Warfield, *The Inspiration and Authority of the Bible*, ed. by Samuel Craig, Philadelphia: The Presbyterian and Reformed Publishing Company, c. 1948, p. 133.

2. *Ibid.*, p. 165.

3. *Ibid.*, p. 131.

4. *Ibid.*, p. 134.

5. *Ibid.*, p. 113.

6. Clark H. Pinnock, *A Defense of Biblical Infallibility*, Philadelphia: Presbyterian and Reformed Publishing Company, c. 1967, p. 16.

7. See Ramm's discussion of *"inner forma"* and *"outer former"* Bernard Ramm, *Special Revelation and The Word of God*, Grand Rapids: William B. Eerdmans Publishing Company, c. 1961, pp. 196-198.

8. R. Laird Harris, *Inspiration and Canonicity of the Bible*, Grand Rapids: Zondervan Publishing House, c. 1957, p. 21.

9. H. D. McDonald, *Theories of Revelation*, London: George Allen & Unwin LTD, c. 1963, p. 196.

10. *Ibid.*, p. 218.

11. *Ibid.*, pp. 284, 285.

12. Milton S. Terry, *Biblical Hermeneutics*, Grand Rapids: Zondervan Publishing House (a Zondervan Reprint Classic), p. 203.

13. *Ibid.*

14. E. R. Cravens, "Footnote" p. 98, *Revelation* by John Peter Lange in *Lange's Commentary on the Holy Scriptures*, trans. and ed. by Philip Schaff, Grand Rapids: Zondervan Publishing House, n.d.

15. Pinnock, *op. cit.*, p. 1.

16. Everett F. Harrison, "The Phenomena of Scripture" in *Revelation and the Bible* ed. by Carl F. H. Henry, Grand Rapids: Baker Book House, c. 1958, p. 250.

17. Roger Nicole, "New Testament Use of the Old Testament," in *Revelation and the Bible* ed. by Carl F. H. Henry, p. 138.

18. Carl F. H. Henry, "Inspiration" in *Baker's Dictionary of Theology*, ed. by Everett F. Harrison, Grand Rapids: Baker Book House, c. 1960, pp. 288, 289.

19. Laird Harris, "The Problem of Communication" from *The Bible—The Living Word of Revelation*, ed. by Merrill C. Tenney, Grand Rapids: Zondervan Publishing House, c. 1968, pp. 90, 91.

20. Parts of what occur under IV "The authority of Scripture" were taken from Leroy Forlines, *Issues Among Evangelicals* published by the Commission on Theological Liberalism of the National Association of Free Will Baptists, Nashville, Tennessee, 1968, pp. 5-10. The material used was rearranged and rewritten to meet the need for use in this study.

4

Nature and
Attributes of God

When that inescapable question, "Is there a God?" is answered in the affirmative, a question just as inescapable presents itself. What kind of being is God? The answer to this question is of greatest importance. The very fact that He is God means that He is the Sovereign Ruler and the Lord and Judge of my life. My relationship to Him is the most important of all my relationships. His nature and attributes form the foundation of the only valid value system. It is the value system by which I will be judged. It is the value system by which I must live if I am to have harmony within. My system of thought must acknowledge Him and must reflect a commitment to Divine values.

In this chapter, I plan to discuss God as God, i.e., things that are equally true of each member of the Trinity. It is a mistake to understand the discussion of the nature and attributes of God to be a discussion of God the Father as distinguished from God the Son and God the Holy Spirit. What is true with regard to the nature and attributes of God is equally true of all members of the Trinity.

I. THE BASIC NATURE OF GOD

By the basic nature of God, I mean what God is within Himself apart from any consideration of His relationship with His creation. These facts about God are important considerations when thinking about His relationship with His creation, but we can think of them without thinking of His relationship to His creation.

A. God is Spirit

God is a spirit-being (John 4:24) as distinguished from a

material being. It is proper to think of God as having an essence or substance, but the substance is immaterial rather than material. Our minds are so accustomed to thinking of material substance that it is hard for us to think of a substance that is immaterial. Yet, we must think of immaterial substance if we are to think of the spirit-essence of God, or if we are to think of our own human spirit or the spirit-essence of angels.

There are two logical consequences of the fact that God is spirit: (1) He is incorporeal. (2) He is invisible.

By incorporeal is meant that God does not possess a physical body. It is of the very nature of spirit that it does not have flesh and bones (Luke 24:39). It is true that the Bible speaks of God as having hands, feet, eyes, ears, etc. (Isaiah 59:2; Genesis 3:8; 1 Peter 3:12; and others). These are to be understood as metaphorical expressions that serve as aids in communication. When Isaiah said, "Behold, the LORD's hand is not shortened, that it cannot save" (59:1), we do not think of the Lord as having a long arm with which He saves. What these anthropomorphic terms (terms describing God with human characteristics) do is to speak of God figuratively in terms of the organ with which we perform functions similar to those functions being ascribed to God. In view of the frequent use that we make of figurative language, it should not seem strange that such language would be used of God.

In accord with the fact that God is incorporeal, He is invisible. Jesus said, "No man hath seen God at any time" (John 1:18). Some problem is created by Genesis 32:30; Exodus 24:10; 33:18-23; Judges 13:22; and others. In these appearances God assumed some visible form, but in the light of Jesus' statement we must conclude that this was less than viewing the very essence of God.

B. God is Personal

In speaking of God as God, I prefer to say He is personal rather than say He is a person. "He is a person" would be appropriate to speak of one person. Since there are three persons in the Godhead, it is better to speak of God as personal. By personal we mean that He is a being who thinks, feels, and acts. That the God of the Bible thinks, feels, and acts is too obvious to require scriptural documentation.

The fact that God is personal means that He is the living God. He is separated from idols who can neither see, hear, speak, nor act (Deuteronomy 4:28; Psalm 115:5, 8; and others).

The fact that God is personal separates Him from the impersonal God of philosophy. He is not an impersonal object to be found by our searching. He is a personal God who cares and has declared Himself.

The fact that God is personal is not an observation to be made

36

and passed over quickly. It deserves much thought in order to see and appreciate its far reaching implications. If God were impersonal, our relationship with Him (or better, It) would either be an unintelligible mystical relationship, or simply a relationship to laws. With God as personal, the ultimate relationship is personal. As personal beings we need personal relationships. We need to know that the highest of all beings cares for us. A personal relationship can be a warm relationship.

The doctrine of revelation is a logical outgrowth and depends upon the fact that God is personal. A personal God who speaks makes the difference between having a "sure word of prophecy" (2 Peter 1:19) and being tossed about on the uncertain sea of philosophical speculation.

Miracles are no problem to a personal God who created and rules the universe. He is not locked in by the laws of nature. He does not have to suspend the laws of nature to work a miracle. He simply acts directly. His activity may counteract the laws of nature, but He does not have to suspend them. If a small child is riding with us and we have to stop suddenly, we reach out our hand to hold him to keep him from falling. If we had not reached out our hand and held him, the laws of nature in operation would have caused him to fall. As persons, we reach out the hand and introduce another law of nature that counteracts the law of nature that would have caused the child to fall. We did not suspend the law of nature. If we, as persons, can counteract one law of nature by another law of nature, cannot the personal Ruler of the universe interpose His own activity without suspending the laws of nature? Is He not free to do so?

The question of when to work miracles is a matter that is solely within God's control. The logical possibility of miracles is clearly present when we have a personal God. In our study of the Bible, we dare not be guided by a view of reality that in principle rules out the possibility of miracles. This is the mental attitude that many have had who have sought to deny or explain away the miraculous in the Bible.

C. God is Independent

God is not dependent upon anything outside Himself for His existence. He is the grounds of His own existence. We speak of the self-existence or aseity of God. God is not the cause of His existence because that which did not begin cannot be caused. God is an uncaused Being.

As Dr. Fred H. Klooster explains:

The independence of God includes more than the idea of God's *aseity* of self-existence. His independence characterizes not only His existence, but His whole being and His attributes, His decrees and His works of creation, providence, and redemption.[1]

There is no force or person outside of God that poses any threat to God or forces Him to take a particular path of action. God's actions are in accord with His own nature and His own plan.

God's independence does not mean that He has not entered into personal relationships with the persons whom He has created, nor that He does not use them in His work. It does mean that the idea of these relationships and the use of those He has created to do His work was His own, not one imposed on Him. His independence does not mean that He is not opposed, but it does mean that He is not in danger of being defeated by His foes. He can and does deal with them according to His own plans and purposes. When He chooses, He will call a halt to His opposition. His independence does not mean that He will not respond to us, but it does mean that the response is in keeping with His own nature, promises, and plans. We do not force God to respond to us.

D. God is Infinite in Relation to Space

God's infinity in relation to space is usually spoken of by the term immensity. Immensity refers to the infinity of God's essence in relation to space (1 Kings 8:27; Acts 17:24). The immensity of God forms the basis of His omnipresence which will be discussed later.

E. God is Infinite in Relation to Time

God is eternal. He had no beginning and He will have no end (Deuteronomy 33:27; Job 36:26; Psalm 41:13; 90:2; Isaiah 43:13; 57:15; Romans 1:20; and others).

To some extent we can comprehend eternity future. We can imagine a being not having an end. We cannot comprehend the eternity past of God. We cannot comprehend the idea of a Being without a beginning. Yet, we cannot comprehend God as having a beginning. It is non-imaginable that *nothing* could have produced God. Stephen Charnock's words are appropriate here:

> Though we cannot comprehend eternity, yet we may comprehend that there is an eternity; as though we cannot comprehend the essence of God, what he is, yet we may comprehend that he is; we may understand the notion of his existence, though we cannot understand the infiniteness of his nature.[2]

The most common way theologians describe God's eternity is to refer to it as timelessness. It is said that God has no past and no future. Everything with God is one eternal now. Time is said to be a creation of God and will be terminated by Him. Time is characterized by past, present, and future and has succession of events. Eternity has only the present, thus no succession of events.

Concerning God's relationship to time, Strong, who supports the eternal now view comments:

> Yet, we are far from saying that time, now that it exists, has no objective reality to God. To him, past, present, and future are 'one eternal now,' not in the sense that there is no distinction between them, but only in the sense that he sees past and future as vividly as he sees the present. With creation time began, and since the succession of history are veritable successions, he who sees according to truth must recognize them.[3]

This explanation by Strong of God's relation to time would find general support among theologians holding to the eternal now view. It is my contention that to say the " . . . past, present, and future are 'one eternal now,' . . . only in the sense that he sees the past and future as vividly as he sees the present" contradicts the eternal now view. It confuses omniscience with the eternal now. To see with equal vividness with the present that which God recognizes to be past and future is not the same as saying they are all now to Him.

I think a person has to make a choice between believing in eternal now and believing that God can observe human experiences as past, present, and future. If to God, eternity is one now, all human experiences are one now to Him. It is not the same as saying God sees the past and future as vividly as He sees the present. To Him, what to us is past and future must be viewed as occurring now. This would be a consistent presentation of the eternal now view. It is only when it is consistently presented that it can rightly be spoken of as eternal now.

As I see it, when the eternal now view is consistently presented, it cannot stand. The present moment for me is the only moment that has objective reality. Yesterday had objective reality. Tomorrow will have objective reality. If my yesterday and my tomorrow are objectively real to God, He would have a different standard of objective reality as it relates to me for Himself than He has given to me for myself. This is inconceivable.

Some have argued that just as God fills all space, He fills all eternity, or just as His infinity fills one, it fills the other. Such a conclusion is not necessary. There is a vast amount of difference in the space filled by an elephant and a flea, but now is the same to both.

39

The essence of God fills space. Eternity cannot be filled in the same way. God is eternal in that He has no beginning and no end. The plain language of Scripture tells us that God has duration; a past, a present, and a future (Psalm 90:2; 102:12; Ephesians 3:21; Hebrews 13:8; and others). The question of the vividness with which God sees the past and future will be discussed under omniscience.

Some have sought support for the eternal now view from 2 Peter 3:8: "But, beloved, be not ignorant of this one thing, that one day is with the Lord as a thousand years, and a thousand years as one day." It is not meant that God sees no objective difference between a day and a thousand years. The meaning of the verse is explained in Psalm 90:4: "For a thousand years in thy sight are but as yesterday when it is past, and as a watch in the night."

It is obvious from Psalm 90:4 that it is the subjective experience of time that is under discussion. Objectively, time is the same for a child and an older person. Subjectively, it seems that time passes much more quickly with age. To us a thousand years seems like a long time. To God it does not.

Revelation 10:6 has been used to support the termination of time. The angel said " . . . There should be time no longer." This is to be understood to mean that there will be no further delay. There is nothing in the passage to indicate that it has reference to an ending of time as such.

Part of the whole problem seems to be the problem of thinking of time as having a beginning and an end. Time usually is viewed as the succession of events. On the basis of this definition, it is thought that time began with creation.

Dr. Buswell's definition of time helps at this point. He says, "Time therefore should be defined as the *mere abstract possibility of relationship in durational sequence.*"[4]

Viewed from this angle, time is the possibility of succession of events. The possibility exists whether the events are present or not. Looking at it from this viewpoint, there is no reason for not believing time to be eternal.

Following the same principle, *"Space is the mere abstract possibility of dimensional relationships."*[5] Space would be eternal. Space would not have to be created. Only objects needed to be created.

Dr. Buswell, as one who rejects the eternal now view, says:

> If the past is not past for God as well as man, then we are yet in our sins; Christ has not come and never will come, for He is Deity and therefore timeless. But He is said to have come in the fullness of time *(chronos)* and 'in due time *(kairos).*' If the past is not past for God, we are yet under the wrath and curse of a righteous Judge.[6]

The view of time and eternity that has been set forth has no difficulty recognizing God as the God of history. It has no difficulty seeing the redemptive acts of God in history. It sees God as the King of Kings and Lord of Lords and the Supreme Judge of the universe, but He is not the wholly other whose revelation is an irrational break through as neo-orthodox theologians say.

I am well aware of the fact that the majority of conservative theologians believe in some form of the eternal now view. I do not accuse them of having neo-orthodox tendencies for this reason. The eternal now view is much older than neo-orthodoxy. However, I do raise the question: For one who holds the eternal now view, are there not some logical difficulties in avoiding the view of revelation that the neo-orthodox sets forth in connection with his view of eternity and time? In coping with these difficulties, does one not in effect explain away the eternal now view?

F. God is Immutable

By the immutability of God is meant that He is unchangeable in His essence and attributes. This unchangeableness of God is clearly taught in Scripture (Numbers 23:19; 1 Samuel 15:29; Psalm 33:11; 119: 89-91; Malachi 3:6; Hebrews 6:17; James 1:17; and others).

Some problem is created by verses that speak of God as repenting (Genesis 6:6; Exodus 34:12; 2 Samuel 24:16; Jonah 3:10). Some verses like these are to be explained by the difficulty of describing God and His acts in human language. The experience of human beings that most nearly approximate the Divine experience referred to may be repentance. Yet, some aspects of the human experience may not be applicable to the Divine experience. This would be the case in Genesis 6:6 where " . . . it repented the LORD that he had made man . . . . " Second Samuel 24:16 would also be explained this way.

In other places, repentance represents a change of attitude on the part of God in response to a change of attitude on the part of people. This is in full harmony with His unchangeableness. He is unchangeably committed to change His attitude toward those who change their attitude toward Him. He is also unchangeably committed to answer prayer under certain conditions. Such a change of attitude, instead of representing a change in His essence and attributes, actually demonstrates His unchangeableness in His essence and attributes. Exodus 34:12 and Jonah 3:10 would be explained this way.

Dr. Henry C. Thiessen's comment is helpful at this point:

God's immutability is not like that of a stone that does not respond to changes about it, but like that of a column of mercury which rises and falls according as the temper-

41

ature changes. His immutability consists in His always doing the right and in adapting the treatment of His creatures to the variations in their character and conduct.7

II. THE NATURAL ATTRIBUTES OF GOD

In distinguishing attributes from the basic nature of God, I am viewing the attributes of God as the Divine characteristics that in our conception of them, involve His relationship to His creation. I am not suggesting that He did not have these characteristics before He created. I am saying that in our understanding of them we tend to always think of His relationship to His creation. Any division that we choose to discuss God will have its shortcomings. No approach has all the advantages.

A. God is Omnipresent

Frequently, there is no distinction made between omnipresence and immensity. When a distinction is made, immensity refers to the infinity of God's essence. Omnipresence speaks of God as being present everywhere for a relationship to His creation. It is the immensity of God that forms the basis for His omnipresence.

Wherever we go, God is there (Psalm 139:7-12; Jeremiah 23:23; Acts 17:24-28; and others). We cannot run from His presence to flee His judgment. We will never find ourselves at a place where He is not when we need Him. He is the ever present One.

B. God is Omniscient

When we speak of God as omniscient, we mean that His knowledge is infinite. There is nothing that has existed, does exist, or will exist outside His knowledge. As Thiessen explains:

He knows Himself and all other things, whether they be actual or merely possible, whether they be past, present, or future, and that He knows them perfectly and from all eternity. He knows things immediately, simultaneously, exhaustively and truly.8

Our knowledge is known on two levels. We have a very limited amount of knowledge that is in our conscious mind. The majority of what we know exists in our sub-conscious mind. Some of it is available for instant recall for our conscious mind. Some of it is not recalled so readily. There is no sub-consciousness with God. As

42

Thiessen says, "He knows things immediately."

The scriptural support of God's omniscience is abundant. The following are some selected passages: 1 Kings 8:39; 1 Chronicles 28:9; Job 34:21, 22; 42:2; Psalm 44:21; 147:4, 5; Isaiah 29:15; 40:27, 28; 46:10; Acts 15:18; Hebrews 4:13.

Now, let us pick up the discussion of the vividness with which God knows the past and future that was postponed from our discussion of God's eternity. God sees the past and future as vividly as He sees the present. This is a logical necessity if God is to be omniscient. However, only the present is objectively real to God. The past was objectively real. The future will be objectively real.

When we say that God sees the past and future with a vividness equal to His knowledge of the present, we are thinking about knowledge in two ways: (1) knowledge of facts, and (2) knowledge as subjective reality.

In considering God's knowledge of facts, there is nothing about the past that God knew then, that He does not know now. There is nothing about the present that God knows now, that He did not know in the past. He will not know more about the future when it becomes present than He knows now and has always known.

When we speak of knowing vividly, we are not only thinking of knowing facts, but also of knowing subjectively. The subjective experience of God's knowing the past is the same that it was when it was present. His subjective experience of the present is the same that it was when it was future. His subjective knowledge of the future is the same now that it will be when the future becomes present.

An illustration of subjective reality, where the objective reality is not present, is what happens when we relive an event of the past. The objective reality of the event is gone, but we still view it with subjective reality. The same could be said about anticipation of a future event.

God's factual knowledge of past, present, and future is exhaustive. The subjective reality of past, present, and future knows no difference. Yet, only the present is objectively real to God. We can say, then, that God views the past, present, and future with equal vividness. This is not the same as speaking of all things as being one eternal now with God. To me it is far easier to comprehend. It accords with all scriptural evidence. It is more acceptable.

C. God is Omnipotent

By God's omnipotence, we mean that God can perform any act consistent with His nature. He is never limited in an activity by lack of power (Genesis 17:1; 18:14; Job 42:2; Matthew 19:26; Acts 26:8; Revelation 19:6; and others).

By omnipotence, we do not mean that God can do the

ridiculous and the absurd. There are some things that God cannot do. He cannot lie (Titus 1:2). He cannot make a square circle.

Frequently, in theological discussions, we hear the statement made, "I don't want to limit God." Certainly, we want to be careful, but we do not have to refuse to say under any circumstances, "God cannot do thus and so." Ominpotence does not preclude the possibility that there are some things that God cannot do. It does preclude the possibility that He is ever limited by lack of power. The very nature of His being precludes the possibility that He could do some things.

III. THE MORAL ATTRIBUTES OF GOD

A. God is Holy

One of the main themes of the Old Testament is a declaration and demonstration of the fact that God is holy (Exodus 15:11; Leviticus 19:2; 1 Samuel 2:2; 6:20; Job 34:10; Psalm 47:8; 89:35; 119:9; Isaiah 6:3; 57:15; and others). This theme continues in the New Testament (John 17:11; James 1:13; 1 Peter 1:15, 16; 1 John 1:5; Revelation 4:8; 15:4; and others).

When we think of God as holy, we think of Him as being absolutely free from sin in thought, word, and deed. There is not the slightest taint of sin in Him. He is absolutely pure. As John says, "God is light, and in him is no darkness at all" (1 John 1:5). He cannot in any way condone sin. As Habakkuk says, "Thou art of purer eyes than to behold evil, and canst not look on iniquity . . ." (Habakkuk 1:13).

God as a holy God will not tolerate sin. It is because of God's holiness that "the wrath of God is revealed from heaven against all ungodliness and unrighteousness of men, who hold the truth in unrighteousness" (Romans 1:18). The first revelation of God's holiness is a revelation of judgment. He said to Adam and Eve, "But of the tree of the knowledge of good and evil, thou shalt not eat of it: for in the day that thou eatest thereof thou shalt surely die" (Genesis 2:17). God's judgment against sin reveals His determination to remain holy.

The acts of judgment in Biblical history bear testimony of God's hatred toward sin and His determination to remain holy. The flood, Sodom and Gomorrah, and the many other acts of judgment in the Scriptures leave us no doubt where God stands on the sin issue.

The eternal punishment of the wicked reveals the intolerant attitude of God toward sin. The Bible speaks of the punishment of the wicked with such expressions as, "outer darkness" (Matthew 8:12; 22:13; and 25:30), "furnace of fire" (Matthew 13:42, 50),

44

"everlasting fire" (Matthew 18:8 and 25:41), "everlasting punishment" (Matthew 25:46), "fire unquenchable" (Mark 9:43-48), "everlasting destruction from the presence of the Lord, and from the glory of his power" (2 Thessalonians 1:9), and "the lake which burneth with fire and brimstone: which is the second death" (Revelation 21:8).

The cross of Jesus Christ also reveals God's determination to remain holy. The cross of Christ is an eternal testimony of the fact that God will not forgive sin unless it is first punished. If we see in God a pattern of purity and righteousness but fail to see His hatred of sin, we have failed to understand the Biblical view of holiness.9

God's holy will is an expression of God's holy nature. As Thiessen says: "In God we have purity of being before purity of willing. God does not will the good because it is good, nor is the good good because God wills it; else there would be a good above God or the good would be arbitrary and changeable. Instead, God's will is the expression of his nature, which is holy." 10

We are not to imagine that God can by an arbitrary act of will declare a thing to be holy and it be holy. His will must be a true expression of His nature. It is incompatible with God's nature to declare one person obligated to the morality of the Ten Commandments and to declare a reverse morality for another. Under such an arrangement, God could reign by whim and fancy. We would not know what to expect next.

Thanks to the fact that God's will is an expression of His holy nature, there is a reasonableness to morality. We can discover principles from our study of Scripture and apply them to things not mentioned in the Bible.

Holiness is the basic or fundamental attribute of God. As Thiessen explains: "Because of the fundamental character of this attribute, the holiness of God rather than the love, the power, or the will of God should be given first place. Holiness is the regulative principle of all three of them; for the throne is established on the basis of His *holiness* (Psalm 47:8; 89:14; 97:2).11

This is one of the most important observations to be made in a doctrinal study. When love is made the basic attribute of God, it leads to the idea of universal salvation—an idea that finds no support whatever in Scripture. It also leads to compromise in moral issues. Love that is not subject to holiness is too ready to modify and compromise. It is only when holiness, not love, is seen to be the basic attribute of God that the Biblical doctrines of Hell and atonement can be maintained. It is holiness, not love, that sends sinners to Hell. It is holiness, not love, that demanded that sin be punished before God would forgive sin.

Righteousness and justice flow from God's holiness. When we speak of God as righteous, we mean that He is right in all that He does. Righteousness is an overall term that refers to all of God's

45

dealing as being right.

Justice is an aspect of righteousness. It refers to the fact that God is righteous in His judicial proceedings in handing out punishments and rewards. Remunerative justice is the justice of God that guarantees that obedience will receive its appropriate reward. Retributive justice is the justice of God that guarantees that disobedience will receive its appropriate punishment. Justice is the guardian of God's holiness.

B. God is Loving

That God is a God of love is made abundantly clear in Scripture (Deuteronomy 4:37; 7:7, 8; Psalms 42:8; 63:3; 89:33; 103:13; Jeremiah 31:3; Hosea 11:1; John 3:16; Romans 5:8; 1 John 3:1; 4:8-10; and others). By God's love is meant His affectionate concern. It is expressed in the Scriptures through the words "love," "lovingkindness," "compassion," and "mercy." This love is expressed in God's concern for both man's temporal and his eternal welfare.

The loving concern of God is evidenced in the Old Testament, particularly in the Psalms, but the revelation of God's love reaches a high point with Jesus. Jesus had compassion in action. He was moved with compassion when He saw the sick, the bereaved, and the hungry. One of the most heart-moving scenes in the Scriptures is described for us when Matthew relates the lament of Jesus over Jerusalem: "O Jerusalem, Jerusalem, thou that killest the prophets, and stonest them which are sent unto thee, how often would I have gathered thy children together, even as a hen gathereth her chickens under her wings, and ye would not!" (Matthew 23:37).

As moving as the show of compassion was in the life of Christ, the high point in the revelation of God's love did not come in the life of Christ. The highest point in the revelation of God's love came at the Cross. As Paul tells us, "But God commendeth his love toward us, in that, while we were yet sinners, Christ died for us" (Romans 5:8).

The death that Jesus died for sinners was not just an ordinary death. It was a death in which He paid the penalty for man's sin. He suffered the full wrath of God for man's sin. For the sinless Son of God to pay the full penalty for our sins in order that we who had sinned might be saved was the highest possible manifestation of God's love. God's love for us is real. It is love in action. It is love at a cost. 12

The love of God manifests the deep feeling of concern that God has for us. Some have denied that there is any feeling in God. I am in agreement with Thiessen's comment when he says:

Philosophers frequently deny feeling to God, saying that

46

feeling implies passivity and susceptibility of impression from without, and that such a possibility is incompatible with the idea of the immutability of God. But immutability does not mean immobility. True love necessarily involves feeling, and if there be no feeling in God, then there is no love of God. 13

God feels His love toward us. He feels His wrath toward sin. Explanations of God which deny that He is personal and deny that He has feeling make us think He is not approachable. It is hard for us to believe that He could or would care for us. I believe that such explanations of God grow out of the idea that reason divorced from the rest of our personality has a special gift for finding the truth. I think the reverse is true. We do not set our reason aside, but it functions as a part of our total personality.

When God's love is manifested toward those in misery and distress, we call it mercy. When God's love is manifested toward the ill-deserving, we call it grace because the stress is on the fact that it is unmerited. God's love toward sinners is mercy in that they are in misery and distress. It is grace in that they are ill-deserving.

To be technical, grace is not an attribute of God as such. Grace is a provision of God made possible through atonement. God could not save sinners simply by exercising an attribute of grace. This would be incompatible with His holiness. He can exercise grace only in accord with the provision of atonement and the application of that atonement on the condition of faith.

It is also of interest to note that grace gets its characteristic not only from love, but from holiness. The fact that grace is offered is owed to the love of God. The fact that it is free is owed to the holiness of God. The same holiness which demanded that the full penalty of sin be paid before man could be forgiven also demanded that no more could be collected. Holiness will not tolerate an underpayment nor an overcharge. To charge more than what Christ paid through atonement for our forgiveness would have been an overcharge. Holiness would not tolerate this. Therefore, the characteristic of grace that describes it as an unmerited gift owes its origin to holiness.

The love of God as it is manifested to the good and bad alike is called benevolence. It was this kind of love that Jesus had in mind when He said, "For he maketh his sun to rise on the evil and on the good, and sendeth rain on the just and on the unjust" (Matthew 5:45).

C. God is Wise

The Bible says a lot about the wisdom of God (Proverbs 3:19;

Daniel 2:20, 21; Luke 2:40, 52; 11:49; Romans 11:33; 1 Corinthians 1:24; Ephesians 3:10; and others). I am aware of the fact that it is not customary to list wisdom as a moral attribute of God. As a rule, it gets brief mention in connection with omniscience.

While it is not out of place to consider wisdom in connection with omniscience, I believe it belongs more logically under the moral attributes of God. It is only then that it will be given its proper significance. Consider the value that God places upon wisdom in the following references: Job 28:12-28; Proverbs 3:13-18; 4:5-9; 8:11-21; 16:16, 20-24. A study of God should call attention to the importance of God's wisdom and the fact that there is a corresponding responsibility in us to exercise wisdom. Yet, it is almost passed over in most studies of the attributes of God.

I believe wisdom should be considered under the moral attributes of God because it is impossible to consider wisdom apart from its moral tone. Strong says, "Omniscience, as qualified by holy will, is in Scripture denominated 'wisdom.' In virtue of his wisdom God chooses the highest ends and uses the fittest means to accomplish them." [14]

The following observations from Charnock show that wisdom is moral through and through. He explains:

But in particular, wisdom consists,
1. In acting for a right end. The chiefest part of prudence is in fixing a right end, and in choosing fit means, and directing them to that scope. . . .
2. Wisdom consists in observing all circumstances for action. He is counted a wise man that lays hold of the fittest opportunity to bring his designs about. . . .
3. Wisdom consists, in willing and acting according to the right reason, according to a right judgment of things.[15]

Dr. Anthony A. Hoekema explains: "Wisdom means the application of knowledge to the reaching of a goal. God's wisdom implies that God uses the best possible means to reach the goals He has set for Himself." [16]

God's wisdom works in full harmony with His holiness and love. It sees to it that the best possible interests are carried out. Yet, the moral tone of wisdom is not simply that it acts in accord with holiness and love. The ability to achieve ends under complex circumstances is itself a virtue or a value. The exercise of wisdom is a moral obligation.

Wisdom is one of the most admirable characteristics of God. By His wisdom God is able to direct the affairs of the universe so that His plan will be carried out. This takes into account the freedom of man and the existence of evil. The sovereignty of God is maintained without constant reliance on the brute force of His omnipotence. By

48

God's wisdom He created man a person and allows him the freedom inherent in being a person without forfeiting His sovereignty. It was the wisdom of God that arranged a plan whereby the holiness of God could be satisfied and the love of God could provide redemption for fallen man.

When we begin to see the wisdom of God in proper perspective, we heartily join with Paul when he said, "O the depth of the riches both of the widsom and knowledge of God! how unsearchable are his judgments, and his ways past finding out!" (Romans 11:33).

D. Holiness, Love, and Wisdom are Interrelated

There is a sense in which holiness, love, and wisdom each embrace the other. To subtract love or wisdom from holiness would corrupt holiness. To subtract holiness or wisdom from love would corrupt love. To subtract holiness or love from wisdom would corrupt wisdom. Yet, they are distinct. We do not think of compassion as growing out of holiness. We do not think of wrath as growing out of love. We think of wisdom as arranging the plan of redemption. We think of love as providing it.

IV. THE OVERALL CHARACTERISTICS OF GOD

Some of what I will discuss as overall characteristics of God are usually considered attributes of God. I choose to treat them here because they seem to characterize God as a whole rather than describe a particular characteristic of God.

A. God is a True God and is the God of Truth

God is not a lie as idols are (Romans 1:25). He is real. He exists. He speaks and He acts. Everything He says is true (Titus 1:2). All that is true depends upon Him. Nothing that is true can be fully and ultimately explained without a reference to God.

B. God is Good

Goodness is frequently used to head the category of God's moral attributes. Others have tended to restrict it more to a category under which to consider love and related attributes.

I would agree that goodness embraces both the qualities of holiness and love, but it goes beyond that. It embraces all the qualities of an ideal person. Holiness and love are specific terms that

49

carry great force. Goodness is a general term. It does not seem to do justice to holiness and love to consider them as subpoints under a general term such as goodness. I would prefer to consider it as an overall characteristic of God embracing all the characteristics of an ideal person.

C. God is Glorious

When we think of the glory of God, we think of His splendor. We stand before Him in amazement and wonder. We are awed by His presence. We praise Him. We honor Him. We worship Him.

D. God is Majestic

When we think of the majesty of God, we think of His royal dignity. He is King of kings. He is kingly in the fullest possible sense of the word.

E. God is Perfect

Perfect means complete. Every quality of an ideal person is present in God. None of these qualities exist in short measure in Him.

V. CONCLUDING OBSERVATIONS

What we believe about the nature and attributes of God is of utmost importance. It pervades every area of life and thought. Any thought and any action that is not consistent with the nature and attributes of God will not stand the test.

The four basic values of holiness, love, wisdom, and ideals find their foundation in God. Holiness, love, and wisdom find their foundation in the moral attributes of God. Ideals find their foundation in the overall characteristics of goodness and perfection. God has woven these values into the fabric of truth. If we ignore them, we do it to our own hurt. If our life and thought are guided by them, they form the foundation for true thought and a happy life.

CHAPTER FOUR
NOTES

1. Fred H. Klooster, "The Attributes of God: The Incommunicable Attributes," *Basic Christian Doctrines,* edited by Carl F. H. Henry, New York: Holt, Rinehart and Winston, c. 1962, p. 24.

2. Stephen Charnock, *The Existence and Attributes of God,* Grand Rapids: Kregel Publications, 1958 (a reprint), p. 72.

3. Augustus Hopkins Strong, *Systematic Theology,* three volumes in one, Philadelphia: The Judson Press, c. 1907, seventeenth printing, 1953, p. 277.

4. James Oliver Buswell, Jr., *A Christian View of Being and Knowing,* Grand Rapids: Zondervan Publishing House, c. 1960, p. 47.

5. *Ibid.,* p. 41.

6. James Oliver Buswell, Jr., *A Systematic Theology of the Christian Religion,* Volume I, 2 volumes, Grand Rapids: Zondervan Publishing House, c. 1962, p. 47.

7. Henry Clarence Thiessen, *Introductory Lectures in Systematic Theology,* Grand Rapids: William B. Eerdmans Publishing Company, c. 1949, p. 128.

8. *Ibid.,* p. 124.

9. The material under "God is Holy" up to this point was taken from Leroy Forlines, *Biblical Ethics,* Nashville: Randall House Publications, c. 1973, pp. 10-12. Changes and additions have been made to suit the use in this study.

10. Thiessen, *op. cit.,* p. 129.

11. *Ibid.*

12. The material under "God is Loving" up to this point was taken from Leroy Forlines, *op. cit.,* pp. 12-14. It was adapted for use in this study.

13. Thiessen, *op. cit.,* p. 131.

14. Strong, *op. cit.,* p. 286.

15. Charnock, *op. cit.,* p. 269.

16. Anthony A. Hoekema, "The Attributes of God: The Communicable Attributes," *Basic Christian Doctrines,* edited by Carl F. H. Henry, p. 29.

The Trinity

What we know about God, we know through revelation. We know something of the basic nature of God through general revelation. Since God is a personal being, plus the fact that He does not come within the view of the five senses, we are dependent upon special revelation if we are to know some things about Him. Our knowledge of the fact that God is a Trinity fits into this category. As Warfield observes: "In point of fact, the doctrine of the Trinity is purely a revealed doctrine. That is to say, it embodies a truth which has never been discovered, and is indiscoverable, by natural reason."1

Our belief in the Trinity is not the product of our reason. On the other hand, our reason knows of nothing about the Trinity that is in contradiction to reason. There is no contradiction between "one" and "three" applying to God unless we mean one and three in the same sense. Reason does not have to originate what it believes. Neither does it have to see how it could have originated, on its own, what is received by revelation before it believes it. Reason does not need to fully comprehend what it believes. In fact, in the vast realm of reality, reason expects to encounter difficulty in comprehending some things. It is incomprehensible that our finite minds could completely comprehend every truth. Reason needs to see that what is believed does not contradict reason, and that it forms a part of a vital system of knowledge. Each truth must be seen as a part of an organic whole.

I. THERE IS ONLY ONE GOD

One of the burdens of the Old Testament was to firmly establish in the minds of God's people that there is only one God (Deuteronomy 6:4, 5; 1 Kings 8:60; Isaiah 45:5, 6; 14:18; 46:9).

This conviction is also clearly adhered to in the New Testament (Mark 12:29; 1 Corinthians 8:4-6; James 2:19).

By the very nature of things, there could not be but one who could in the fullest sense of the word be God. We ascribe infinity to God. There can be only one infinite being. The idea of two infinite beings is a logical contradiction. If we try to conceive of two unlimited beings, we run into the problem that if one cannot control the other he is not infinite in power. If he can control the other, the one he controls is not infinite in power. In trying to conceive of two infinite beings, we either conclude that neither is infinite, or we conclude that only one is infinite. We cannot attribute infinity to both. Both Scripture and logic support the conclusion that there is only one God.

The fact that there is only one God rules out the possibility of tritheism which teaches there are three gods, each having a distinct and separate essence. Tritheism has had very few adherents in the history of the church. It mainly serves as an error with which we contrast the proper understanding of the Trinity. Tritheism would maintain that the unity of the Godhead is in purpose and endeavor. We do not question that there is unity of purpose and endeavor between the three persons in the Godhead. However, this is not what we mean when we talk about one God.

When we say that there is one God, we mean that there is only one Being. There is only one essense. There is only one spirit-essence that is shared fully by all three persons.

II. FATHER, SON, AND HOLY SPIRIT ARE EACH DEITY

A. The Father is Deity

Since there is no debate over the deity of the Father, I will mention only a few references in support and will not proceed to develop the argument (2 Corinthians 1:3; Ephesians 1:3; 5:20; Colossians 1:3; and others).

B. The Son is Deity

One of the most seriously contested truths in the history of the church is the deity of Christ. Yet, it is clearly and unquestionably taught in Scripture both by direct statement and by necessary inference.

He is called God (John 1:1; 20:28; Titus 2:13; Hebrews 1:8; and others). The Jehovahs' Witnesses, who deny the deity of Christ, have insisted that John 1:1 cannot be used in support of the deity of Christ. In the statement " . . . the Word was God," there is no article in the Greek before the word God. They insist that it should be translated "The Word was a god."

To insist on the translation "a god" will not stand for the following reasons: (1) It would contradict the clear teachings of Scripture in other places which clearly indicate that Jesus is God in the fullest sense of the word. (2) It shows a lack of understanding the use of the article and the absence of the article in Greek. As Dana and Mantey explain: "The articular construction emphasizes *identity;* the anarthrous [without the article] construction emphasizes *character.*" On the basis of this distinction they explain that the Greek construction without the article in the word was God "emphasizes Christ's participation in the essence of the divine nature." 2 The emphasis is on the Divine nature of the Word. This understanding is true to the Greek and consistent with the whole of Scripture. It should also be pointed out that the presence of the article with "Word" and the absence of the article with God make it clear that "The Word" is the subject of the sentence. (3) There are many clear-cut references to deity where the article is not used. There are so many that it is hard to conceive of the idea that anyone would conclude that the absence of the article in John 1:1 would indicate that Jesus was less than God in the full sense of the word. Some references from John in which the reference is clearly to deity, which have no article in the Greek before God, should be adequate in rebuttal to such claims (John 1:6, 12, 18; 3:2 (first occurrence of the word "God" in the verse); and 16:30).

Some may want to question the use of Titus 2:13 as a claim that Jesus is called God. They may want to say "the great God and our Saviour Jesus Christ" refers to two persons rather than one. Dana and Mantey quote Granville Sharp, who explains:

> When the copulative *kai* connects two nouns of the same case, if the article *ho* or any of its cases precedes the first of the said nouns or participles, and is not repeated before the second noun or participle, the latter always relates to the same person that is expressed or described by the first noun or participle; i.e., it denotes a farther description of the first-named person.3

Dana and Mantey proceed to point out that the same Greek construction referred to by Granville Sharp is found in 2 Peter 2:20 where it indicates that Jesus is both Lord and Savior. They also point to 2 Peter 1:1 where it means that Jesus is our God and Savior and to Titus 2:13 where it is asserted that Jesus is our great God and Savior.4

In furthering our proof of the deity of Christ, we observe that He is called the Son of God (Matthew 14:33; 16:16; 17:5; Mark 1:1; 5:7; 14:61, 62; 15:39; Luke 9:35; 10:22; John 1:34; 3:16; 9:35-37; 20:31; and others).

It is clear that Jews understood Jesus to be claiming to be deity when He claimed to be the Son of God. We read: "Therefore the Jews sought the more to kill him, because he not only had broken the sabbath, but said also that God was his Father, making himself equal with God" (John 5:18). It is also clear from their charge and Jesus' answer in John 10:33-36 that they equated the claim of being the Son of God with being God. Jesus did not deny the charge. Rather, He defended His right to make the claim (John 10:34-38).

Warfield observes:

> It may be very natural to see in the designation 'Son' an intimation of subordination and derivation of Being, . . . But it is quite certain that this was not the denotation . . . in the Semitic consciousness, which underlies the phraseology of Scripture; and it may be thought doubtful whether it was included even in their remote suggestions. What underlies the conception of sonship in Scriptural speech is just 'likeness'; whatever the father is that the son is also. The emphatic application of the term 'Son' to one of the Trinitarian Persons, accordingly, asserts rather His equality with the Father than His subordination to the Father.5

A third proof of Jesus' deity is the fact that He had the power to forgive sins. In Mark 2:1-11, Jesus said to the paralytic, "Son, thy sins be forgiven thee" (verse 5). The scribes objected saying, "Why doth this man thus speak blasphemies? Who can forgive sins but God only?" (verse 7).

Jesus did not deny their charge that no one but God could forgive sins. Rather, He said:

Whether is it easier to say to the sick of the palsy, Thy sins be forgiven thee; or to say, Arise, and take up thy bed, and walk? But that ye may know that the Son of man hath power on earth to forgive sins, (he saith to the sick of the palsy,) I say unto thee, Arise, and take up thy bed, and go thy way into thine house (verses 9-11).

Another proof of Jesus' deity is the fact that He was and is the object of worship (Matthew 2:2; 9:18; 14:33; 15:25; 20:20; 28:9; Mark 5:6; Luke 24:52; John 5:23; Revelation 5:8-14; and others). The Scriptures make it clear that only God is to be worshiped. Yet, Jesus was worshiped. He never denounced anyone for worshiping Him. He accepted it.

In the temptation, Jesus made it clear that God and God alone was the object of worship. He said to Satan, " . . . For it is written, Thou shalt worship the Lord thy God, and him only shalt thou serve" (Matthew 4:10).

After the healing of a crippled man in Lystra, the people thought Paul and Barnabas were gods and were going to offer sacrifices to them. At such a thought as receiving worship, Paul and Barnabas rent their clothes and assured the people that they were fellow human beings and were not to be worshiped (Acts 14:8-18).

In the Book of Revelation, on two occasions John was going to worship an angel that was speaking to him. The angel assured John that he was a fellowservant and was not to be worshiped (Revelation 19:9, 10; 22:8, 9).

In Acts 12, we read of the fate of Herod who was ready to be acclaimed a god after delivering an oration. "And immediately the angel of the Lord smote him, because he gave not God the glory: and he was eaten of worms, and gave up the ghost" (Acts 12:23).

In the light of the above observations, there can be no doubt that the fact that Jesus is a proper object of worship is an unquestionable proof of His deity. He made no refusal like Paul, Barnabas, and the angel John was about to worship. He met with no fate such as Herod. Truly, He is God!

A fifth proof of His deity is the fact that He has existed from all eternity (Micah 5:2; John 1:1-3; and Colossians 1:17). Only God exists from eternity. Yet, Jesus has existed from eternity. Therefore, He is God.

Other proofs could be added, but the case already built is more than adequate. There can be no justification for denying the deity of Christ, or understanding the term to have any less or any different significance when applied to the Son than when applied to the Father.

C. The Holy Spirit is Deity

The main issue concerning the Divine nature of the members of the Trinity has always centered in Jesus. There does not seem to have been any widescale attempt to advocate a binitarian view of the Godhead consisting of the Father and Son, but failing to grant deity to the Holy Spirit. Therefore, I will give only limited attention to supporting the deity of the Holy Spirit.

When we see the Holy Spirit in Scripture, we always receive the impression that He is a member of the Godhead. The reference to the Holy Spirit in Matthew 28:19 and 2 Corinthians 13:14 view the Holy Spirit as being equal with the Father and the Son.

The strongest support for the deity of the Holy Spirit comes from references in which He is called God. In Acts 5:3 Peter asked Ananias, "Why hath Satan filled thine heart to lie to the Holy Ghost?" In Acts 5:4, Peter said to Ananias, " . . . Thou hast not lied unto men, but unto God." In 1 Corinthians 3:16 Paul says, "Know ye not that ye are the temple of God, and that the Spirit of God dwelleth in you?" The Spirit of God dwells in the temple of God. It is clear that the Spirit of God is viewed as God. In 1 Corinthians

12:4-11, Paul elaborates on the various ways the Holy Spirit works in us through bestowing gifts upon us. In verse 6 with reference to this work of the Holy Spirit, Paul explains: "And there are diversities of operations, but it is the same God which worketh all in all." The Holy Spirit is clearly referred to here as God.

III. FATHER, SON, AND HOLY SPIRIT ARE EACH DISTINCT PERSONS

A. Modalism Fails to see Three Persons in the Godhead

The support presented above for the belief in one God and for the belief in the deity of the Father, the Son, and the Holy Spirit has been acceptable to some who have fallen short of a Trinitarian view of the Godhead. The view known as modalism was introduced into the third century by Sabellius. Sabellius believed in a Trinity of revelation, not an ontological Trinity. (An ontological Trinity is a Trinity of being. God is a Trinity in the very nature of His being.)

There have been varying shades of modalism, but there are basically two types: (1) The names of God are names for particular periods in the history of revelation: The Father in creation and the giving of the Law, the Son in redemption, and the Holy Spirit in regeneration and sanctification. Some might say He was Father in the Old Testament, Son in the Gospels, and the Holy Spirit in Acts and continuing in the church. (2) The names are understood as titles relating to the different functions such as one person may be a father, husband, and businessman. This is similar to the first, but differs in that God can be viewed as all three at the same time.

Before setting forth the positive teaching of Scripture that will support Trinitarianism and show the fallacy of modalism, let us first take a look at two suggested proofs of modalism. In John 10:30, Jesus said, "I and my Father are one." It is felt by some that they have found irrefutable proof that Jesus taught that the Father and the Son were one person.

A very interesting parallel is found in 1 Corinthians 3:8, "Now he that planteth and he that watereth are one." The Greek for "are one" is *hen eisin* in 1 Corinthians 3:8. The Greek for "are one" in John 10:30 is *hen esmen*. The construction is identical except that in 1 Corinthians 3:8 *eisin* is third person plural to correspond with the subject, "he that planteth and he that watereth." In John 10:30 *esmen* is first person plural to correspond with the subject, "I and my Father."

In 1 Corinthians 3:8, "he that planteth and he that watereth" definitely refer to two persons; namely, Paul and Apollos. If 1 Corinthians refers to two persons as "one," there is no reason whatever that the Father and Son cannot be two persons who are said to be one. The very fact that Jesus said, "My Father" makes it far more suitable to think of them as being two persons instead of one person.

In what sense were Paul and Apollos one? They were one in that there was no division among them. They were in agreement. The church was becoming divided over Paul and Apollos; yet, Paul and Apollos were in agreement. They were one.

Jesus and the Father are one in that they are in total agreement, but the oneness goes much deeper than that. That could be true in Tritheism. They are one in that they have the same essence.

The singular use of the word "name" in Matthew 28:19 has frequently been urged as proof that "the Father, Son, and Holy Spirit" are all one person in this verse. The name of this person is said to be Jesus.

A case cannot be built for the conclusion that the singular use of the word "name" requires that the Father, Son, and Holy Spirit all have one name. In 1 Samuel 14:49, the first occurrence of the word "name" is in the plural in the English translation, but in the Hebrew it is singular, yet it is followed by two names. The same thing happens in 1 Samuel 17:13. The singular is used of the word "name" and it is followed by three names. It is not impossible that something similar to this could have happened in Matthew 28:19.

Though the above explanation shows that one cannot build a conclusive case from the singular use of "name" for saying that there must be one name applied to the Father, Son, and Holy Spirit, I think there is a more probable explanation for the verse. The use of the word "name" in Scripture, as can be seen by the use of a concordance, is not limited to the designation by which a person is called. "Name" refers to the person, his character, his reputation, his power, his authority, etc. When Proverbs 22:1 says, "A good name is rather to be chosen than great riches . . ." it is clear that it is not referring to a good first name, nor a good last name, but a good reputation based on good character. When Peter said in Acts 3:16, "And his name through faith in his name hath made this man strong," he meant the power and authority of Jesus Christ.

In keeping with the Biblical use of the word "name," which also finds parallels in our own use of the word, it seems best not to understand "name" in Matthew 28:19 as a designation, whether thinking of one or three, by which a person (or persons) is called. Rather, the name refers to the character, power, and authority of the Father, Son, and Holy Spirit.

B. The Father, Son, and Holy Spirit have Objective Relationships one to Another

The Father says, "This is my beloved Son" (Matthew 3:17).

58

The Father sent the Son (John 3:34; 14:24). The Father loves the Son (John 13:35). The Father sent the Holy Spirit (John 14:16, 26).

The Son prayed to the Father (John 17). The Son went to the Father (John 16:16). The Son sent the Holy Spirit (John 16:7).

The Holy Spirit testifies of the Son (John 15:26). The Holy Spirit glorifies the Son (John 16:14).

The interrelationships within the members of the Godhead rule out that form of modalism that sees the names Father, Son, and Holy Spirit as titles relating to the different functions of God. It is true that one person may be father, husband, and businessman, but he does not in these roles experience inter-personal relationships. All of us have more than one role in life, but a writing of our autobiography or biography would not lead people to think one of us as being two or more sane, intelligent persons. We cannot escape the fact that in the New Testament we see God as three distinct persons.

C. The Father, Son, and Holy Spirit are Concurrent

All three were present at the baptism of Jesus (Matthew 3:16, 17; Mark 1:10, 11; Luke 3:21, 22). The reference to the Father, Son, and Holy Spirit in Matthew 28:19 and 2 Corinthians 13:14 also indicate that the Father, Son, and the Holy Spirit are concurrent.

The concurrence of the Father, Son, and Holy Spirit rule out the modalism which says that the names of God are names for particular periods in the history of revelation.

An error is commonly made by Trinitarians when they speak of the Father being revealed in the Old Testament, the Son in the Gospels, and the Holy Spirit in Acts and the epistles. In the Old Testament, God was revealed as God without reference to which person was being revealed. In the New Testament, we have the revelation of the Trinity. It is true that Jesus is the center of the gospels, but it is also the time of the revelation of the Father and Holy Spirit as distinct members of the Godhead. It is true that we receive a greater understanding of the Holy Spirit beginning with Acts, but the Son continues to be the central person so far as the focus of redemptive revelation is concerned.

We know less about the doctrine of the Father, so far as His distinct role is concerned, than we do about the roles of the Son and Holy Spirit. In a few books, the section dealing with nature and attributes of God is called the doctrine of the Father. This is an error. What is said about the nature and attributes of God is equally true of the Father, Son, and Holy Spirit. Some books may make a few specific statements about the Father, but this does not justify calling the section the doctrine of the Father.

I am not aware of any well-developed doctrine of God the

Father. Perhaps, this is not as unfortunate as it seems in view of the roles of the Son and Holy Spirit in redemption and our need of knowledge of these roles. Part of the reason for the lack of a well-developed doctrine of God the Father is the fact that His role is not always as easily distinguished as that of the Son and Holy Spirit. Perhaps, for that reason, we are about as well off to have our discussion of the Father interwoven with our discussion of the Son and Holy Spirit.

IV. THE TRINITY IS INTIMATED IN THE OLD TESTAMENT

Without the aid of the New Testament revelation, no one would read a Trinitarian concept out of the Old Testament. However, once the Trinity is revealed we can with the aid of that revelation see that some statements of the Old Testament are better understood in the light of the Trinitarian revelation. As Warfield explains:

> The Old Testament may be likened to a chamber richly furnished but dimly lighted; the introduction of light brings into it nothing which was not in it before; but it brings out into clearer view much of what is in it but was only dimly or even not at all perceived before. The mystery of the Trinity is not revealed in the Old Testament; but the mystery of the Trinity underlies the Old Testament revelation, and here and there almost comes into view. [6]

A. There are Clear Intimations of the Trinity in the Old Testament

In speaking, God uses the plural pronoun "us" (Genesis 1:26; 3:22; 11:7). Once the revelation of the Trinity has been made known, it seems clear that we should understand the "us" in these references as referring to the persons in the Trinity.

Having seen the revelation of the Son in the New Testament, we would naturally interpret the Father and Son in Psalm 2:7 which reads: "I will declare the decree: the LORD hath said unto me, Thou art my Son; this day have I begotten thee." Having seen the Holy Spirit as a distinct person in the New Testament, we would interpret references such as Genesis 1:2; 6:3; and Psalm 51:11 as making references to the Holy Spirit.

In Hosea 1:7, it seems that we see two Divine persons rather than one. "But I will have mercy upon the house of Judah, and will save them by the LORD their God." "I" and "the LORD their God" seem to be, in the light of the Trinitarian revelation, a reference to two persons in the Trinity.

B. Some Suggested Intimations of the Trinity in the Old Testament Seem to be Invalid

One of the most commonly suggested intimations of the Trinity in the Old Testament is the use of the plural name for God, Elohim. Though it is plural it is used with a singular verb in Genesis 1:1, 26, and 48:15. The use of a plural, I think, is properly understood by Dr. G. F. Oehler. After rejecting various interpretations of the plural, among them being that it implies the Trinity, he explains:

> It is much better to explain Elohim as the *quantitative plural*, which is used to denote unlimited greatness in *shamayim* [heavens] and *mayim* [waters]. The plural signifies *infinite fulness* of the might and power which lies in the Divine Being, and thus passes over into the *intensive plural*, as Delitzsch has named it.[7]

Another illustration of the intensive plural is found in Isaiah 53:9. The word "death" is plural in the Hebrew. The plural was used to show that this was not just an ordinary death.

There is justification for using the intensive plural to show the greatness of God. To seek to show the plurality of persons by using the plural for the name *God* would run the risk of Tritheism.

What is referred to as the Trisagia (an expression where the word "holy" is repeated three times with reference to God) in Isaiah 6:3 is thought by some to be an intimation of the Trinity. I fail to see in the repetition of the word holy three times any reference to three persons. It seems far more likely that it is intended to magnify the holiness of God.

Some see in the threefold blessing of the Aaronic benediction in Numbers 6:24-26 a blessing from each member of the Trinity. Again, I see no connection. The only connection is in three blessings and there are three persons in the Trinity. It seems to take more connection than that to read an inference of the Trinity from the passage.

V. HOW DO WE EXPLAIN THE TRINITY?

Frequently, though he has a clear faith in the Trinity, a person will tend to drift toward Tritheism or Modalism in his attempt to explain the Trinity. For this reason, we must consider a person's training and ability to express himself before we judge him a heretic on the basis of the way he explains the Trinity. The explanation that explains the oneness of God as unity of purpose and endeavor does not distinguish itself properly from Tritheism. There is unity of purpose and endeavor between the persons in the Godhead, but that is not what is meant by the fact that God is one God. When we say that there is only one God, we mean that there is only one Divine essence. Each person shares the entire Divine essence.

We have to be careful when we explain the Trinity by saying that there are three personal manifestations. That could mean three persons who manifest themselves, or it could mean one person who manifests himself three ways as in modalism. It is better to use the word "persons" rather than personal manifestations to avoid confusion.

The word "person" is better than the word "personality." Though it is possible to use person and personality in the same way, there is a tendency to think of personality more in terms of personality traits. If we say that there are three personalities in the Godhead, we run the risk of someone taking us to mean that the Father, Son, and Holy Spirit have different personality traits. This is not the case. The use of the word person helps avoid this misunderstanding.

The main thing to keep in mind is that there are three persons in one essence. As additional clarifying statements, we can say each person shares the entire essence. The personal distinctions are eternal. The persons are equal. Each person can say "I." With reference to others, He can address them as "Thou," or He can refer to each of the others as "He."

Illustrations of the Trinity are risky. They either illustrate Tritheism or Modalism. The one egg made up of yolk, white, and shell illustrates Tritheism because the yolk, white, and shell each have a different essence. The illustration of the 3 members of a family making up one family illustrates Tritheism because each member has a different essence. The illustration of water, steam, and ice illustrates Modalism because, though they have the same substance or essence, they are not concurrent. No illustration properly illustrates both the oneness and threeness of God.

VI. HOW ARE WE TO UNDERSTAND THE NAMES FATHER, SON, AND HOLY SPIRIT?

Do the names have an ontological significance? Another way of putting it is: Is there something in the very nature of the Trinity that causes the Father by His nature to be called Father, the Son by His nature to be called Son, and the Holy Spirit by His nature to be called Holy Spirit? Or are the names Father, Son, and Holy Spirit related to their functions in the economy of redemption?

Since there should be less difficulty in making the decision, let us begin with the name Holy Spirit. Is there something about the very nature of the Holy Spirit that causes Him to be called Holy Spirit rather than one of the others, or is it because of His function?

If the word "Spirit" is in His name because He has a spirit-essence, the same is equally true of the other members of the Trinity. If the word "Holy" is in His name because He is holy, the same is equally true of the other members of the Trinity. Is He not called the Holy Spirit because of His special ministry to convict us of sin, draw people to Christ, regenerate those who believe, and continue the work of sanctification in believers? In short, He is to work in us to make us holy people.

If we can accept the view of functional significance with reference to the name Holy Spirit, it should not be so painful to do the same with reference to the Father and Son. The problem here comes from the doctrine of the eternal generation of the Son from the Father.

Origen introduced the doctrine of the eternal generation of the Son in the third century. It has been generally accepted by orthodox theologians. There are some, however, who disagree. After carefully examining what is thought to be scriptural support for the doctrine of the eternal generation of the Son, Dr. Buswell comments:

> We have above examined all the instances in which 'begotten' or 'born' or related words are applied to Christ, and we can say with confidence that the Bible has nothing whatsoever to say about 'begetting' as an eternal relationship between the Father and the Son.
>
> The suggestion that we completely drop the doctrine of eternal generation of the Son is somewhat revolutionary. We might be misunderstood . . . . Yet I do believe that the 'eternal generation' doctrine should be dropped.[8]

The eternal generation of the Son from the Father refers to an eternal emanation of the Son from the Father. It is not an emanation or generation of the essence because He has the same essence as the Father. It is a generation of the person. This is not supposed to mean that the Father was before the Son because the generation was eternal. Those who hold to this view consider the generation of the Son by the Father to be the basis of the names Father and Son. The names Father and Son are thus considered to have an ontological significance.

After referring to John 3:16; 5:26; 10:38; 14:11; 17:21; and Hebrews 1:3 as verses used to support the eternal generation of the Son, Dr. Loraine Boettner remarks:

> The present writer feels constrained to say, however, that in his opinion the verses quoted do not teach the doctrine in question. He feels that the primary purpose of these verses is to teach that Christ is intimately associated with the Father, that He is equal with the Father in power

and glory, that He is, in fact, full Deity, rather than to teach that His Person is generated by or originates in an eternal process which is going on in the Godhead. Even though the attempt is made to safeguard the essential equality of the Son by saying that the process by which He is generated is eternal and necessary, he does not feel that the attempt is successful.9

To me the expression "eternal generation" is self-contradictory. Generation implies a process that has a beginning. Eternal denies the idea of beginning. To try to modify generation by eternal attempts to deny the idea of beginning. The whole idea of an eternal generation is incomprehensible. It is not incomprehensible simply because it is beyond comprehension, but because it speaks of a process that implies beginning as though it has no beginning.

We do not refuse to believe an idea because it is incomprehensible, but when it is incomprehensible because it appears self-contradictory, it would require unquestionable support in the Biblical revelation before we should be expected to believe it. The verses cited above along with Psalm 2:7 fail to make such an impression on me. For those who would like a thorough examination of the main verses used to support eternal generation, I would recommend Dr. Buswell's treatment cited above, pages 106-11.

At this point attention needs also to be given to the eternal procession from the Father and Son of the Holy Spirit. It is basically the same as the eternal generation of the Son except the Son is generated from the Father while the Holy Spirit proceeds from the Father and the Son.

John 15:26 is the verse used to support the eternal procession of the Holy Spirit. The words "proceedeth from the Father" are adequately understood as being sent by the Father as He was sent on the day of Pentecost. I would present the same case against the eternal procession of the Holy Spirit that I did against the eternal generation of the Son. It is doubtful that anyone believes in the eternal procession of the Holy Spirit who does not believe in the eternal generation of the Son. Both Dr. Buswell and Dr. Boettner reject the doctrine of the eternal procession of the Holy Spirit.

I have already pointed out that I think the name Holy Spirit is a functional name rather than an ontological name. The name Holy Spirit is fully consistent with the ontological nature of the Holy Spirit, but the same could also be said about the Father and Son.

If the doctrine of the eternal generation of the Son from the Father fails, there are no grounds for granting an ontological significance to the name Father and Son as members of the Trinity. There is nothing in the names Father and Son that is contrary to the ontological nature of the Father and the Son, but there is nothing distinctive in the ontological nature of each that would make the names more appropriate for one than the other.

The names Father and Son seem to have been chosen for the members of the Trinity designated Father and Son because their functional relationship in redemption, particularly as it relates to the incarnation, somewhat parallels a father and son relationship. There is certainly no ontological subordination of one member of the Trinity to another, but there is some voluntary functional subordination in some developments in the economy of redemption. There is a voluntary subordination of the Son to the Father (John 6:38, 39; Luke 22:41, 42; and others). The fact that the Holy Spirit is sent by the Father and Son (John 14:16, 26; 15:26) implies some functional subordinations.

Warfield observes:

> It may be natural to assume that a subordination in modes of operation rests on a subordination in modes of subsistence; that the reason why it is the Father that sends the Son and the Son sends the Spirit is that the Son is subordinate to the Father, and the Spirit to the Son. But we are bound to bear in mind that these relations of subordination in modes of operation may just as well be due to a convention, and agreement, between the Persons of the Trinity—a 'covenant' as it is technically called—by virtue of which a distinct function in the work of redemption is voluntarily assumed by each. [10]

As long as we realize that the subordination refers to a voluntary arrangement, and not an ontological subordination, there is no inequality implied.

One more question remains: Are the names Father, Son, and Holy Spirit eternal names of the persons? I would say, yes, not based on ontological significance, but based on the fact that the redemptive plan is an eternal plan. In eternal anticipation of the functions ascribed to each member of the Trinity they have been eternally Father, Son, and Holy Spirit.

CHAPTER FIVE
NOTES

1. B. B. Warfield, *Biblical Foundation*, Grand Rapids: William B. Eerdmans Publishing Company, 1958, p. 79.

2. H. E. Dana and Julius R. Mantey, *A Manual Grammar of the Greek New Testament*, New York: The MacMillan Company, c. 1927, renewed in 1955, p. 140.

3. *Ibid.*, p. 147.

4. *Ibid.*

5. Warfield, *op. cit.*, p. 109.

6. *Ibid.*, pp. 87, 88.

7. Gustav Friedrich Oehler, *Theology of the Old Testament*, a revision of the translation in Clark's Theological Library by George E. Day, Grand Rapids: Zondervan Publishing House, a reprint of the 1873 edition, p. 88.

8. James Oliver Buswell, Jr., *A Systematic Theology of the Christian Religion*, Volume I, 2 volumes, Grand Rapids: Zondervan Publishing House, c. 1962, pp. 111, 112.

9. Loraine Boettner, *Studies In Theology*, Grand Rapids: William B. Eerdmans Publishing Company, c. 1947, p. 121.

10. Warfield, *op. cit.*, p. 111.

Why We Believe in God and the Bible

Since God does not fall within the view of the five senses, the question, "Why do we believe in God?" is an important one. At times it may be a troublesome question. It is troublesome if someone raises a question for which we do not have the answer. Questions may arise from within us for which we do not have ready answers.

Part of the problem is that we are talking about "faith-knowledge," rather than "sight-knowledge" or "sense-knowledge" (that known through the five senses), when we talk about believing in God. In faith-knowledge, we believe something to be true that does not fall within the view of our five senses.

Even in our daily experiences we have faith-knowledge. We believe something to be true that does not, at the time of our believing it, fall within the view of the five senses. It may, however, in principle be capable of being observed, but we believe it before it is observed.

Faith-knowledge is illustrated by what took place when some men took me 'coon (racoon) hunting once. The dogs barked which indicated that they had treed something. I was a novice at 'coon hunting, but my partners were old hands at it. They assured me that there was a 'coon up the tree. I did not see it, neither did they because the leaves were too thick on the tree. One of the men did see what looked like a reflection from the eye of an animal when he shined his flashlight up the tree. They assured me that there was a 'coon up the tree on the following grounds: (1) The dogs would not continue to bark if they were not sure that something was up the tree. (2) The tree was larger than 'possums (oppossum) usually climbed, but not too large for a 'coon. (3) If there were need for proof, the reflection of light was a sure indication that an animal was up the tree. Based on the integrity of the hunters, their experience in coon hunting, and their confidence in the dogs, I, too, believed that there was a 'coon up the tree. That was faith-knowledge because I did not see a 'coon.

It will be observed that while my knowledge of a 'coon up the tree was faith-knowledge, it was not without an involvement of reason. The reasons did not furnish absolute proof of the fact that there was a 'coon up the tree, but the reasons did make believing completely compatible with reason.

I realize that my faith-knowledge in God differs from my faith-knowledge of the 'coon in the tree. These men had seen 'coons up trees. No person has seen God. Yet, I think the mere fact that I was believing something I did not see, hear, touch, taste, or smell means that there are at least some comparisons. The main comparisons with which I am concerned are: (1) We do make use of faith-knowledge. (2) Reason is involved in faith-knowledge.

I. THE RELATIONSHIP BETWEEN REASON AND FAITH

There are various opinions regarding the relationship between reason and faith. They range anywhere from complete confidence in reason to support faith to a total rejection of any possible involvement in faith.

By faith as we are using it now, we are referring to faith in God and the Bible, or to speak more broadly, religious faith, or knowledge of what is in the upper story. This would be using the divisions lower story and upper story as used by Francis A. Schaeffer in *Escape From Reason*. (Reference was made to Schaeffer's use of the upper and lower stories in chapter 2 under the heading: "The Current Scene.")

A. Complete Confidence in Reason To Support Faith

Some are boldly confident that the arguments for the existence of God offer absolute proof that God exists. The arguments are foolproof.

B. Reason Not Involved in Faith

This view restricts the working area of reason to the lower story. Reason only works with sense data. Reason does not apply to the upper story. The upper story is irrational. Faith, with reference to the upper story, is neither produced by reason, nor is it subject to examination by reason.

68

C. A Distrust in Reason

This view does not accept the idea that what is in the upper story is irrational, but it does distrust the reasoning power of man, especially as it is affected by the fall of man into sin. The advocates of this view do not hesitate to use reason when it seems to be of value, but they retreat into distrust for reason when difficulty arises. They call attention to verses like 1 Corinthians 1:21 where Paul said: "For after that in the wisdom of God the world by wisdom knew not God, it pleased God by the foolishness of preaching to save them that believe." They also call attention to 1 Corinthians 2:14 which reads: "But the natural man receiveth not the things of the Spirit of God: for they are foolishness unto him: neither can he know them, because they are spiritually discerned."

D. Reason Involved in Faith

This view differs from the first view in that it does not propose to give absolute proof for faith-knowledge. It differs from the second view in that it has a place for reason in upper story knowledge. The difference between this view and the third view vary from person to person depending on the degree of distrust the person has of reason. Since the third view does not make a complete rejection of reason in faith-knowledge, there will be some likeness. The use the third view makes of reason will be far more in accord with the fourth view than the first view. At times those who distrust reason make it sound as if reason has no place at all in faith. In fact, they make it sound as if reason is an enemy of faith. At other times they use reason.

I think the proper relationship between reason and faith is seen in the fourth view. There is a caution given in Scripture. A limitation is placed on the ability of reason. Paul refers to this in 1 Corinthians 1:21 and 2:9. I do not think these verses can be explained simply as speaking against fallacious reasoning. They definitely place limits on reason. The world by widsom (reason) did not arrive at a knowledge of God (1 Corinthians 1:21). The scientific and philosophical approach to knowledge cannot discover redemptive truth (1 Corinthians 2:9). These observations do not nullify the validity of the use of reason in these areas of thought, but they do limit the use of reason.

I do not believe that the view which places complete confidence in reason to give absolute proof for faith-knowledge is consistent with the limitation imposed on reason in the verses referred to previously. Also, I do not believe the proofs given for believing in God and the Bible offer absolute proof. This will be seen when we examine these proofs.

I believe the second and third views are untenable in view of the make-up of man. We are so constructed that we cannot possibly set reason aside. Even those who propose to set reason aside give reasons for it. If John says, "I saw Joe at the airport," we subconsciously test the statement to see if it is reasonable to accept it as true. If John knows Joe; if John is an honest person; if we know of no reason to doubt that Joe was at the airport; and if we know of no bad motives John could have for saying he saw Joe at the airport if he were not; we accept his statement as true. If John does not know Joe well; if John's veracity is in question; if we had good reason to believe Joe was somewhere else; or if we know of a motive John would have for lying about whether Joe was at the airport; we will question John's statement or reject it altogether. If the answer is not immediately obvious, we will analyze it in our conscious mind. We cannot hear John say, "I saw Joe at the airport" and give no rational thought whatsoever to it. If the answer is not immediately obvious, we may decide it is not important enough for us to settle, but that, too, will be a rational decision.

I have used the illustration above to show how our rational minds are continually at work judging, analyzing, and assessing. It cannot be otherwise. Our decision to try to deliberately turn off our reason is itself a decision made by reason. Those who distrust reason use it anyway. Those who try to deny reason a place in some areas of knowledge never fully succeed. The very effort to crush the reasoning process in us is painful and creates problems. Our inner being cries out for meaning and purpose in life. We long to see truth as a unified whole.

When we say that reason is involved in faith, we are not saying that reason gives absolute proof for faith. We are saying that reason considers what is believed in faith-knowledge to be reasonable. It is safe for believing. Taken in the total context of life and reality, what we believe in faith-knowledge may be the only alternative that we feel to be safe. We may feel compelled to believe it, but we do not do so on the grounds that we have answered all the questions.

II. AN EXAMINATION OF THE ARGUMENTS
FOR THE EXISTENCE OF GOD

At this point, my interest is to state the arguments and show that they do not prove in the absolute sense of the word. The positive value from the reasoning involved will be set forth later when I discuss why we believe in God.

A. The Cosmological Argument

This is probably the most widely used of all the arguments for God's existence. It argues from effect to cause. Every thing that has a

70

beginning is an effect, and therefore, must have a cause. That cause is God.

The problem is: How do we know the universe had a beginning? Can we prove it? Does not our confidence that the universe had a beginning belong in the category of faith-knowledge? If we work on the assumption that the universe did have a beginning, how do we know that the cause that produced the universe was not itself the product of another cause? This type reasoning could go on endlessly. It is easy enough to know what we believe about whether the universe had a beginning. It is easy to reject the idea of endless causes, but have we proved our point in each case?

B. The Teleological Argument

The teleological argument argues from the presence of design in the universe to the existence of a designer. The presence of order, harmony, and signs of purpose in the universe are said to argue for the existence of an intelligent cause who is God. This argument presupposes the effect to cause argument involved in the cosmological argument. It would, therefore, have all the weakness of the cosmological argument.

While the presence of order and harmony are impressive, one could raise the question: What about the presence of disorder and disharmony? Do they tell us something about the originating cause? We may feel that we have an answer to this question, but we must admit the problem.

C. The Moral Argument

This is another effect to cause argument. The effect in this case is the feeling of moral imperative in man. Since man would like at times to escape this moral imperative, it does not seem adequate to think of it as self-imposed. The existence of God as a Lawgiver is considered the cause of the moral imperative.

Without relying upon Divine revelation, can we prove, in the sense of absolute proof, that morality is not the product of culture? Can we prove that moral ideas have not originated from the interaction of people in society? These are not my ideas, but I do recognize the problem of proving them to be an impossible alternative so far as proving things goes.

D. The Ontological Argument

This argument requires more thought to be grasped than the

71

previous ones. It is stated thus:

We have the idea of an absolutely perfect being. Existence is an attribute of perfection. Therefore, an absolutely perfect being must exist.

This argument is very fascinating. It is harder to cope with from a logical viewpoint than the others. Yet, it seems to be less convincing. It is saying that the only way we can think of an absolutely perfect being is to think of it as existing. The very idea of a perfect being is said to involve the idea of its existence. To think of a perfect being and not think of its existence is to think of something less than a perfect being. The problem in my mind is this: Can we not logically have the idea of an absolutely perfect being and think of its existence as a part of that perfection, and then deny the reality of the whole idea? The difficulty in getting a hold of this argument would mean, to say the least, that it would not be the reason for the faith of many people.

A variation of this argument simply says that since we have the idea of a perfect being, the only adequate explanation of this idea is that God exists and is the cause of our having this idea. It is argued that imperfect beings would not originate the idea of a perfect being. Certainly, the existence of God is a good explanation for the idea of a perfect being, but can we prove that it would be impossible for the idea to have originated from imperfect beings?

There have been variations of these arguments, and other arguments have been given, but what has been given above illustrates the principle involved in the problem of proof. Varying values have been placed on these "so-called proofs."

Concerning the value of the arguments for the existence of God, Dr. Buswell explains:

In approaching the theistic arguments we must first of all ask ourselves the purpose of the arguments . . . . Facts are observed and implications of facts are inferred, leading to more or less probability in conclusions, with more or less cogency. There is no argument known to us which, as an argument, leads to more than a probable (highly probable) conclusion . . . . The theistic arguments are no exception to the rule that *all* inductive arguments about what exists are probability arguments. This is as far as the arguments, qua arguments, claim to go.[1]

Berkhof says concerning their value:

They have some value for believers themselves, but should be called *testimonia* rather than arguments. They are important as interpretations of God's general revelation and as exhibiting the reasonableness of belief in a divine

Being. Moreover, they can render some service in meeting the adversary. While they do not prove the existence of God beyond the possibility of doubt, so as to compel assent, they can be so construed as to establish a strong probability and thereby silence many unbelievers.2

Dr. Addison H. Leitch explains with reference to the arguments:

They have been subjected to much criticism and therefore to considerable refinement in the history of thought. In spite of such criticism, however, they keep cropping up in one form or another, one argument, or one way of stating the argument, appealing to one generation more than another; but none of the arguments ever quite disappears. That these arguments keep reviving is probably a reason for their fundamental strength; men feel under some duress to define what they know must be true about God from the evidence of the external world.3

It is usually conceded that the arguments for the existence of God do not prove in the absolute sense of the word. However, they are frequently mentioned without this clarification. Some would take them to prove in the absolute sense.

III. WHY WE BELIEVE IN GOD

A. Our Constitution and Our Belief in God

I do not believe that the knowledge of God is innate. This would imply that we are born with a knowledge of God. I believe we are made to believe in God. It is natural for us to believe in God, but it requires the proper environment or circumstances for us to believe in God.

It is natural for a grain of corn to sprout and produce a stalk of corn. However, it will do so only under the right environment. It must be in the soil, having the proper content of moisture, and the temperature must be right. If a grain of corn is placed on top of a table, it will never sprout because the right environment does not exist. This is the case regardless of the fact that it is natural for it to sprout. When the grain of corn is placed in the ground, it becomes activated by the soil, moisture, and temperature, and thus a sprout comes forth which will grow into a stalk.

If a member of the race from birth were to grow up in isolation, it is doubtful that he would believe in God. In one sense, he would be less than human. He would, so to speak, have all the parts that go to make up a human being. The problem is he would not be in the environment that would activate him into being what a functioning human being is.

A human being cannot be described purely in terms of being an individual. He is a member of a group. He is a relationship-creature. The grain of corn depends upon its relationships with soil, moisture and temperature for it to be its fullest and truest nature. A human being is dependent upon other members of the race, the created order, and God for him to be his truest and fullest self. The mention of God comes from other human beings. The normal procedure is for a human being through interaction with other people, reflection upon the created order, and interaction with God to be activated into believing in God. It is his total experience that is brought to bear upon his believing, not just logical reflection. The process of logical reflection comes into play as a safeguard to protect us from believing that which is false. When we try to make logical reflection our only basis for believing an idea, it ceases to serve as a safeguard to protect us from believing that which is false and causes us to fail to believe that which is true. As I have said before, I am not suggesting that we set aside rationality, but I am suggesting that it function in the context of our total experience.

It is true that some people do not profess to believe in God. It is my opinion that such people do so to their own hurt. It introduces malfunction into their experience. I think this will be seen in further discussion following.

B. A Case for Our Belief in God

One of the most important points to be made in building a case for believing in God is that we must make a choice between alternatives. We do not simply refuse to believe in God. We must choose an alternative. Before we reject our belief in God because of problems, we would do well to examine the alternatives to see what problems they have. We must believe in God, be an agnostic, or be a naturalist. There are many shades of belief, but they would fall into one of these categories.

Naturalism is the positive statement while atheism is the negative statement of the view. We dare not let the atheist get by by tearing down our view without supporting his own. I was in the audience in the fall of 1973, when the well-known atheist, Madilyn Murray O'Hare, was debating on television against belief in the existence of God. When an opportunity was given for questions, I asked Mrs. O'Hare if she could prove that there was no God. Her answer was, "No." She felt no obligation to prove her position. She felt obliged, only, to tear down belief in God. When I insisted that she held to her position by faith, she denied that this was the case.

I prefer the term naturalism to atheism, though both terms

must be used, because naturalism tells us that the advocates attribute everything to natural causes. We have let the naturalist get by too often by putting us on the defensive and pointing out our problems. We need to put the naturalist on the defensive. We need to expose the inadequacy of naturalism as a system of thought.

Naturalism is forced to believe that matter is eternal. From the viewpoint of naturalism either matter is eternal or "nothing" created matter out of nothing. The latter is unthinkable. There can be no proof that matter is eternal, but in naturalism it is a logical necessity.

The next problem is that either life must have been eternal, or it must have originated from lifeless matter. It is quite a burden to be borne by the intellect, but the usual belief of the naturalist is that life originated from lifeless matter. This is considered to be an easier burden on the mind than believing that life has been eternal.

Naturalism is in effect giving many of the attributes and activities usually ascribed to deity to matter. Matter is eternal. Matter is the creator. Does matter seem to be capable of all this?

Another weak point of naturalism is that it gives no adequate explanation for the presence of the inescapable questions of life and for the concerns which are represented by these questions. Why the question, "Is there a God?" if there is no God? Naturalism is mute on questions like: Is there life after death? If so, how can I prepare for it? Why am I so concerned about right and wrong? How can I know what is right and wrong? Why are men so prone to be religious? Why is it that we cannot just turn these questions off? Naturalism has no satisfactory answer to these questions nor to why we have these questions. Naturalism leaves us lost on the sea of reality.

In chapter 2, I gave the following criteria for testing a system of thought that proposes to explain the whole of reality: (1) Is there internal consistency, i.e., is the structure logically related to the foundation? Do all the parts fit consistently together? (2) Is there internal sufficiency, i.e., are the causes adequate to produce the effects attributed to them? (3) Does it conform to that which is undeniably true? (4) Does it answer the inescapable question of life?

I will call attention to the second and fourth criteria. Naturalism is woefully lacking in internal sufficiency. Matter is the creator without having the attributes of a creator ascribed to it. Disorganized matter is not capable of organizing itself into an organized universe. Yet, it had to if naturalism be true. According to naturalism, matter is eternal, but the universe is not.

Matter is not described as being capable of creating life out of lifeless matter. Yet, it had to if naturalism be true. Matter is not pictured as being capable of creating personality. Yet, it had to if naturalism be true. Naturalism woefully fails for lack of internal sufficiency. It has the work of deity without deity.

Concerning the fourth criterion, the discussion earlier mentioned about naturalism and the inescapable questions of life makes it clear that naturalism flunks the test at this point. At the point where our need is the greatest, naturalism comes forth with negation, silence, and inadequate and unsatisfactory answers. If naturalism be true, there is no meaning and purpose to life. The truth does not make us free. To know the truth is to be in despair and depression. This cannot be. Surely life has more to offer than this. For the naturalist who wants to deny the charges in this paragraph, let him come forth with his proof.

Agnosticism has all of the weaknesses of naturalism. For all practical purposes, it is naturalism because it restricts knowledge to natural causes and effects as known through sense data. Whatever may exist outside of the natural is unknowable and furnishes no basis of comfort. It is inconceivable that man could have the inescapable questions of life so indelibly written in his constitution if it were not possible to know the answers to these questions.

In addition to the fallacies of naturalism, agnosticism is guilty of self-contradiction. The foundation says you cannot know. Yet, the statement itself affirms knowledge. If you cannot know, it is a contradiction to affirm that you cannot know.

The irrational leap of "faith" into the upper story is a form of agnosticism and illustrates its inadequacy as an approach. The human constitution will not tolerate the denial of the possibility of upper story knowledge. We are deeply rational, yet the compelling desire for upper story knowledge and experience makes many take a leap into the dark and lay hold on something irrational to satisfy that need. They have been told that they cannot have rational knowledge of anything beyond what can be known through sense data. They cannot limit life's experiences and knowledge to the lower story. When a being so deeply rational as a human being, feels compelled to take a leap into the dark and lay hold on the irrational, the need must be great. The problem is: Can a deeply rational being find satisfaction in such an experience? I cannot. One that offers a unified view of knowledge appeals far more to me.

Our knowledge of God comes to us as a "given." It is presented to us. We examine it for validity. We do not examine the mere idea of God to decide if He exists. We examine a particular view of God. It is for this reason that I presented my view of God before discussing why we believe in God. Also, our belief in God must not be considered alone. It must be considered in the context of a system of thought.

Naturalism and agnosticism leave a void in our experience as it relates to the inescapable questions of life. At this point our belief in God comes in strong. To the question, "Is there a God?" the answer is yes. To the question, "How can we know Him?" the answer is through general revelation, the Bible, and Jesus Christ. To the

76

question, "Is there life after death?" the answer is yes. To the question, "How can we prepare for life after death?" the answer is through faith in our Lord and Savior Jesus Christ. To the question, "How can we know what is right and what is wrong?" the answer is through our moral constitution and the moral revelation of God in the Bible.

These answers bring peace and satisfaction to the deepest longings of our innermost being. We expect any system of truth that attempts to explain the whole of reality to do this. This makes us citizens of a rational universe. Inescapable questions have answers. These questions are not there to tantalize and confuse. They are there to prepare us to expect and receive the true answers. Just as thirst prepares one for water and hunger prepares one for food, these questions and the longings they represent prepare us for a knowledge of God and an experience with God.

I am aware of the fact that what I am saying does not prove that there is a God. It does show that belief in God is reasonable. We are not dealing simply with cause and effect at this point. We are not simply saying that God is the cause and the inescapable questions are the effect. That is true, but these observations involve more than that.

In a system we have not only cause and effect, but also "togetherness," "cohesiveness," and "interrelatedness." Truth is a functioning system. Ideas fit together. To believe in God answers the questions of our innermost being and fills the longings of our deepest being in such a way that these ideas and experiences fit together to form a part of a functioning system of truth. There is togetherness, cohesiveness, and interrelatedness.

These observations do not prove that God exists, but if we live in an intelligent universe we can certainly reject as false any system of thought that does not adequately deal with the inescapable questions of life. We can reject any system of thought that does not have this togetherness, cohesiveness, and interrelatedness. In fact, it would not be a system. We certainly have a right to believe a system if it passes the test of all the criteria for testing a system of thought. In fact, we will likely feel compelled to believe such a system.

We do not stand outside the Christian system and prove that there is a God as set forth in the system. We are a deeply involved part of the system. We look at the system from within and apply the test. The basics of the system come to us as given ideas. They are given to us for our examination. We do not show how we could have originated these ideas apart from having them given to us.

A system of truth must meet the need of our total personality, i.e., our mind, heart, and will, not just our minds. It is for this reason that I started with the criterion of answering the inescapable questions of life. Truth must meet these needs. If a system does not speak to these needs, it is not worthy of consideration. We dare not accept a system that does not adequately deal with these needs. However, we must keep in mind that our rational mind is a part of our total personality. Therefore, there are some other tests to which a system must be subjected other than whether it speaks to our inner being. I think it was appropriate to begin with this test since truth is for life and only that which speaks to life is worthy of being considered.

Let us now apply the criterion: Is there internal sufficiency? Here again Christianity with its belief in God passes the test. God, as described in Christian doctrine, is fully capable of creating the universe and its inhabitants. It makes sense to think of the universe and its inhabitants as being an effect and God as being the cause. Here again we see togetherness, cohesiveness, and interrelatedness. It all fits together as a part of a system of truth. To try to argue from effect to cause, as in the cosmological argument, may not be the proper application of reason to our belief in God. It appears to be better to examine the cause and effect relationship between God and the universe for reasonableness as a part of a system of thought. It makes sense to think of God as the cause and the universe as the effect.

It makes far more sense to look at God as an eternal Being who created matter out of nothing than it does to think of matter as being eternal and thus the creator of the universe, life, and personality. There may be some difficulty in grasping the idea that God has existed from eternity past, but there is no difficulty in believing it. If we believe in God, we cannot conceive of God as being other than without beginning. It goes with the idea of God to believe in His eternity past. It does not go with our understanding of matter to believe it to have no beginning. It fits the idea of God to believe that He has created matter, the universe, life, and personality. It does not fit the idea of matter to attribute the work of creator of the universe, life, and personality to it. This is why we hear so little about it from those who propose to believe it. It is intellectually embarrassing to make matter the creator.

The same basic reasoning can be applied to the facts of the teleological argument. It is not the correct use of the data to argue from the presence of order and design to the existence of God as an intelligent cause. To view God as the intelligent cause of the order and design in the universe makes sense. It forms a part of a system of thought that is internally sufficient and consistent. God as creator is an adequate explanation for the presence of purpose and order in the universe. If the question of disorder be raised, Christianity is not without an adequate cause. It is not to be attributed to God, but to Satan and the presence of sin. Here again we see internal sufficiency and consistency. Also, it passes the test of conforming to that which is undeniably true. It is undeniably true that there is disorder in the universe. The Christian system has an adequate cause without attributing this disorder to God. The answer is found in Satan and sin.

The same basic principles that have been applied to the data used in the cosmological argument and the teleological argument also apply to the data in the moral argument. How do we account for the inescapable presence of the moral imperative in man? A holy God who is man's creator and the moral Lawgiver and Judge of the universe is an adequate answer. It makes sense to believe that God created man with a moral constitution from which man cannot totally escape. We never totally escape the categories of right and wrong. The moral imperative is too strong to be self-imposed. It is too strong to be culturally imposed. It may, up to a point, be culturally conditioned, but it is too deep within us to find its total answer in culture. It makes sense to believe that our moral imperative is related to a moral relationship and a moral accountability to the holy Creator, Lawgiver, and Judge of the universe.

The cause and effect relationship between God and man as it relates to the moral imperative is very important. It is rationally sound, but its impact is based on the fact that it meets an experiential need within us. We have no need in our total existence that is more real to us then our moral need. We need an adequate explanation of why this need is so great within us. The Christian system with its belief in God is an adequate explanation. We need a moral authority from which we can receive moral laws, moral guidelines, and moral principles. The Christian system with its belief in the Bible meets this need. We need an answer to moral guilt. The Christian system gives us the answer through Jesus Christ. It also helps us distinguish false guilt from true guilt as we study its moral teachings.

Here again we see togetherness, cohesiveness, and inter-relatedness. Our rational minds are satisfied. The needs of our innermost being are met. We dare not settle for less.

The Christian system of truth would present the existence of God and His relationship to man as the cause of the existence of the idea of God. Here again we have a cause and effect relationship that is not only rationally sound, but also meets the needs of our innermost being. It speaks to the needs of life. It not only explains adequately the existence of the idea of God, but also the fact that man is so deeply religious.

It is an undeniable fact that some people say that they do not believe in God, and many others do not worship the true God. Any system of truth must have an adequate answer for this. The Bible is fully aware of the problem. We are not caught off guard by this fact. The answer is found in sin and Satan. Sin has placed man in an awful predicament. Man is so deeply moral in his constitution that he cannot escape the categories of right and wrong. Yet, sin makes him want to cast off moral restraint. He wants to do that which he cannot do with total success. Man, because of sin, wants to cast off authority. It is to be expected that some will try to do so by trying to deny the existence of God while others will seek a god more to their own liking. Our observations of those who have tried these alternatives show us that they have not found satisfaction.

The Christian system is internally sufficient both to explain why most people believe in God and some do not. A place for the undeniable fact that some do not believe in God is found in the system. Again, we see togetherness, cohesiveness, and inter-relatedness.

Our examination of the Christian system of truth with its belief in God has shown that it passes the test of the criteria: (1) It is internally consistent. (2) There is internal sufficiency. (3) It conforms to that which is undeniably true. (4) It answers the inescapable questions of life. Belief in God passes all the tests of reasonableness. When we let our total personality be a part of our believing, I believe we will be compelled to believe in God. There is no other alternative to believing in God that meets the deepest needs of our personality. To reject belief in God is a course that cannot be followed without great loss. To reject belief in God means to be lost in the sea of life.

To believe in God through Jesus Christ opens the door to a rationally and experientially satisfying life. It opens the way for unified knowledge of the lower and upper stories. It makes it so man can be an intelligent, functioning citizen of the lower story and the upper story.

To believe in God or not to believe in God is not a choice between faith-knowledge and sight-knowledge (or sense-knowledge). Naturalism is faith-knowledge. Nobody has observed that matter is eternal. Nobody has observed that matter is the creator of the universe, life, and personality. To believe in God or not to believe in God are both faith-knowledge. We have two choices: (1) To have faith-knowledge in a system that forms the basis for unified knowledge of the whole of reality, satisfies our mind and meets the deepest needs of our personality. (2) To have faith-knowledge in a view that in the basic questions of origins is rationally unsatisfactory, and leaves one lost on the sea of life when it comes to the deepest needs of the personality. As for me, I will continue in the faith-knowledge that meets the needs of my total personality.

IV. WHY WE BELIEVE IN THE BIBLE

The basic principles of what has been said earlier are applicable to our belief in the Bible. We cannot offer absolute proof that the Bible is the Word of God. We can show that it properly fits into a system of thought that has togetherness, cohesiveness, and inter-relatedness. We can show that it is reasonable to believe in the Bible.

A. An Examination of the Arguments for the Divine Inspiration of the Bible

We will first examine the argument based on the indestruct-ibility of the Bible. The Bible has survived in the midst of adversity. Many attempts have been made to destroy it, but all attempts have failed. It is felt that this survival in spite of attempts to destroy it is evidence (some would speak of it as proof) of the supernatural origin of Scripture.

At present, I will simply show the weakness in these arguments as I did the arguments for God's existence. The positive value of the data will be mentioned later.

The fact that the Bible is still with us proves that it has not been destroyed, but it does not prove that it cannot be destroyed. There can be no proof that the Bible cannot be destroyed. We believe that it cannot be destroyed, but that is based on our faith in its own testimony (Matthew 5:18; 24:35). We could not prove to an unbeliever that the Bible is indestructible and then use it as a base from which to build our case.

Another problem with this argument is: If we found another book that had withstood the same attempts to destroy it, would we believe it to be the Word of God for that reason? Doubtless, that would not convince us.

A second argument that is frequently used is the argument from the character of the Bible. The Bible is characterized by unity and nobility of thought. It is so characterized to those of us who believe it and love it, but unbelievers frequently challenge its unity and nobility of thought. An argument based on the character of the Bible would not be convincing to such a person. The unity and nobility of thought of the Bible is knowledge that is shared by believers, but not the critics of Scripture.

We can raise the questions at this point: If we discover a book that is characterized by unity and nobility of thought, would we of necessity believe it to be Divinely inspired? I think not.

A third argument is based on the influence of the Bible. Wherever the Bible has been, it has had an uplifting influence upon society. It is felt by many that this evidences the Divine inspiration of Scripture.

The same problems can be raised about this argument that has about the others. Many people do not believe that the Bible has had a good influence. With such people, we could not use this information to prove the Divine origin of Scripture. Again, I raise the question: Would we believe some other book to be of Divine origin if it had a good influence?

A fourth argument is based on fulfilled prophecy of the Bible, particularly that which was fulfilled within the Biblical period. The believer does believe the Bible sets forth a lot of prophecy and its fulfillment. He also believes that any unfulfilled prophecy will be fulfilled in the future. The problem is that some people either explain away the prophetic statements of Scripture or consider them as history instead of prophecy. To such people there would be no proving value from what we call fulfilled prophecy. Another problem is the fact that through satanic influence some predictions are made that come true. We do not grant, then, in every case that a predictive utterance that turns out to be true is of God.

The data used in these arguments are useful in showing the reasonableness of our faith as we will see later. It is a mistake to use the data to construct arguments of proof. We do not prove a system to be true by starting with some commonly accepted major premise or premises and proving that the basic ideas of the system are seen to be a necessary logical conclusion. Rather, we subject a system to certain tests. To test for validity is not the same as proving something to be a logical necessity. Also, we must be concerned with necessity other than logical necessity.

B. The Starting Point of our Faith in the Divine Origin of Scripture

We do not find God's revelation. It finds us and identifies itself to us. This is the only way it can be. We would certainly expect a revelation from God to so identify itself to us. We could not conceive of a revelation from God not bearing the marks of self-authentication. We do not expect every part to bear the label, but we do expect the whole to be adequately labeled as a revelation from God. It is only then that we will consider any message or book to be a Divine revelation. The marks of self-authentication have been set forth in chapter three under the heading, "Divine Authorship" and need not be repeated here.

Why be concerned over a Book that claims to be the Word of God? It has a message for us. It makes demands upon us. Our interest is not kindled simply because it proposes to be a message for us that makes demands upon us. Our interest is kindled because of the inescapable questions which represent unquenchable longings. The message of the Bible sounds like what our innermost being needs. In the Bible we see answers to our inescapable questions. In the Bible we see provisions for our needed experiences. It speaks to our total personality. We see it as the alleviation of our lostness.

As a man who thinks he has a dreaded disease finds a sudden

interest in that which claims to be a cure, we find ourselves interested in that which proposes to be a message from God and an answer to our questions and our needs. The man with the disease must be concerned with the validity of the claims of the cure. The claims must be subjected to the proper tests. So it is with that which claims to be the Word of God. It must be subjected to tests.

C. The Claims of Scripture Under Testing

It is my conviction that in some way God has placed in our constitution certain ideas that are self-evident truths about any book that is truly a Divine revelation. These are placed within us by God to help us keep from being led astray.

It is a self-evident truth that a book that would be a Divine revelation would be indestructible. The fact that the Bible has withstood up to this point means that it passes this test in the only way it could. From this standpoint, the Bible is safe for believing as a Divine revelation.

It is a self-evident truth that a book that would be a Divine revelation would be characterized by unity and nobility of thought. To me the Bible passes this test. I believe it will for others if they come at it with the right attitude of heart and mind. If they develop a critical attitude toward Scripture that blinds them to this unity and nobility of thought, they will reject it as a Divine revelation. They will reject it as a Divine revelation because they believe it to be a self-evident truth that a Divine revelation will be characterized by unity and nobility of thought. There must be a willingness to see the truth before it can be seen (John 7:17). It is my conviction that those who come at the Scripture with the right attitude do see this unity and nobility of thought. For such people, the Bible passes this test and is safe for believing so far as this test is concerned.

It is a self-evident truth that a book which would be a Divine revelation would have a good influence. For me the Bible passes this test. I believe it does for others who look at it with the right attitude. The same further elaboration, in principle, could be made about this self-evident truth as for the others. The Bible passes this test.

It is a self-evident truth that a significant amount of fulfilled prophecy would have to have a supernatural source. If it is constantly associated with good and is consistently related to the rest of the system of truth, the supernatural source would be God. It is my conviction that to those who approach the Bible with the right attitude, it passes this test.

I have used the same data in these tests that were used in the arguments to prove the Divine origin of Scripture. I think there can be far fewer problems and objections raised against these tests than can be raised against the arguments based on the same data. If anyone wants to raise any objections against calling these self-evident truths by which to test a Divine revelation, I would ask, "Would you believe a book to be a Divine revelation if it did not pass these tests?"

The reasonableness of our faith in Scripture is also shown by the fact that the Bible fits into a functioning system of truth. When we believe in God, the Bible, Jesus Christ, and man with his needs, it all fits together. There is togetherness, cohesiveness, and inter-relatedness. If we were to take the Bible out of this system of thought, it would, in effect, be destroyed. The Bible is integrally related to God, Jesus Christ, and the needs of man. We expect truth to have this togetherness, cohesiveness, and interrelatedness.

We should single out for separate consideration the testimony of Jesus Christ concerning the Scripture (Matthew 5:17, 18; John 10:35; and others). Jesus Christ bears witness of the Divine origin and truthfulness of Scripture. The Bible also bears witness of the truth of the claims of Jesus Christ (John 5:39). In a sense we believe the Bible because of Jesus Christ and Jesus Christ because of the Bible. To believe in one is to believe in the other.

Some immediately charge: "This is circular reasoning." There is nothing wrong with circular reasoning as long as it is not presented as proof. Circular reasoning is all right as long as it is used to demonstrate togetherness, cohesiveness, and interrelatedness. A system will present many opportunities for circular reasoning. It is not circular reasoning that is wrong. It is making wrong claims for circular reasoning that is wrong.

Our belief in the Bible as a part of the Christian system of truth passes the tests of the criteria we have given for testing a system.

(1) It is internally consistent. There is consistency between believing in the Bible, God, and the other parts of the system. There is consistency in the Bible.

(2) It is internally sufficient. The God of the Bible is fully capable of revealing the truth of the Bible and inspiring the writers to write the Bible. The causes set forth in the Bible are capable of producing the effects ascribed to them.

(3) It conforms to that which is undeniably true. There is no fact of reality which is undeniably true that is contradicted by the Bible. There may be some things that may be questioned, but they do not stand as undeniably true and in contradiction to the Bible.

(4) It answers the inescapable questions of life. The Bible comes through strong at this point. It meets the needs of our total personality. To reject it is to be lost on the sea of reality.

When we say that we cannot offer absolute proof of the existence of God and the Divine origin of Scripture, that is not to say that we have a weak case. It simply says that the very nature of reality is such that some things are not subject to absolute proof. There are some things that are true that cannot be proved in the absolute sense. There are some things that are false that cannot be proved in the absolute sense. It is my conviction that the only way to test any system that proposes to explain the whole of reality is the way I have tested the Christian system in this chapter.

It is a serious mistake to work on the assumption that our belief in God and the Bible is capable of absolute proof. Some have, no doubt, had their confidence in God and the Bible built up on the assumption that they had proof of their conviction. However, they were on risky ground. If they were definitely resting upon their proof, all it would take to seriously damage or wreck their faith would be for someone to come along and show the fallacies in their proofs. Also, to claim to be able to prove makes it difficult for some unbelievers to come to faith if they get the idea that faith is supposed to be capable of absolute proof. It is the wrong attitude about proof and disproof that causes many to lose their faith when encountered by unbelievers.

The approach used in this chapter is very satisfying to me. God and the Bible meet every test of reasonableness. My faith in God and the Bible meets my personal needs. I do not feel threatened by any other system. To me they fail woefully both from a rational viewpoint and from the standpoint of meeting the needs of the total personality. I wholeheartedly recommend God, the Bible, and Jesus Christ to every human being.

CHAPTER SIX
NOTES

1. James Oliver Buswell, Jr., *A Systematic Theology of the Christian Religion*, Vol. I, 2 vols., Grand Rapids: Zondervan Publishing House, c. 1962, p. 72.

2. L. Berkhof, *Systematic Theology*, Grand Rapids: William B. Eerdmans Publishing Company, c. 1941, p. 28.

3. Addison H. Leitch, "The Knowledge of God: General and Special Revelation," in *Basic Christian Doctrines*, ed. by Carl F. H. Henry, New York: Holt, Rinehart, and Winston, c. 1962, p. 2.

The Creation of Man

One of the inescapable questions of life is: Who am I? We know our name, but we need help in knowing our full identity. What is the real nature of man? Knowledge of the full nature of man is tied in with his origin. As those who are committed to the Christian system of truth, we are committed to what the Divine revelation says about the origin of man. This knowledge comes to us as a given in the Divine revelation. It is integrally related to the Christian system. Our first obligation is to study the data of revelation to find out what it says about the origin of man.

I. THE BIBLICAL TEACHING CONCERNING THE ORIGIN OF MAN

A. The Creation of Man

The Bible clearly attributes the origin of man to be a creative act of God. Genesis 1:27 reads: "So God created man in his own image, in the image of God created he him; male and female created he them." Genesis 2:7 reads, "And the LORD God formed man of the dust of the ground, and breathed into his nostrils the breath of life."

There can be no debate over whether God is man's creator according to the Bible. The question is: Does the Bible leave room for theistic evolution? According to theistic evolution, God directed the process of evolution and made use of it in bringing man into existence. Physically, man would have an animal ancestry according to theistic evolution. He would have become man when God breathed into his nostrils the breath of life and he became a living soul.

Many have felt compelled by the findings of science to accept theistic evolution. The problem for the Christian is: What does the Divine revelation say? Are the Biblical teachings compatible with theistic evolution? He must apply the laws of language to the Biblical account and see if it be compatible with theistic evolution. If it is not, he must reject it.

It is my conviction that the Biblical account is incompatible with theistic evolution. I shall offer two proofs: (1) The creative days do not allow enough time. (2) The creation of Eve is definitely outside the pattern of evolution.

A word should be said here about proof. When discussing our belief in God and the Bible, I pointed out that we could not prove the existence of God and the Divine origin of Scripture. Now, I am speaking of proof that the Bible is incompatible with evolution. Once a system of thought is accepted as true, we can talk about proving things to people who believe the system to be true. In principle, we can prove that the Bible teaches a view by studying its teachings in the light of the laws of interpretation. It will be proved to those who accept the system of thought as true if they are convinced by the proof. It will have no meaning to those who do not accept the system of thought as true. We may not always succeed, but in principle we can prove things to those who believe the Bible to be the Word of God.

B. The Length of the Creative Days

It is my conviction that the days of the creative week must be understood as literal days. It is true that the Hebrew word *"yom"* (day), like the English word "day," can refer to a period of time longer than a 24 hour day in certain contexts. However, it is my conviction the case is clear cut against long days in Genesis 1. Though it is agreed that *yom* can refer to a period longer than a 24 hour day, it is not agreed by all Hebrew scholars that *yom* is suitable as an equivalent for the word "age." I will not get involved in this discussion since I think the context is against such usage even if the word is suitable in a proper context to mean "age."

The first reason is that the days are qualified as having evening and morning. Evening and morning are the phenomena that make up a solar day. The Hebrew is translated literally, "And there was evening and there was morning."

Day with the qualification of evening and morning can mean nothing other than a solar day. Some have felt that they could give a figurative meaning to evening and morning.

Edwin K. Gedney says:

It is natural for us to think of this as meaning ending

(evening) and beginning (morning), for so it is in our culture. This was not true of Hebrew age. The beginning of the day was evening and it is logical to think that the writer intended that here . . . Evening and morning then have the sense of 'beginning' and 'ending' in the passage.1

Dr. Buswell comments:

It is obvious that if the word 'day' is figurative, the parts of the day would be figurative, as when we say 'a new day is dawning,' meaning, 'a new era is opening.' The Hebrews regarded the new day as beginning at sunset. Thus the words, 'The evening and the morning were the ____th day,' would be equivalent to saying in literal modern words, 'The epoch had its gradual beginning, and gradually merged into the epoch which followed.2

Buswell suggests that if day be taken figuratively it follows that evening and morning must be taken figuratively. I concur with his reasoning, but not his position. I believe that a figurative use of day depends upon a figurative use of evening and morning consistent with the figurative use of the word day. If a figurative use of the words evening and morning cannot be supported that is consistent with the figurative use of the word day, the figurative use of the word day must be rejected. Let us examine the evidence.

The figurative use of the words suggested by Gedney and Buswell are without parallel in the Old Testament. (I base my conclusions upon a study of the occurrences of the Hebrew words for evening and morning listed in *The Englishman's Hebrew and Chaldee Concordance of the Old Testament,* fifth edition, London: Samuel Bagster and Sons, Limited.) *At no place do we find that evening is used figuratively to mean beginning nor that morning is used to mean ending.* In fact, morning did not end the literal day. Morning in the literal day referred to the change from darkness to light, not the last part of the 24 hour day. Morning is never used figuratively to mean ending. *It is used figuratively to mean early.* This is seen by the fact that the Hebrew word for morning is translated "early" in Psalm 46:5; 90:14; and 101:8.

It is of further interest to note that when the Israelites referred to the daylight hours they spoke of them as from morning to evening (Exodus 18:13, 14). From a practical viewpoint they looked at morning as early and evening as being late in spite of the fact that from a technical point the 24 hour day began at evening.

It is quite obvious that to interpret evening figuratively to mean beginning and morning figuratively as ending is contrary to their usage in Scripture. Therefore, the terms evening and morning cannot be fitted into the day-age interpretation. When evening and morning are used in the same context, they can refer to nothing but a solar day.

Further support is seen for the literal-day view in the reference to the creative week in Exodus 20:8-11. Is there any justification for understanding the "six days" of verse 9 to refer to 24 hour days and the "six days" of verse 11 to refer to six ages? I think not.

From an exegetical viewpoint, two problems have been raised for the literal-day view. The first is the fact that the sun was not made to function until the fourth day. First, let it be said that this poses a greater problem for the day-age view than the literal-day view. The literal-day view has a problem for only 72 hours. The day-age view has a problem that could extend into millions or billions of years. It is very doubtful that any holder of the day-age view actually believes that the earth existed that long before the sun began to function.

If we take the view about the sun's function during these days that Dr. Buswell takes, there is no problem with regard to the first three days. He suggests that the sun functioned during the first three days, but was not visible. The light of the sun was diffused through a cloudy atmosphere.3 If that be the case, the sun's function would be adequate to cause the transition from darkness to light and light to darkness during the first three days. There would be no problem whatsoever under such circumstances of thinking of the days as being solar days.

Whatever the case might have been during the first three days, the fact that the words evening and morning are used from the fourth day onward helps us to interpret the previous references. Whether the sun functioned or not on the first three days, there was a division of light from darkness. We are told in Genesis 1:4, "God divided the light from the darkness." It is clear that the sun had its normal function from the fourth day on. The fact that all of the creative days are described, "And there was evening and there was morning," tells us that all were the same kind of day. There can be no reason for understanding the first three days of the creative week to be any different, so far as length is concerned, from the last three.

The other exegetical problem is presented by a reference to the seventh day in Hebrews 4. In verse 4, it is said, "And God did rest the seventh day from all his works." Verse 5 speaks of the rest as having continued until Moses day (and is still continuing). "And in this place again, If they shall enter into my rest." Since the rest is continuing, it is concluded that the day is continuing. This would make the seventh day a long day. If the seventh day of Genesis 1 and 2 were a long day, it would follow that the six were also long days.4

My answer to this problem is that although the rest is continuing, the day is not continuing. The day is clearly treated as a fact of history. "And God did rest the seventh day . . . " (Hebrews 4:4). The seventh day is presented as being already finished in the past. The language of Exodus 20:11 and Genesis 2:2, 3 also treat the seventh day as a completed fact of history. If the seventh day is history, there is no basis for interpreting it as a long day.

Dr. H. C. Leupold comments:

> There ought to be no need of refuting the idea that *yom* means period. Reputable dictionaries like Buhl, BDB or K. W. know nothing of this notion. Hebrew dictionaries are our primary source of reliable information concerning Hebrew words. Commentators with critical leanings utter statements that are very decided at this instance. Says Skinner: 'The interpretation of *yom* as aeon, a favorite resource of harmonists of science and revelation, is opposed to the plain sense of the passage and has no warrant in Hebrew usage.' Dillman remarks: 'The reasons advanced by ancient and modern writers for constructing these days to be longer periods of time are inadequate.'[5]

So far as I am concerned, there can be no doubt that the days were literal days. If the description in Genesis 1 is not of literal days, one wonders how it could have been stated so as to clearly mean a literal day. Suppose God did mean these to be understood as literal days, can anyone say that anything was said that would confuse the issue, or anything left out that would be needed to clarify it?

In addition to the fact that the day-age theory cannot be supported as an interpretation of Genesis, another serious problem is raised in connection with it. It fails to really solve the problem of harmonizing scientific opinions on geology and paleontology with Scripture.

Those who hold to the day-age theory generally conclude that each day represents a geological age and that these ages are in the same order as given in Genesis. However, many believe that this is not the case. Dr. Carl F. H. Henry, though not an advocate of the literal-day view, in discussing the difficulties of the day-age theory points out that " . . . the Genesis days do not harmonize fully with the chronology proposed by modern science . . . . "[6]

Dr. Bernard Ramm, though rejecting the literal-day theory, also rejects the day-age theory because to accept the long-day view and to accept the order in which they appear could not be squared with science. He illustrates the problem by pointing out: "We have a botanical creation with no animals and a mammalian creation with no creation of plants, yet the science of biology tells us how intimately related plants, animals, and insects are in the order of nature."[7]

The only real thing that the day-age theory does is allow for more time, but the order of what happened still fails to fit in with modern science. Therefore, it fails as a means of bringing about harmony.

Another observation is that the day-age theory offers no help at all in the problem of how long man has been on the earth. The question of the antiquity of man is studied by scientists in connection with fossils. It is obvious that wherever fossils are found death has occurred. It is equally obvious that regardless of the length of the creative days that men did not die until after the sixth creative day. Surely, no one would place Genesis 3 in the sixth day. Death occurred in the human race after Genesis 3. This means that all fossil remains of human beings must be accounted for after the sixth creative day was finished. The person who believes in the day-age theory and the person who believes in the literal-day theory would have to look for a way to scripturally account for the age of man through exactly the same possibilities.

Apparently, Fetzer overlooked the fact mentioned above in making the following observation: "By taking the age-day interpretation of Genesis and by realizing that the genealogical tables of Genesis have gaps in them, we free ourselves from any notion that man was made 4004 B. C."[8]

The possibility of gaps in the genealogies may help give an earlier date for the origin (this will be discussed later), but the day-age theory cannot be used to increase the time man has been on earth one bit more than the literal-day view. Again the day-age view is seen to fail to offer any aid.

Another problem that one encounters, when he by the day-age theory or some other view tries to allow enormous lengths of time for the six creative days, is the type of conditions that must have prevailed during this time. The geological strata require catastrophic conditions, and the fossils of animals require death.

Ramm shows an awareness of this when he remarks: "There was disease and death and bloodshed in Nature long before man sinned."[9]
He further comments:

> Outside of the Garden of Eden were death, disease, weeds, thistles, thorns, carnivores, deadly serpents, and intemperate weather. To think otherwise is to run counter to an immense avalanche of fact. Part of the blessedness of man was that he was spared all of these things in his Paradise, and part of the judgment of man was that he had to forsake such a Paradise and enter the world as it was outside of the Garden, where thistles grew and weeds were abundant and where wild animals roamed and where life was only possible by the sweat of man's brow. [10]

Many would not be willing to go along with Ramm in ascribing such conditions to earth and animals before man sinned. However, one must admit conditions of this kind before he can hope to get any help from the day-age theory.

We may not know what the exact conditions were before man sinned, but one can hardly reconcile most of what Ramm says above with what God said to Adam when He said, "Cursed is the ground for thy sake; in sorrow shalt thou eat of it all the days of thy life; Thorns also and thistles shall it bring forth to thee . . . " (Genesis 3:17, 18).

Also, with regard to this statement: "Part of the blessedness of man was that he was spared all of these things in Paradise, and part of the judgment of man was that he had to forsake such a Paradise and enter the world as it was outside the Garden." Ramm is overlooking the fact that man's responsibility to God would have taken him outside the Garden even if he had not sinned. This is seen in the fact that man, before he sinned was commanded to "have dominion over the fish of the sea, and over the fowl of the air, and over the cattle, and over all the earth, and over every creeping thing that creepeth upon the earth" (Genesis 1:26).

We may not know the exact conditions of the earth before man sinned, but we must conclude that the earth is different now as a result of the curse. We must also conclude that man would have gone into all the earth if he had never sinned.

Those who want to resort to a view that seeks to explain fossils and geological changes by placing them within the six days of creation must ask if they can reconcile the conditions that would have produced these with the Genesis account. Special attention should be given to the fact that at the close of days 3-5 it reads, "And God saw . . . that . . . it was good." The statement at the end of the sixth day is made to include the whole creation. "And God saw every thing that he had made, and, behold, it was very good" (Genesis 1:31).

If the days of the creative week are literal 24 hour days, there can be no harmony between the Bible and evolution. This is true since man was created on the sixth day. Twenty-four hours is not enough time for evolution. In my opinion the case is clear for the literal-day interpretation; therefore, I see no possibility of evolution.

C. The Creation of Eve by God

As has already been stated, if one accepts the literal-day view he cannot accept evolution. However, theistic evolution has not won its case with those who believe the Bible even if the day-age theory were a proved fact. There are many who accept the day-age view that do reject evolution. They reject it on other grounds. The account of the creation of Eve in Genesis 2:21, 22 requires one to believe that the creation of Eve was instantaneous and by a direct act of God that bypassed natural processes. No one can hope to escape by claiming that this is poetic or symbolic. If the language is capable of being understood at all, it means that God took something from Adam and by a direct act made Eve. Those who advocate theistic evolution would not be willing to grant that Eve was created by a special act of God. Those who grant that Eve was created by a special act also grant that Adam was.

Another problem with theistic evolution is that it has the same forces at work in the world today that were at work in the creative week. If so, what is meant by, "And on the seventh day God ended his work which he had made" (Genesis 2:2)? There can be no finished creation, nor can there be any ceasing of creative activity in theistic evolution because it fails to distinguish in essence, between creative activity and the activity of providence.

After examining Genesis 1 and 2, one feels like asking, "If God used the evolutionary process to bring man into existence, why did He make it so hard for one to believe in evolution after studying Genesis 1 and 2?"

II. THE INFLUENCE OF THE THEORY OF EVOLUTION

One might ask: Why all the concern over evolution? The biggest reason is that it is unscriptural. However, one might ask: In view of all the bad interpretation that has received much lighter treatment, why not be easier on those who feel that evolution is in harmony with Genesis 1 and 2? The problem is that there is a philosophy of life that often accompanies evolution which has had devastating effects on Christianity and that for which Christianity stands.

Of course it could be said that evangelicals who accept evolution do not accept the evolutionary philosophy of life. It could be said in reply that this may be true in particular cases, but it will hardly remain true. Respect for the scholarship of geologists and paleontologists seems to have been one of the chief reasons that most who have accepted theistic evolution did so. Those who set forth the evolutionary philosophy of life or the evolutionary philosophy of the origin of religion are as learned in their fields of study as the geologists and paleontologists are in theirs. Shall we accept the conclusions of one out of respect to his scholarship and reject the conclusions of another though his scholarship is just as respectable?

Those who are motivated by respect for the scholarship of others will eventually accept the total evolutionary view including the philosophy of life. Those who stay with the Scripture will have to do so at the cost of rejecting much of what is called respectable scholarship. This is not intended to cast reflection upon scholarship as such. However, it is intended to make it clear that we cannot accept the Christian system of thought without turning down much of what is known as respectable scholarship in other systems of thought. Are we any worse if we reject the conclusions of geologists and paleontologists than we are when we reject what some other scholars say?

I am well aware of the fact that an evangelical who holds to theistic evolution would not go along with most of the things that will be pointed out as the products of evolutionary thinking. However, I do believe that the tide moves in that direction and that many who take the step of theistic evolution will in varying degrees move in these directions.

Dr. Carl Henry gives a frank account of the past influence of evolution. He explains:

> This evolutionary speculation challenged not only the dignity of man on the basis of creation; it challenged also the fact of his fall and sinfulness. For both these conceptions, evolutionary philosophy substituted the dogma of human progress and perfectibility. Hence it eliminated the doctrine of man's need of supernatural redemption. The intellectual movement of the past century portrays a loss of faith in the Apostles' Creed simultaneous with a rise of faith in the evolutionary creed. The new importance of change whetted the destructive assault on Holy Scripture as a divinely given revelation, and on Jesus Christ as an absolute divine incarnation.[11]

The theory of biological evolution brought into prominence the principle of change and progress. When this view became deeply embedded in the minds of scholars, they became convinced that every area of life must submit to the principle of change and progress. Religion and morals were not to be exempted.

When applied to the realm of religion, detrimental results immediately appeared. The origin and development of religion was to be studied within the framework of an evolutionary philosophy. The beginning of religion was to be found on a very low level such as superstition or ancestor worship. Through a gradual development Christianity finally emerged on the scene. Until this is recognized there can be no intelligent understanding of liberalism.

In liberalism the evolutionary principle became the interpretive principle in interpreting the Old Testament. Some of the results of this have been (1) a denial of the Mosaic authorship of the Pentateuch; (2) the view that monotheism had its beginning with Amos; and (3) the dating of the origin of the law after the Babylonian captivity.

There is also a denial of the historicity of the account of sinless Adam and Eve placed in the Garden of Eden, and the account of the fall. The evolutionary philosophy has no place for a sinless state because the earlier state of man is thought to be below the present state. It has no place for a fall because man is on the upward climb. It is easy to see how destructive this could be on Christian doctrine.

Neo-orthodoxy, because of its allegiance to evolution, has denied the fact that Adam and Eve were historical persons. It has rejected the optimism of liberalism, but its respect for evolution would not allow an orthodox position on Adam and Eve.

The application of the principle of change and progress to the realm of morals is quite obvious. There can be no looking back to a set of morals revealed in a Bible that was written in the long ago. There can be no doubt that this has been the greatest reason for the moral decay that has given respectability in many circles to gross immorality.

Dr. Henry says:

> Triumph of the evolutionary philosophy actually engendered one of the most staggering moral declensions in the history of the world. Deterioration reached its widest extremes with the speculative dogma that man is an animal only, and with the application of the ancient Greek doctrine of change to all fields of study, religion included.[12]

It is true that in the past Christians have rejected, for a time, some of the things we all now accept, for example, the fact that the earth is round. However, there has not been any such viewpoint that has had such a devastating effect on Christianity when it was accepted.

It would be exceeding strange if God would use a method in creation, that when finally discovered by man, would have such effects in the first century of its acceptance as evolution has had. Should it be thought strange that so many have found evolution unacceptable within the Christian faith?

III. SUGGESTIONS FOR COPING WITH THE PROBLEMS

Anyone would either be ignorant or less than honest to deny that there are problems. On the one hand, the Bible, as I understand it, rules out any possibility of an animal ancestry of man. Man came into existence by a creative act of God. Also, as has been stated above, Christianity has suffered immensely from the influence of the evolutionary philosophy of life that usually accompanies biological evolution. On the other hand, we live in a world when men, competent in their field, insist on the evolutionary hypothesis of man's origin and a time period of several hundred thousand years or more for man's existence on earth. How do we cope with all this?

A. The Latitude Allowed by Scripture

The beginning place for the Christian is to examine the Scripture and see how much latitude he has to accomodate himself to scientific thought. He must operate within the framework of these limitations. To fail to do so would be to be less than honest and would violate his rationality as a person who is committed to the Christian system of thought.

A few things have already been decided up to this point that help set the limits of this framework of possibilities. (1) There can be no room for considering the evolutionary view of the origin of man. (2) Any attempt to lengthen the time of man on earth beyond the time of about 6,000 years must be found after the sixth day of creation. It was pointed out that this is just as true of the day-age theory as it is the literal-day theory. This is true since death would have occurred after the sixth day regardless of the length of that day. All fossils of man, therefore, must be placed in the period of history after the sixth day. The day-age theory would offer a possibility of a longer animal history and more time for geological ages, but the conditions that must have existed during that time are, so far as I am concerned, impossible to reconcile with the Biblical account in Genesis 1 and 2. (See earlier discussion on this point under "The Length of the Creative days.")

There are two more subjects that need to be discussed that shed light on the Biblical limits on how much latitude can be allowed: (1) The possibility of gaps in genealogies. (2) The meaning of "kinds" in Genesis 1.

The only way of allowing any significant amount of time beyond the 4004 B.C., according to Usher's date, is through the possibility of gaps in the genealogies in Genesis 5 and 11. It is an established fact, determined by comparing different accounts of the same genealogy, that there are some names left out of some genealogies. (See James Oliver Buswell, Jr., *A Systematic Theology of the Christian Religion*, Vol. 1, 2 vols., Grand Rapids: Zondervan Publishing House, c. 1962, pp. 329—339 for a discussion on gaps in genealogies.)

It should be pointed out that the fact that there are gaps in some genealogies only creates the possibility that there are gaps in other genealogies, not the necessity. However, it does mean that the possibility of gaps cannot be ruled out. This gives one the right to speculate about such possibilities. If there were gaps, it would obviously lengthen the time since man's creation. Also, if there were gaps in Genesis 5 the amount of time that would have transpired for each name left out would be greater than would be accounted for by a life span in our day since the people lived to be considerably older then than now.

Some have taken the position that if there were gaps we can

consider any date of man's origin that might be conjectured by scientists. Their reasoning is that an unknown number of gaps of unknown duration could possibly account for any number of years. A word of caution needs to be sounded here. It may be granted that the unknowns keep a person from dogmatically stating the exact limitation of how far back one could go. However, it is a strain upon the elasticity of a reason controlled imagination to believe that these unknown and unknowable gaps could allow for any imaginable age of the human race short of infinity.

We could with caution consider the possibility of a few thousand years added to the 4004 B.C. But we cannot go hundreds of thousands of years.

It might be well to bear in mind that while we can consider gaps as a possibility for lengthening the antiquity of man, we must keep in mind facts cited by Ramm as he wrestles with this difficulty.

He seems to be caught in a dilemma between scientific thought and the facts of the Bible at this point. He brings out some of the problems in accepting an early date for the origin of man. He explains:

> The chief problem with an origin of man at 500,000 B.C. is the connection of Genesis 3 and Genesis 4. We might stretch the tables of ancestors a few thousand years, but can we stretch 'hem 200,000 years? In the fourth and fifth chapters of Genesis we have lists of names, ages of people, towns, agriculture, metallurgy, and music. This implies the ability to write, to count, to build, to farm, to smelt, and to compose. Further, these were done by the immediate descendants of Adam. Civilization does not reveal any evidence of its existence till about 8,000 B.C. or, to some 16,000 B.C. We can hardly push it back to 500,000 B.C. It is problematic to interpret Adam as having been created 200,000 B.C. or earlier, with civilization not coming into existence till say 8,000 B.C. [13]

Another point to keep in mind is that it places considerable strain upon us to believe that between the redemptive promise of Genesis 3:15 and the coming of Christ there would have been hundreds of thousands of years. We expect in some way to be able to interpret Biblical history so as to show a movement from Genesis 3:15 to the Cross. This problem presents enough difficulty in thinking about a few thousand years. What explanation does one offer for hundreds of thousands of years between the first redemptive promise and the coming of Christ?

Now we turn our attention to the problem of the meaning of the word "kinds." The zoological classification into phyla, classes, orders, families, genera, and species was not existent when Moses wrote the Pentateuch. There are no exegetical grounds for equating kind with species. This is true whether they are to be equated in fact or not. The Hebrew word for kind means form or shape. The limits of each kind is set, but there is no way of proving that the limitation is equated with species. There may be a variation within the kind, but each kind would remain within its own boundaries.

The position that the "kinds" of Genesis need not be equated with the modern term species has been accepted among staunch conservatives. There is coupled with this the admission that new species have arisen since the creation.

John W. Klotz says, "We shall certainly have to admit that there have been new species." 14

> Henry M. Morris states: "Nothing in the account [Genesis] indicates how many original 'species' there were, or what consitutes a 'species' . . . The only biological unit indentified therein is called a *kind* . . . the various types of living creatures were to bring forth 'after their kind.' This states, quite plainly, that there were to be definite limits to possible biological change . . . . But within those limits, it can surely be inferred that variation and speciation [origin of new species] are possible." 15

I am not qualified to speak on the question of whether new species can arise or have arisen. However, when men such as John W. Klotz and Henry M. Morris, who show no desire to give strained interpretations of Scripture to harmonize with scientific opinions, do believe that new species have arisen, I am inclined to believe that new species have arisen. However, one should move with caution at this point since it is doubtful that the literal-day view leaves time for very much development within kinds.

When we talk about the possibility of new species, we are not talking about man, but plants and animals. A limited amount of variation from what was created is permissible, so far as Scripture is concerned, since we have no proof the species and kinds are to be equated.

Some people have looked for help in reconciling science and Scripture by a gap of time between Genesis 1:1 and 1:2. Not all are agreed that there was a gap. Such a gap would permit time for geological ages, but it would offer no help in allowing for geological ages where fossils are embedded in the rock unless one wants to believe in an animal creation prior to the creative week of Genesis that was destroyed. Personally, I am not impressed by the idea of an animal creation prior to the creative week. There is certainly no Biblical evidence for it.

There is some problem over the exact point in Genesis 1:1-3 where the first day of the creative week began. It does not appear to have started at verse 1. If it did not, we have no way of knowing how long the earth was in the shape described in verse 2 before the first day began. It could have been a very short time, or it could have been a long time. If it were a long time, it could help in thinking about an older earth, but it would be of no help with regard to the age of fossils.

B. Observations About the Use of the Scientific Method to Study the Origin of Man

Let us first look at the assumption of the person who proposes to study the origin of man through the scientific method.

1. The person who makes a scientific investigation assumes that that which is the object of his investigation was produced by natural causes.

2. The only kind of data that is allowable is sense data. Biblical statements cannot be considered as data because they do not fall in the category of sense data.

3. The uniformity of nature is assumed for the past, including man's origin. The same system of cause and effect in operation today was in operation and brought man into existence.

In the broad sense, the word "science" would include any field of study whenever it proceeds on principles in keeping with good scholarship. In the restricted sense, science is limited to the realm of nature that can be studied through the five senses. It is science in the restricted sense that proposes to study the origin of man.

All logical thinking requires a person to find one or more unbending principles with which all else must harmonize. The person who makes a scientific study to determine the origin of man has accepted as an unbending principle: "Man's origin can be accounted for by natural causes."

A few conclusions are now beginning to be obvious. (1) If the answer to man's origin is to be found through science, the answer will not be a Divine act of creation. This is true since Divine activity is in the category of the supernatural, not the natural. (2) This same observation viewed from the other side tells us that if the answer to man's origin is to be found in a Divine act of creation, it is not discoverable by science since science finds answers only among natural causes. (3) If life had a beginning, it must be found on a low level. It is very difficult for anybody to believe that life came into being from lifeless matter by natural causes. If one is going to believe such, it is obvious that he will want to reduce his difficulty as much as possible by thinking the first life to be one cell life. No one could believe that natural causes could give sudden rise to a human being from lifeless matter. (4) Some form of evolution is presupposed by those who believe man has come into being by natural causes.

100

Natural causes could not suddenly take one cell life and change it into a fully developed human being. Dr. Robert T. Clark and Dr. James D. Bales in their book, *Why Scientists Accept Evolution* say in the "Preface," "If it was decided that all must be explained naturally, then obviously one would have to accept some hypothesis of evolution regardless of whether it was scientifically established." [16] In this well-documented book, they proceed to show that it was this commitment to naturalism before, during, and after Darwin that actually gave rise to and formed the basis of the acceptance of evolution. For those who want a documented case in addition to the logical case I have presented on this point, I highly recommend this book. (5) It is obvious that it would take a slow, drawn-out process. An enormously long period of time would have been required.

It is important to remember that the above observations are necessary conclusions on the part of the person who seeks the answer to man's origin in science. These conclusions are inherent in the approach before the first bit of evidence is examined. There are only two things left for evidence to do: (1) to describe the pattern of development, and (2) if the evidence be adequate, to give support to the preconceived conclusions inherent in the approach.

Another important observation is that to believe natural causes gave rise to the origin of the universe, life, and the development of life is a conclusion of faith. There is no proof nor can there be any proof that natural causes explain everything within the scope of our experience and observation. This statement is not made on the basis of whether natural causes do or do not explain everything. It is made because it does not lend itself to proof. Those who take the scientific approach cannot get away with the denial that their system is based on faith. If their faith be wrong, their system is wrong.

The only way a person can take the whole package of science on the origin of man and the age of the earth is to accept naturalism as the system of thought that explains the whole of reality. If God has acted, His acts are not the subject of scientific investigation. I am not suggesting that nothing dealing with the length of human history is subject to scientific investigation. I am saying that science cannot settle either for or against creation by a supernatural act. I am saying that if we believe in God we will have to let revelation tell us whether God created and what the limits of scientific investigation are.

C. Observations About the Theological Approach
to Study the Origin of Man

Let us look at the assumptions of those who look for the origin of man through the theological approach:

1. God exists.

2. God has revealed Himself and His plan in an inerrant Bible.

3. There is a supernatural realm and a natural realm. These are interrelated, but are distinct.

4. Whatever the Bible sets forth as belonging to the supernatural must be so accepted.

Theologically, the origin of man is accounted for as taking place by a direct act of God in a period of time not longer than twenty-four hours. The evidence for this position, based on the assumptions stated above, has already been given in this chapter.

The point is simply this: If the theological method be a valid approach for studying the origin of man, the scientific method is not. If the scientific method be a valid approach for studying the origin of man, the theological method is not. An individual may choose either one he prefers, but an evangelical Christian must accept the theological approach.

This approach is not intended to be anti-science. It only seeks to find proper limits for science. We do accept the uniformity of nature, but we do not place the whole realm of reality in nature. In such realms as medicine, chemistry, physics, etc., we would use the same approach any scientist would. However, when the Bible attributes something to a direct act of God, we dare not consider it an object of scientific investigation. Science ceases to be science when it seeks to enter the sphere of the supernatural.

In its proper sphere, we should have a very high regard for the scientific method. No generation has ever been so blessed by scientific research as ours.

A Christian view of science does not discuss the conclusions of science as its starting point. It simply limits science to be sphere of the natural. This limitation makes it as Christian as we could think of any non-biblical field of study as being. Of course, the Christian recognizes the realm of nature as being the creation of God.

After the limitation of science is made, the chief difference between the Christian and the non-Christian is: When the Christian discovers the marvelous wonders of nature, he feels like singing, "How Great Thou Art." The non-Christian feels like singing, "How Great I Am," or "How Great We Are," or "How Great Man Is."

The problem with most efforts to harmonize the Bible and science is that they have started at the wrong place. Science is not Christian because of its conclusions. It is Christian when it lets revelation determine what is supernatural, therefore, not an object of scientific investigation. It is very obvious that the ideas on the origin of man that comes from scientific investigation will not be the same as that which comes from the theological approach. If we accept the conclusions of scientists on the origin of man, it becomes quite obvious that the Biblical account must be twisted to fit. When the proper limitation is placed on science, there is no difficulty. In the realm of what we consider the sphere of the natural, there is no

102

difference in the approach of Christian and non-Christian to scientific study.

Our discussion so far has centered around the problem of the origin of man. It is equally clear that scientific research cannot discover the age of the earth if the theological assumptions are correct.

According to the Bible there are three universal events which do not fall in the category of events caused by natural causes.

1. The creation
2. The curse
3. The flood

We have no way of knowing what the earth looked like immediately after creation. We have no way of measuring creative activity.

We know that the curse affected the earth, but we know of no way to determine exactly how it affected it.

We know that there was a flood that was very devastating in its results. We can do some interesting speculation, but we cannot with any degree of assurance know the results of the flood beyond what is stated in the Bible.

Scientific study, when based on naturalistic assumptions, overlooks all three of the things mentioned above. If these things are true, and if our theological assumptions are true, it is impossible to discover the age of the earth because we would not know how to make proper allowances for the three events. Also, any attempt to discover the age of the earth which attributes it to natural causes will necessarily give a much older age for the earth than it actually is.

We may illustrate our point this way. Suppose we had seen some of the water that Jesus turned to wine (John 2), but had not known that it was turned into wine by a miracle, we would have assumed that it was made by natural processes. If anyone had asked us how long it took to make the wine, we would have told them the length of time it takes to make wine by natural processes. We would have been wrong. Why? Because of our failure to take into account that it was miraculously made.

If our theological assumptions are true, it is easy to see why those who do not take creation by a direct act of God, the curse, and the flood into account, will come up with the wrong answer on the age of the earth. We can rest assured that the earth is younger than scientists tell us. However, we cannot know the exact age of the earth because the Bible does not tell us.

Henry M. Morris makes observations along the same line as stated above. He explains:

> The Biblical framework involves three major facts of history, each of tremendous inportance with respect to the scientific study of data bearing on these problems. These

facts are of such obvious significance that to ignore them means that one is arbitrarily rejecting even the possibility that God could have given a genuine revelation of beginnings in His Book of Beginnings. The three facts are: (1) a real creation; (2) the fall of man and resultant curse on the earth; and (3) the universal deluge in the days of Noah. 17

With reference to creation, he remarks:

Now this can only mean that, since nothing in the world has been created since the end of the creation period, everything must *then* have been created by means of processes which are no longer in operation and which we therefore cannot study by any means or methods of science. We are limited exclusively to divine revelation as to the date of creation, the duration of creation, the method of creation, and every other question concerning the creation *necessarily* involves creation of an 'appearance of age.' It is impossible to imagine a genuine creation of anything without that entity having an appearance of age at the instant of its creation. 18

Perhaps the most vexing problem to the Christian is the problem of fossils. Fossils of men would have come after the curse. Probably the same can be said of animals. Granting that fossils occurred after the creation and curse, only one of the events mentioned above occurred during fossil history, that is the flood. The flood would have something to do with the distribution of fossils, but I am not prepared to say whether it would have affected the aging process of fossils.

Those who have the scientific qualifications to pursue this matter should consider such matters as the flood and fossils; things that affect the aging processes; and the accuracy of dating methods. It must also be kept in mind that while the Christian would like to see a later date for fossils, the scientist is favorable toward the idea of extremely old fossils. This is true because his system requires an extreme antiquity of life on the earth. We have as much right to look for the possibilities of dating fossils late as they do to look for possibilities of dating them early.

It is interesting to observe that the vast majority of the scientific study done on the age of fossils has been done by people who believed in naturalism. They believed that man's origin and development must be accounted for by natural causes. This caused them to look for evidence for a long history of man on the earth. It also caused them to interpret the available data with a favor toward a long history of man on the earth. Is it not resonable to believe that the bias of naturalism could have caused the scientist to overlook evidence that might have supported a younger date for fossils? Is it not reasonable to believe that if enough people who believed in special creation and a younger history of man and animals had been studying the evidence that they might have more answers to perplexing problems about the age of life on earth?

C. Concluding Observations

It is best for most of us to admit that we do not have a ready answer that refutes the scientific estimates on the age of fossils. Most of us are not prepared to discuss the subject intelligently from a scientific viewpoint. Those who are capable may be able to make a few observations, but they cannot remove all the difficulty.

Since we cannot readily show from scientific data that fossils must be given a young date compatible with the Scriptures, what will we do with our faith in the Biblical view of man? One lesson I have learned in life is that we will never believe anything if we cannot believe in spite of the fact that we do not have answers for all the problems.

Lest we let the evolutionist upset us and intimidate us when we admit we believe with problems, let us call attention to some of his problems. First, he must believe in the eternity of matter in some form. He has no proof of this. It is believed out of necessity. It must be a rather embarrassing point because we seldom hear it mentioned.

The spontaneous generation of life out of lifeless matter places a great strain on the intellect. There is no proof for it. There can be no proof for it. Even if scientists would create life out of matter, it would not prove that life originated spontaneously out of lifeless matter. If men after thousands upon thousands of hours over a period of several years would finally create life out of matter, it would not prove that it could have happened without all the minds, equipment, and controlled conditions. Yet, in spite of all the difficulty, those who look to natural causes for the answer must believe that life originated that way.

What about this belief in naturalism? There is no proof for it. There can be none. It must be a matter of faith. The naturalist has a heap of problems, but he believes anyway. He may be able to point to a vast number of learned men and learned works that support his position. This is not much comfort though when such a view introduces him into bankruptcy when it comes to the answers to the basic questions of life. The more the traces of Biblical influence are removed from those who believe in naturalism, the more bankrupt they become on basic issues.

Theism is accepted by faith too. However, it is not embarrassed by it. Neither does it try to cover up the place of faith. It readily admits the place of faith. Those who follow naturalism try to avoid admitting the place of faith in their system.

There are problems in believing the Biblical view of creation. However, there are also problems in believing in evolution and explaining life on the basis of natural causes. Naturalism bankrupts a person in the place where it counts the most—the moral and the spiritual. It leaves him on the sea of life without a compass, guide, or North Star. Theism and the Biblical explanation of the origin of man and God's relationship to man open the door to riches in the areas that count the most—the moral and the spiritual. Is it not reasonable to believe that the truth about the origin of man and knowledge for life will not be contradictory? Shall we not expect that same source of truth that tells us how to face life to also tell us the real answer to man's origin?

Truth is for life. All truth must ultimately fit together so as to make a sytematic whole. It would be a strange world if truth left man without answers to the inescapable questions of life. Biblical truth meets man's needs by answering these questions and giving practical guidance in life. Would we not also expect it to give an accurate answer regarding man's origin? Yes, there are problems, but the evolutionary answer has problems too. Let us stick with the answer that also prepares us for life. 19

CHAPTER SEVEN
NOTES

1. Edwin K. Gedney, "Geology and the Bible," *Modern Science and Christian Faith*, ed. by F. Alton Everest, Wheaton: Van Kampen Press, c. 1948, p. 66.

2. James Oliver Buswell, Jr., *A Systematic Theology of the Christian Religion*, Vol. 1, 2 vols., Grand Rapids: Zondervan Publishing House, c. 1962, p. 146.

3. *Ibid.*, p. 144.

4. *Ibid.*, pp. 145, 146.

5. H. C. Leupold, *Exposition of Genesis*, Vol. 1, 2 vols., Grand Rapids: Baker Book House, c. 1942, p. 57.

6. Carl F. H. Henry, "Science and Religion," *Contemporary Evangelical Thought*, ed. by Carl F. H. Henry, New York: Harper and Brothers, c. 1957, p. 277.

7. Bernard Ramm, *The Christian View of Science and Scripture*, Grand Rapids: William B. Eerdmans Publishing Company, c. 1955, p. 221.

8. Smalley and Fetzer, "A Christian View of Anthropology," *Modern Science and Christian Faith*, ed. by Alton Everest, second edition: Wheaton: Van Kampen Press, 1950, p. 161, referred to in Ramm, *The Christian View of Science and Scripture*, p. 334.

9. Ramm, *op. cit.*, p. 334.

10. *Ibid.*, p. 335.

11. Carl F. H. Henry, "Theology and Evolution," *Evolution and Christian Thought Today*, ed. by Russell L. Mixter, Grand Rapids: William B. Eerdmans Publishing Company, c. 1955, pp. 217, 218.

12. *Ibid.*, p. 218.

13. Ramm, *op. cit.*, p. 327.

14. John W. Klotz, From *"Genes, Genesis, and Evolution,"* Second revised edition, St. Louis, Mo.: Concordia Publishing House, c. 1955, 1970, p. 70. Used by permission.

15. Henry M. Morris, *The Twilight of Evolution*, Grand Rapids: Baker Book House, c. 1963, p. 42.

16. Robert T. Clark and James D. Bales, *Why Scientists Accept Evolution*, Grand Rapids: Baker Book House, c. 1966, p. 6.

17. *Ibid.*, pp. 55, 56.

18. *Ibid.*, p. 56.

19. Much of the material used in this chapter was from *Issues Among Evangelicals* by Leroy Forlines published by The Commission on Theological Liberalism of the National Association of Free Will Baptists, Nashville, Tennessee, 1968, pp. 22-57. The material was rearranged and rewritten with additions and deletions to meet the need of this study. A small amount of the material was taken from the booklet *Evolution* by Leroy Forlines published by Randall House Publications, Nashville, Tennessee, c. 1973, pp. 3, 4, 8-10.

The Nature of Man

The Psalmist asks one of the most important questions ever to be raised by a man when he asked; "What is man, that thou art mindful of him? and the son of man, that thou visitest him?" (Psalm 8:4). The answer to this question is not simply an exercise in mental curiosity by those seated at the intellectual round table.

Proper indentification is important. Even a machine requires proper identification. A motor requires proper identification in order that the right fuel may be used, the proper function may be understood, the right adjustments may be made, the right parts may be ordered for replacement, etc. Improper identification can have serious results. The same things can be said of plants. What may be fatal to one plant may not be harmful at all to another. The same can be said of animals. Improper identification can be dangerous and even fatal because improper identification can result in an improper prescription.

It seems absurd, in a way, to even talk about improper identification of man since we are each human. We observe others and are observed by others. The problem rests in the danger of an improper description of man. There are two conflicting views of man that demand our attention. One view describes man as being related to the animal world. He has an animal history. He has the needs of an animal of his type. The other view describes man as created by God in God's image. He is accountable to God.

It is obvious that the prescriptions written for man's needs will differ greatly according to which of these views a person subscribes. If the wrong prescription can cause malfunction, and even disastrous results for a machine, it should be more obvious that the wrong prescription for a man can have the most serious consequences. We need a proper prescription for our lives. Proper prescriptions can come only after we have proper identification. It is only when we have a prescription based on our design that we can know true happiness.

Revelation takes the guess work out of identification. Indentification comes to us as a "given" from the Creator Himself. The real nature of man's personality and what it takes to meet those needs will never be discovered by observation and experimentation. It must come to us as a "given."

I am not suggesting that the whole picture of man comes so fully amplified that there is no room for study. I am saying, however, that revelation does give us the basics and that all amplification of details must arise out of reflection upon the data of revelation. Also we must be constantly subjecting whatever may be known through research and observation to the authority of revelation.

One of the important things to observe about a system is that nothing in a system can be fully identified without reference to other parts of the system. Every part of a system is tied into the system by relationships to other parts. These relationships must be touched on in identifying a part. The matter of relationship in identification is clearly revealed in the statement: "Man is created in the image of God." To identify man without identifying God and then elaborating the meaning of "the image of God" is disastrous.

I. MAN AS CREATED

A. Created In The Image of God

That man is created in the image of God is declared in Genesis 1:26, 27. The meaning is that man is patterned after God. In what sense is man patterned after God? That it was not a physical likeness is too obvious to require proof in view of our study of the nature of God.

We get clues from Colossians 3:10 and Ephesians 4:24 regarding what is involved in being created in God's image. In Colossians 3:10 we read: "And have put on the new man, which is renewed in knowledge after the image of him that created him." The image of the Creator in man is linked to rationality. Therefore, we conclude that being created in the image of God involves the fact that man is rational.

In Ephesians 4:24 Paul wrote: "And that ye put on the new man, which after God is created in righteousness and true holiness." Therefore, we conclude that the image of God in man includes the fact that man is a moral creature.

The one word that sums up the idea of rationality and morality is the word "person." God is personal. Man is personal. The basic thrust of the idea of being created in the image of God is seen in the fact that man is a personal being.

A person is one who thinks, feels, and acts. We think with our mind. The mind is referred to in Matthew 22:37; Romans 14:5; and Hebrews 8:10. The words "think," "reason," and "understanding" are used too often in Scripture to require a list of proof texts. We think with our minds. In the mind we group ideas. We reason. We make judgments. We draw conclusions. We size up situations.

The heart is referred to in Matthew 22:37; Romans 10:1, 9; Hebrews 8:10; and others. We feel with our hearts. The heart is the seat of the emotions. With the heart we feel the reality of the truth that we know with our mind. The heart registers the value we place on things. It is with the heart that we feel sorrow and sadness. Sorrow and sadness reflect feelings of negative value or disvalue. Feelings of positive value are joy, happiness, satisfaction, peace, and contentment. Heart involvement represents the involvement of our deepest inner self.

The New Testament does not use the noun form of will to refer to the faculty or organ of choice in man. However, the verb form is used (Matthew 16:24; Matthew 21:29; 23:37; Mark 8:34; John 7:17; Revelation 22:17; and others). By will we mean power of choice. Every command, every prohibition, every exhortation, and every entreaty made in the Bible to people presupposes that they are capable of making choices.

Whether we want to think of the act of willing as the function of a faculty of the person or simply the person making a choice, the fact remains that the ability of choice is part of being a person. That ability of choice we call will. In his totality, man is a thinking, feeling, acting being. He thinks with his mind, feels with his heart, and acts with his will.

What has been said about man as a personal, rational, moral creature is frequently referred to as the formal likeness of God in man.[1] I prefer to speak of it as the constitutional likeness of God in man. The image of God in man at creation included more than constitutional likeness; it also included functional likeness (also referred to as material content[2]). The functional likeness means that man, as created, thought, felt, and acted in a way that was pleasing to God.

I think the distinction between constitutional and functional likeness is made clearer if we divide the scope of person into "personhood" and "personality." Personhood would embrace the constitutional likeness of God, i.e., all the elements that go together to constitute a person. Personality refers to the way a person thinks, feels and acts. At times person and personality are used synonymously, but there is usually a difference. In this study, personality will be used as defined above. Man as created was in the likeness of God both with respect to his personhood and his personality.

We need to go a step further. The functioning of personality occurs on two levels: the conscious level and the subconscious level.

110

Man as created and as he developed after creation, up to the time of the fall, functioned both on the conscious and subconscious level in the likeness of God.

The subconscious mind is programmed with ideas, attitudes, and responses. Mind, as it is referred to here, is used in the broad sense to include mind, heart, and will. It is this use of the word mind that we employ when we say, "I have made up my mind to do so and so." Mind in this instance involves more than the reasoning, thinking mind. It involves our total personality: our mind, heart, and will.

Through study, thought, observation, and meditation, we store knowledge or ideas into our subconscious mind. Only a very limited part of our knowledge is at any given moment in our conscious mind. It is stored for recall in our subconscious mind. The storage of ideas is much like the programming of a computer. Our mind is programmed with a vast store of ideas that can be brought to the surface with differing degrees of speed.

In the process of meditation, ideas to which we are committed take on the appropriate attitudes in the heart. We are programmed to think and feel a certain way under certain circumstances. The programming of the subconscious mind of Adam and Eve with ideas and attitudes was in the likeness of God before the fall. In their innermost being they were like God.

Inherent in the constitutional likeness of God in man and demonstrated in the functional likeness is the fact that man is relationship oriented. Man cannot be adequately described apart from these relationships. In fact, he will die, suffer malfunction, or be less than human according to what relationship (relationships) is involved and depending upon the extent he is deprived or deprives himself of these relationships. The relationships are: (1) his relationship to God; (2) his relationship to other people; (3) his relationship to the created order; and (4) his relationship to himself.

His relationship to God is seen in his responsibility to God. After we are told of the creation of man by God, we read, "And God blessed them, and God said unto them, Be fruitful, and multiply, and replenish the earth, and subdue it: and have dominion over the fish of the sea, and over the fowl of the air, and over every living thing that moveth upon the earth" (Genesis 1:28). We read also of man's moral responsibility when God said, "But of the tree of the knowledge of good and evil, thou shalt not eat of it: for in the day that thou eatest thereof thou shalt surely die" (Genesis 2:17). From the reference to God walking in the garden immediately after the fall, we would infer that He had done so before and that they had fellowship with God. Before the fall they functioned properly and in a way that was becoming to God in their relationship with God.

Man was designed for social relationships. In Genesis 2:18, God said, "It is not good that the man should be alone; I will make him an help meet for him." While the direct reference here is to making a wife for Adam, in view of the fact that man is a member of a race, it is obvious that social relationships are a part of the design of God. Man's needs for reciprocal social relationships are no less real than his need for air, water, and food. This need was created in our basic design and cannot be ignored without being followed by serious consequences.

Man was designed for a relationship to the created order (Genesis 1:26, 28-30; Psalm 8:6-8). Man was designed for the responsibility of using the earth, plants, and animals to serve his purpose. Work was a part of the original plan of God for man. It did not involve the undesirable aspects that it does now, but work has always been a part of the Divine plan.

Man was designed for a relationship with himself. Anytime there is responsibility and challenge, there is also a place for self-examination. How did I do? How can I face the challenge that is before me? There were two clear illustrations of responsibility: (1) the responsibility to refrain from eating of the tree of the knowledge of good and evil (Genesis 2:17); (2) to exercise dominion over the earth and its inhabitants.

To eat of the forbidden fruit was to reap the consequences of death. It would also make man guilty. Guilt when recognized by the person becomes self-judgment on the negative side. To refrain from eating would have been self-acceptance on the positive side. The responsibility to exercise dominion over the earth has the same basic results so far as self-judgment and self-acceptance are concerned. The moral tone may not be as strong, but the same basic principles are involved.

In connection with the responsibility placed upon man and the challenge given to him, we see that man is goal-oriented. Achievement with its rewards and failure to achieve with its losses are inescapably a part of a human being that was designed in him by the Creator.

B. The Importance Of The Fact That Man Is Created In The Image Of God

The image of God in man places a sense of worth on man. Man is of far greater worth than animals. Jesus said, "Behold the fowls of the air: for they sow not, neither do they reap, nor gather into barns; yet your heavenly Father feedeth them. Are ye not much better than they?" (Matthew 6:26). It was the greater worth of man than animals that Jesus appealed to when He defended His healing of the man with a withered hand on the sabbath day. "And he said unto them, What man shall there be among you, that shall have one sheep, and if it fall into a pit on the sabbath day, will he not lay hold on it, and lift it out? How much then is a man better than a sheep?

112

Wherefore it is lawful to do well on the sabbath days" (Matthew 12:11, 12).

Sin against our fellow man is viewed to be serious because of the fact that man is made in the image of God. In Genesis 9:6 we see the fact that man is made in the image of God is the basis for capital punishment. In James 3:9 we see the fact that man is made "after the similitude of God" makes slanderous talk about a fellow human being a serious matter.

Fellow human beings regardless of race, nationality, or sex must all be viewed as having special worth as having been created in the image of God. It is this basic respect that forms the beginning point of a right relationship with people.

The fact that man is created in the image of God means that man is characterized by both dependence and independence. The fact that man is created by God means that he is dependent upon God. The fact that he is a member of a race, not just an individual, means that people are interdependent upon each other. The fact that man is a person means that he has a measure of independence.

There must be some sense in which his actions are his own—under his control. If this be not the case, he is less than a person. Yet, the fact that he is a relationship creature means that his actions cannot be explained as independent in the absolute sense. Influence is brought to bear on his actions. Influence in personal decisions can never be equated with cause as in mechanical cause and effect relationships. Influence and response are more appropriate terms, where persons make decisions, than the terms cause and effect.

In many of our decisions, we are both active and acted upon. To have to make a choice between active and passive is to equate personal relationships with mechanical cause and effect relationships. These principles relate both to our relationships to God and our relationship to other human beings.

It is only when we see the full meaning of man as a personal, rational, moral being along with the fact that man is designed for the four basic relationships that we can determine what man's needs are according to his design. The design of man represents not only possibilities, but needs. It is not only possible for us to be rational and moral but to have functioning relationships. We *need* to function rationally and morally, and properly in the framework of the four basic relationships. Failure in any of these areas means loss. All rational, moral, and spiritual functions are functions of the personality. A Christian psychology, sociology, and system of ethics must have as a part of its foundation an acquaintance with what it means to be made in the image of God.

Government, both secular and church government, should allow the degree of freedom required for man to develop his personality and prepare to meet God. On the one hand, there must be

113

government. On the other hand, there must be freedom.

One of the most important facts related to man's being made in the image of God is that it made the incarnation possible. There could have been no incarnation with a non-rational, non-moral, sub-personal animal. The possibility of redemption is closely related to the fact that man is made in the image of God.

C. Man Created A Dichotomous Being

There has been much debate over whether man is a dichotomous being or a trichotomous being. To say that man is a dichotomous being is to say that he consists of a body (material part) and spirit (some use soul and spirit interchangeably). To say that man is a trichotomous being is to say that man consists of a material body and two immaterial parts—soul and spirit.

Dr. A. H. Strong gives the following explanation of dichotomy:

> We conclude that the immaterial part of man, viewed as an individual and conscious life, capable of possessing and animating a physical organism, is called *psuche* (soul); viewed as a rational and moral agent, susceptible of divine influence and indwelling, this same immaterial part is called *pneuma* (spirit). The *pneuma* (spirit), then is man's nature looking Godward, and capable of receiving and manifesting the *Pneuma Hagion* (Holy Spirit); the *psuche* (soul) is man's nature looking earthward, and touching the world of sense. The *pneuma* (spirit) is man's higher part, as related to spiritual realities or as capable of such relation; the *psuche* is man's higher part, as related to body, or as capable of such relation.[3]

As Strong presents it, soul and spirit are different terms referring to the same immaterial substance. These terms each speak of the same immaterial part from a different viewpoint of function. Some trichotomists refer about the same function to soul and spirit, but use them to refer to two different immaterial parts.

I think the real problem centers around trying to think of the soul in terms of being a "part" of man. An examination of the Hebrew word *nephesh* and the Greek word *psuche* as used in the Bible does not seem to support the idea that it refers to an immaterial substance of man.

In Genesis 2:7; 14:21; 17:14, *nephesh* means being, individual, or person. The use in these verses would not make sense if *nephesh* referred to a part of man. It is the person, not a part of the person, that is in view. *Nephesh* is translated person several times (Exodus

114

16:16; Leviticus 27:2; Numbers 19:18; Joshua 20:3, 9; and others). In Genesis 19:17; Exodus 4:19; 21:23; Leviticus 17:14; and many others, it is translated life. In these passages it would not fit to think of *nephesh* as being to the immaterial part of man. In Leviticus 26:11, 15; Psalm 42:2; and other similar uses the reference is to the innermost being. In these cases it would be possible for *nephesh* to refer to the immaterial part of man, but it is not necessary. Also, one wonders why Psalm 42:2 did not use the word "spirit" if the usual distinctions made between soul and spirit by both dichotomists and trichotomists are valid. The meaning of *nephesh* in Numbers 16:50 is "self." It is translated "yourselves" in Deuteronomy 4:15.

In the New Testament the word *psuche* at times clearly means individual or person (Acts 2:41; 7:14; 37:37; Romans 13:1). In Luke 1:46 and John 12:27 *psuche* refers to the innermost being. Again one wonders why the word spirit instead of soul did not appear in Luke 1:46 based on the usual distinctions. In Ephesians 6:6, *psuche* is translated heart. Luke 12:19 is a clear case of where the meaning of the word *psuche* is self.

A study of the evidence supports the conclusion that soul does not refer to an immaterial part of man. Soul refers to a self-conscious individual; the innermost being; the self; the life; the person.

Psalm 31:5; Ecclesiastes 3:21; 12:7; and Zechariah 12:1 are clear references to the Hebrew word *ruach* (spirit) in which the reference is to the immaterial part of man. John 3:6 is a clear reference where the Greek word *pneuma* (spirit) refers to the immaterial part of man. Man's basic nature is in his spirit (John 3:6; Romans 1:9; 2 Corinthians 2:13; and Hebrews 12:23). Functions and states that are attributed to man's spirit do not always require it to be a reference to the immaterial part of man, but they are always consistent with that idea (Genesis 41:8; Exodus 6:9; 1 Kings 21:5; Psalm 34:18; Acts 17:16; 18:5, 25; and Romans 1:9). These observations, along with the fact that angels and evil spirits are called spirits, apparently because of their immaterial make-up, lead to the conclusion that the spirit of man is the immaterial part of man and describes it as being spirit rather than physical.

A contrast of the use of soul and spirit will help in what I am meaning by my view of dichotomy. Soul is not an immaterial part of man. Spirit is an immaterial part of man. No occurrence of the word for soul requires it to be a part of man. Many occurrences of the word cannot be understood as a reference to a part of man. All occurrences of the word spirit, unless of course we are talking about the spirit of jealousy, the spirit of wisdom, etc., when referred to man, are capable of being understood as the immaterial part of man. Many occurrences of the word for spirit must be understood as referring to a part of man. A way of saying it that may be a slight oversimplification is: I am a soul. I have a spirit.

It is hard for most of us to think of soul without thinking of a part of our being because we have been accustomed to thinking that way. If we will give soul the same basic meaning as person, that will help get away from thinking of soul as a part of our being. We do not think of person as an immaterial substance, nor a material substance. We are a person. We have a body and a spirit. Also, the words mind, heart, and will do not refer to different immaterial parts of man's being. In the same way we think of these terms, we can train ourselves not to think of soul as an immaterial substance, but the self-conscious individual, the innermost being, the self, the life, or the personality.

My view of dichotomy differs from the traditional view which sees a high degree of interchangeableness between soul and spirit. It may be true that sometimes a person could accomplish his purpose in a sentence by using either, but he would not be saying identically the same thing. At times the purpose in a sentence could not at all be served by one term as well as the other. A choice must be made between the terms. If it is a part of man, it must be spirit. If it is person or individual, it must be soul.

There is a very close relationship between spirit and soul. Without the spirit there would be no soul. In a sense we might think of soul as issuing forth from spirit. To borrow terminology from Berkhof when he explains the difference between nature and person, soul is the terminus to which spirit tends.[4]

I think there are some very definite advantages to the approach I am suggesting. The traditional understanding of soul and spirit, both in dichotomy and trichotomy, make the expression "soul-winning" inacurrate since soul is understood to refer to the lower function of man. To be consistent, one should talk about spirit-winning. In my view, soul-winning is appropriate terminology since it refers to winning the person. Soul embraces all of a person's experiences, both the ordinary experiences of life and our relationship with God.

Another advantage is that it does away with the need of trying to decide what functions are to be attributed to soul and what functions are to be attributed to spirit. By distinguishing between the use of soul and spirit, traditional dichotomy engages in this about as much as trichotomy. The problem is that when we get through we find functions attributed to soul that are supposed to be attributed to spirit. When soul is basically equated with person or personality, any action or attitude can be attributed to it. When soul refers to the lower functions of man, and spirit the higher functions of man, it comes unexpectedly when we read that Mary said, "My soul doth magnify the Lord" (Luke 1:46). It is surprising when we read in Ephesians 6:6 "... doing the will of God from the heart" and discover that the Greek word for heart in this verse is *psuche* (soul). We are puzzled when we read in James 1:21 " ... and receive with meekness the engrafted word, which is able to save your souls." It

116

seems from the usual distinction between soul and spirit that the word spirit should have appeared in these passages, but it did not. However, there is no problem when the meaning I suggest is given to soul.

It is true that the spiritual functions of man are frequently ascribed to the spirit. In such instances, the intention is not to give us the functions of spirit as distinguished from soul, but spirit as distinguished from the body.

We run into another problem when we try to make the distinctions usually made between soul and spirit. Animals, we might expect to have souls, but not spirits. Yet Ecclesiastes 3:21 speaks about animals as having a spirit. I am inclined to agree with Dr. Buswell at this point. He says, "The distinction between man and beasts is qualitative, not substantive. It is not that man has or is a soul, spirit, heart, mind, will, affective being, but that man's non-material being is a person created in the image of God."5

D. The Origin Of The Immaterial Part Of Man

By origin of the immaterial part of man, I am not referring to the original creation by God, but to the origin of the immaterial part as it relates to those who have descended from Adam and Eve. In one sense, this discussion may not belong under the discussion of man as created, but in another sense it does. The design of providing the immaterial part of man is not related to the fall, but was already a part of the Divine plan before the fall. The same plan would have been followed if there had been no fall of man into sin.

There are three approaches: (1) The pre-existence theory which teaches that the immaterial part of man existed prior to the creation of the body. Since this view has never been accepted by orthodox Christians, I do not deem it necessary to deal with it. There are no reasons for anyone to even be confused about whether the Bible supports such a view. (2) The creationist theory teaches that God creates the immaterial part of each person and places it in the body sometime between conception and birth. (3) The traducian theory teaches that the immaterial part of man is transmitted through propagation just as the body is.

One of the main reasons that people have advocated the creationist view is that it is felt that this was the only way for Christ to be born without depravity. It is felt that traducianism would result in a depraved nature for Christ. I would suggest that the same Divine act of conception that could provide Jesus with a body that did not bear the marks of depravity could also sanctify the immaterial part of man.

The most serious objection to the creationists' view is how the immaterial part becomes corrupt. One thought, which is sometimes

117

associated with the federal headship view of Adam's sin and the race, suggests that God created the immaterial part of man corrupt because Adam violated the covenant God made with him when he sinned. I cannot conceive of God as creating anything corrupt. Another view states that God creates the immaterial part sinless but that it becomes corrupt upon contact with the body. There is a close relationship between the spirit and the body, but to blame the total process of perpetuating the depravity of the race on the body is more than can be justified. The depravity of the spirit is far more basic in our depravity than that of the body.

The traducian theory most easily accounts for the perpetuation of depravity in the human race and its effects on the total person. Some are of the opinion that the Bible does not give a clear-cut case for either creationism or traducianism. I do not think this is the case. In Genesis 5:3 we read, "And Adam . . . begat a son in his own likeness, after his image; and called his name Seth." If the creation of man in God's image included the personhood and personality of Adam, certainly the begetting of Seth in Adam's image included Seth's personhood and personality. Personhood and personality cannot be based upon body alone, but must embrace the spirit also. Traducianism offers the only adequate explanation of Adam begetting Seth in his own image.

There are some interesting implications of traducianism. According to traducianism the beginning of a human person takes place at conception. This means that a human being who will live forever has come into existence. This is of some comfort to the woman who has had a miscarriage. All is not lost. There will be a human being who will live with God forever. The implications as they relate to abortion are obvious. Abortion puts to death a human life. The question of when human life begins is not to be settled scientifically by the medical profession, but theologically by those who subscribe to the Bible as God's revelation.

II. MAN AS AFFECTED BY THE FALL

A. The Effect On The Image Of God In Man

Dr. Henry explains: "The fall of man is not destructive of the formal image (man's personality) although it involves the distortion (though not demolition) of the material content of the image."6

As was stated previously when discussing the meaning of being made in the image of God, I prefer "constitutional likeness" to "formal image" and "functional likeness" to "material content," but the meaning is the same whichever way it may be stated. I, further, made a distinction between personhood and personality. This distinction will be particularly helpful in explaining the effect of the fall on the image of God in man.

With reference to the constitutional likeness, the fall did not change this fact. The personhood of man remains intact. He is still a thinking, feeling, acting being. He is still morally constituted. All of the constituent parts of personhood remain intact after the fall. The parts have suffered damage, but they all remain. The damage reflects itself in the personality.

The effect of the fall is seen in the functional likeness. A basic and drastic change occurred in man's personality. Before the fall, man thought, felt, and acted both on the conscious and unconscious level in the likeness of God. After the fall, this is no longer true. Man no longer thinks, feels, and acts in a way that is pleasing to God. This is true both in the conscious and subconscious level.

It is clear that man fell from a state of holiness into a state of sin (Isaiah 53:6 and Romans 3:23). It is clear that sin has placed man under condemnation before God (Romans 6:23 and Revelation 21:8). It is clear that fallen man cannot please God and has no fellowship with God (Ephesians 2:1-3 and Romans 8:7, 8). It is clear that man cannot come to God without the drawing power of the Holy Spirit (John 6:44). It is clear that a work so drastic as to be called a new birth is required for man's salvation (John 3:3-7). But we enter areas where the state and condition of man is not so clearly understood.

Dr. Henry is grappling with the difficulty of a clear statement on the effect of the fall on the functional likeness in man in what he says in the quotation given earlier. He states that while there is a "distortion" there is not a "demolition" of the material content (functional likeness). What we are dealing with here is: How depraved is man? What do we mean when we say that there is not a demolition of the functional likeness?

I am not raising the question of whether man is totally depraved; but rather, what is meant by total depravity. Dr. Charles C. Ryrie makes the following observations about the meaning of total depravity:

> Total depravity is a theological term used to denote the unmeritoriousness of man in the sight of God. Negatively, the concept does not mean (1) that every man has exhibited his depravity as thoroughly as he could; (2) that sinners do not have a conscience of 'naive induction' concerning God; (3) that sinners will indulge in every sin; or (4) that depraved man does not perform actions that are good in the sight of man. Positively, total depravity means (1) that corruption extends to every part of man's nature, including all the faculties of his being; and (2) that there is nothing in man that can commend him to a righteous God.7

119

Why is it that every sinner does not exhibit his depravity as thoroughly as he could? Why is it that every sinner does not commit every sin? Why is it that a degree of moral concern can be found among sinners? Why is it that sinners perform some good deeds? The answer goes back to the fact that sinners still retain personhood. They are still personal, rational, moral beings by constitution and design.

Man did not become non-moral in the fall anymore than he became non-rational. A being must be moral, i.e., morally constituted, to be immoral. He must be rational, i. e., rationally constituted to be irrational. It is the moral constitution of man that Paul is discussing in Romans 2:15 when he speaks about the Gentiles, "Which shew the work of the law written in their hearts . . . ."

The sinner is so constituted that he has the categories of right and wrong. Right is considered a plus factor, and wrong is considered a minus factor. No human being does what he knows to be wrong without to some extent considering it to be a minus factor. This fact cannot be obliterated. Sin has introduced a foreign element in man's being. Man was made for righteousness. He was not made for sin. A human being can never live in sin and have self-acceptance and full harmony of being. Sin has placed man in conflict, contradiction, and confusion. To whatever extent a person has forfeited the morality of the Ten Commandments, to that extent, he is in trouble not only with God but with himself. No person who lives in gross violation of the morality of the Ten Commandments is happy.

Since man cannot totally erase moral concern, he tries to enter into label changing. He tries to place the label "right" on what he wants to do and "wrong" on what he does not want to do. The effort never totally succeeds. Regardless of what may go on in the conscious mind, a person can never accept in his deep inner being the violation of the basic morality of the Ten Commandments. Ten thousand arguments will never make these violations acceptable. Notice the lack of self-respect among those who try this route. Notice the need of alcohol and the need of drugs. Notice the presence of misery, despair, and depression. All of these tell us that the deep inner self is not going along with the attempt to set aside basic Christian morality.

Man is in drastic need of approval both from himself and from others. This fact gives rise to worthy deeds among sinners. Every person feels good when he by conscious choice does what he believes to be right. Every person feels good when he by conscious choice accommodates another person.

The fact that the categories of right and wrong, with right being a plus factor and wrong being a minus factor, are indelibly written in the constitution of man is not totally void of producing some good in the sinner. This good will never provide acceptance before God, neither will it meet the needs of the person himself. It is the presence of this moral constitution in man that provides a point of contact for the gospel. If fallen man were a moral blank, or had the categories of right and wrong reversed, there would be no point of contact for the gospel. There would be no grounds for conviction of sin.

In addition to the influence of man's own moral constitution in curbing his experience with sin and producing some good, there are external restraints that keep people from being as wicked as they would otherwise be. There are the restraints of parents, government, society, and the church.

In assessing the seriousness of the power and influence of depravity, we must keep in mind the fact that the truest picture of sin does not always manifest itself in overt acts. Everyone has in his imagination imagined committing sins that he has not committed. The same capacity that can imagine evil can commit evil. Everyone has kept in check some desire for evil that he has had. With the same capacity we desire evil, we can also commit evil. Sometimes people enjoy seeing sin committed by others. The same capacity that enjoys evil can commit evil.

It is possible and sometimes happens that an unconverted man reaches a measure of decency and uprightness in society. He may perform some humanitarian deeds, but all of these fall far short of meeting Divine approval. The presence of sin in his life still renders him unrighteous before a holy God. The power of sin in his life makes him stand in need of the new birth.

The real controversy over depravity centers around the will. Does the fallen man have a free will? If descendants of Adam do not in some sense have freedom of will, they have lost their personhood. One of the factors involved in being a person is to have power of choice or the ability to will. The will can only choose and act to the extent that it is free. To deprive will of freedom is to deprive it of being a will.

Before proceeding to discuss the effect of depravity on the will, let us make a few things clear about what is and is not meant by freedom of will. The freedom of the will does not mean that forces or influences cannot be brought to bear upon the will. It does not mean that these forces cannot be a determining factor in the exercise of the will. It does mean that these forces cannot guarantee the action of the will. We are dealing with influence and response, not mechanical cause and effect.

Freedom of will is a freedom within the framework of possibilities. It is not absolute freedom. We cannot be God. We cannot be an angel. The freedom of a human being is in the framework of the possibilities provided by human nature. Also, the influences brought to bear on the will have a bearing on the framework of possibilities.

Before Adam and Eve sinned, it was in the framework of possibilities within which they operated to remain in the practice of complete righteousness, or to commit sin. After they sinned, it no longer remained within the framework of possibility for them to practice uninterrupted righteousness. The same is true for fallen man now (Romans 8:7, 8). If anyone reads the meaning of freedom of will to mean that an unconverted person could practice righteousness and not sin, he misunderstands the meaning of freedom of will. The fact that the Scriptures do not teach this to be true is clear from Romans 8:7, 8.

Jesus makes it clear that it does not fall within the framework of possibility for a sinner to respond to the gospel unless he is drawn by the Holy Spirit (John 6:44). The influence of the Holy Spirit working in the heart of the person who hears the gospel brings about a framework of possibilities in which a person can say yes or no to the gospel. If he says, "yes," it is his choice. If he says, "no," it is his choice. To say less than that is to raise serious questions about the existence of real personhood after the fall. If man is not in some sense a self-directed being, he is not a person. The self-direction may have a high degree of dependence at times, but it is still self-direction. As has already been made clear, I am not suggesting that fallen man can choose Christ without the aid of the Holy Spirit. I am saying, however, that no matter how much or how strong the aid of the Holy Spirit may be, the "yes" decision is still a decision that can rightly be called the person's decision. Also, he could have said no.

Faith can be called a gift in the sense that it would not have been made possible without Divine aid. It is not a gift in the sense that it exists outside the person and is given to him, nor is it a gift in the sense that God believes for the person. The person himself does the believing by Divine aid.

I think Calvinism errs in its understanding of "dead in trespasses." Dr. Cornelius Van Til explains the Calvinistic interpretation:

> It was only as a creature of God, made in his image, that man could sin. So, when a sinner, and as such 'dead in trespasses,' unable of himself even to stretch forth his hand to receive salvation, Scripture continues to deal with him as a responsible being. He is called to faith and repentance. Yet faith is a gift of God. Lazarus lay in the tomb. He was dead. Yet Jesus told him to come forth. And he did come forth. [8]

The above interpretation interprets "dead" in "dead in trespasses" (Ephesians 2:1) as meaning lifeless. The dead body of Lazarus had no life in it. It was capable of no action until it was made alive by Jesus. If "dead in trespasses" means dead in the same way, the logic of Calvinism follows. The sinner would be both deaf and speechless. He would know nothing about God, sin, and

122

salvation until God made him alive through the new birth. Then and only then would he be able to hear and to speak.

I think "dead in trespasses and sins" or spiritual death means that man is separated from God, dead in relationship to God. There is no communion and no fellowship with God. The principle is similar to that spoken of by Paul when he said," ... By whom the world is crucified unto me, and I unto the world" (Galatians 6:14). Both Paul and the world were alive in the sense that they were not lifeless. They were not alive so far as a functioning relationship between them was concerned.

Spiritual death, if this be the correct interpretation, refers to the fact that the sinner is cut off from communion and fellowship with God. This is true both because a holy God demands that it be so until sin is taken care of, and also because the bias of the sinner's heart is against God. The fact the sinner is not in communion with God does not mean that he is totally deaf to God's communication. If that were the case, the sinner could not even distort the message of God. You cannot distort that to which you are totally deaf. The fact that a person is a sinner does mean that he does not hear well. He tends to resist and oppose the truth and to distort the truth. The gospel has to go forth against great opposition. The Holy Spirit must work before there can be a successful communication of the gospel to the sinner and conviction and response from the sinner. This approach recognizes the seriousness of sin, the necessity of the enlightening and drawing power of the Holy Spirit, and the personhood of the sinner.

B. The Consequences Upon The Race Of Adam's Sin

The questions to be answered are: (1) Is Adam's sin imputed to the race? (2) If it is imputed, how and why? (3) How is depravity transmitted?

The key passage in deciding the consequences upon the race of Adam's sin is Romans 5:12-19. How do we interpret, " ... death passed upon all men, for all have sinned" in verse 12? "Death passed upon all men" is the effect. "All have sinned" is the cause. Concerning the Greek word translated "have sinned," there are two possibilities so far as Greek grammar is concerned. "Have sinned" is a translation of *hemarton* which is the aorist. If we understand the aorist as a simple aorist, we would translate "all sinned." It would mean that all sinned at some time in the past. This would mean that death passed upon the race because the race sinned at some time in the past.

If we understand the aorist as being a gnomic aorist, we would translate it "all sin." If we understand it to be a culminative aorist, we would translate it "all have sinned." Whether we would understand the Greek to be a gnomic aorist or a culminative aorist, the interpretation would be the same. It would mean that death passes upon all men because all people sin.

If we understand that death passed upon all men because all men sinned at some time in the past, death would pass upon all because all sinned in Adam. If we understand that death passes upon all men because all sin, death would pass upon each person because of his own sins, not the sin of Adam. The context must decide which of these interpretations is right.

I think the chart below will help us see how the context decides the question.

CAUSE	EFFECT
5:12 "All sin" or "all sinned"?	"Death passed upon all men"
5:15 "The offence of one"	"Many be dead"
5:16 "By one [person]"	"Condemnation"
5:17 "One man's offence"	"Death reigned"
5:18 "The offence of one"	"Judgment came upon
(The Greek means "one offense.")	all men to condemnation"

On the "effect" side of the chart, it is obvious that the effect in 5:15-18 is the same as the effect in 5:12. If it is clear what the cause of the effect is in 5:15-18, that should help clarify what the cause is in 5:12. The cause in 5:15-18 is "one person," "one man's offence," and "one offence." Putting that together, it is clear that the cause is the one offense committed by Adam when he ate the forbidden fruit.

If 5:12, 15-18 all give the same effect, it is to be expected that 5:12, 15-18 will all give the same cause. The cause is clear in 5:15-19. This interprets the cause in 5:12. While Greek grammar may allow the statement in 5:12 to refer to each individual's sin, the context decides against it and in favor of the other grammatical possibility. It is clear in the total context that 5:12 is to be interpreted, "all sinned in Adam."

Romans 5:12-19 definitely settles the fact that the sin of Adam is imputed or placed on the account of the whole race. The question to be decided now is how and why was this done? There are two views given on how this is done.

One view would say that the answer is found in the natural headship to the race. The other would declare that while Adam is the natural head of the race, the natural headship did not furnish a grounds for imputing the sin of Adam to the race. Adam was appointed federal head of the race and the grounds of imputation are found in the federal headship of Adam.

According to the view that grounds imputation in the natural headship of Adam, sin is imputed to the race because the race by being in Adam was a part of Adam when he sinned, thus identified with him in his sin and the guilt of that sin. This view accepts the

124

traducian view of the origin of the human spirit. Depravity is transmitted by the process of propagation.

According to the federal headship view, Adam became the representative of the race by Divine appointment. The reason for Adam's being chosen was his natural headship, but natural headship did not of itself involve the race in Adam's sin. God entered into a covenant with Adam promising to bestow eternal life upon him and his posterity if he should obey God, and corruption and death would pass on to his posterity if he should disobey God. It is the covenant relationship of the race with Adam by virtue of his being appointed as the representative of the race that involves the race in the consequences of his sin. Instead of saying the race sinned in Adam, this view would say, "All are accounted as sinners."

Comparison of Natural and Federal Headship Theories

Natural	Federal
1. Traducianist	1. Creationist (As a rule, but not necessarily)
2. Adam representative of the race because the race was in him	2. Adam representative of the race because of Divine appointment
3. Sin imputed because of identification by being in Adam	3. Sin imputed because Adam as appointed representative violated the covenant
4. All sinned	4. All accounted as sinners
5. Spirit transmitted with a depraved nature	5. Spirit immediately created by God with a corrupt and depraved nature, or created without corruption and corrupted by contact with the corrupt body. (A few would go along with the traducian view, but this is not the usual view.)

While a person may be a traducianist and hold to the federal headship view, a creationist must hold to the federal headship view if he believes in the imputation of the sin of Adam to the race. Being in Adam from a physical viewpoint only, would not furnish an adequate basis for imputing the sin of Adam to the race as it relates to the total personality.

125

The federal headship view works on the assumption that the federal headship principles of imputation explain the imputation of the death and righteousness of Christ to the redeemed. It then seeks to build a parallel view of the imputation of Adam's sin to the race.

While there may be some people who accept the federal headship view of Adam that do not accept unconditional election, the federal headship principle fits logically in the Calvinistic system. The covenant made with Adam, because of Adam's disobedience, brought condemnation to all who were in the covenant. In this case, it was the whole race. The covenant made with Christ, because of His obedience in death and righteousness, brought eternal life to all who were in the covenant. In this case, according to Calvinism, it was only those who were unconditionally elected to be parties of the covenant who were in the covenant.

By an act of His own will and based on His own reasons, God chose to include the whole race as the recipient of the guilt and consequences of Adam's sin. He could have chosen to have done otherwise. There was nothing in the nature of things that made it necessary for it to be that way. By an act of His own will and based on His own reasons, God did not choose to elect the whole human race and make them participants in the benefits of Christ's obedience. There was nothing in the nature of the case that required Him to limit the number of the elect. I mention these observations here because in systematic thinking we must see the possible bearing on other parts in a system of the way we interpret principles and their application in a particular place.

Does the Scripture aid in our choice between the natural headship view and the federal headship view? I think it does. The evidence presented above supports the conclusion that Romans 5:12 is to be interpreted as, "All sinned in Adam."

The language of Romans 5:12 is more appropriate for the natural headship view because the language of Romans 5:12 and of the natural headship view are identical. The "all sinned" of Romans 5:12 must be twisted to mean "all are accounted as sinners" for the federal headship view. "All sinned" is in the active voice. "All are accounted as sinners" would require the passive voice.

We have some difficulty in our total being in accepting the conclusion that the whole race was condemned for Adam's sin. This is made far more acceptable when we see that the nature of things made it necessary that the race be charged with Adam's sin than to think that God made the decision in no relationship to necessity. There are those who say in rebuttal, God can do anything. God cannot be limited by necessity. This is to misunderstand the case. God must act in accord with His nature. He has built certain principles and guidelines into the nature of reality. He is obligated to abide by these principles and guidelines in order that He may maintain a rational consistency with His creation. The objectionable features of the creationist view of the origin of the spirit and how it becomes corrupt have already been discussed earlier in the chapter and need not be repeated here.

Let us now return to a further discussion of the natural headship view. We have already seen that it best accords with Scripture. Now let us look at the logical defense.

The race was in Adam and has descended body and spirit from him. The fact that we were in Adam means that we were identified with him in his sin. This necessitates our being a partaker with him in his guilt and condemnation. To say otherwise would say that not all of Adam was condemned because that which was in Adam's loins, which was the race potentially, was as much a part of Adam as any other part. No matter how many subdivisions there may be, the parts never lose their real identification as being a part of the original whole. We have never lost our identification with him in his sin.

I would not accept some of the ideas that have usually been associated with this view. In explaining this view, Dr. A. H. Strong says," . . . The powers which now exist in separate men were then unified and localized in Adam; Adam's will was yet the will of the species. In Adam's free act, the will of the race revolted from God and the nature of the race corrupted itself." [9]

It sounds as if Strong may be saying that the will of every human being acted in Adam's will. I do not think this to be the case. The wills did not exist. Only the potential for these wills existed. Our wills came into being only when we came into being as an individual person. To say that all sinned in Adam must not be understood to say that their wills were active in Adam. We could say that his will was the will of the race since the race was in him and descended from him, but we cannot speak of the wills of the race being combined in his will.

The principle involved in imputation of something from one to another is identification by being in or in union with the person. This is true whether it be sin or whether it be righteousness. The Scripture knows of no other way that the action of one person can be imputed to another. This is the principle involved in the imputation of the death and righteousness of Christ to the believer.

The Bible knows of no imputation from one to another except in a manner that makes it so the action can in some sense be said to be the action of the person himself. Paul said in Galatians 2:20, "I am [or I have been] crucified with Christ." By being in union with Christ, Paul became so identified with Christ that it could be said that he was crucified with Christ. Paul was not actually crucified with Christ in the sense of experiencing the sufferings of Christ. By identification with Christ the death of Christ became his so that he could get credit for its benefits. (For a more thorough explanation of this see the discussion on the union of Christ in connection with the doctrine of justification.)

In a similar sense that the death of Christ is ours, the sin of Adam is ours. We did not perform the sin by an act of our own will, but we were in Adam when he committed the sin. We were identified with him. We were in Adam at the time of his sin. Our connection with him is maintained by an unbroken continuity between Adam and us. We were not in Christ at the time of His crucifixion, but were placed in Him when we exercised faith. We are now in Him.

I think the federal headship principle misinterprets both the imputation of Adam's sin and the imputation of the death and righteousness of Christ. The Scripture knows of only one principle of imputation of the actions of one person to another and that is identification by union. The natural headship view, not the federal headship view, maintains the parallel between Christ and Adam in connection with the principle involved in imputation. (If the reader has problems at this point, I would suggest that he skip over and read what is said about union with Christ as it relates to justification. The whole case is better elaborated there.)

A question that always arises in this connection is: What about those dying in infancy? I will reserve the discussion of this until later. Let me just say at this point, I believe in infant salvation. The discussion belongs more properly to the doctrines of atonement and salvation.

There are two more views that should be mentioned. The theory of mediate imputation denies that the guilt of Adam is imputed to the race. We receive depravity from him, and depravity forms the basis of guilt and condemnation. The sin of Adam is the indirect cause, not the direct cause of the race being charged with guilt. This imputation of guilt precedes personal acts of sin. This view does not accord with Scripture as we have seen from our discussion above.

Another view that is frequently referred to as the Arminian view does not believe that the race is charged with the guilt of Adam's sin. Depravity is inherited from Adam and caused people to sin. They are not condemned before God until they commit individual sin upon becoming responsible persons. The discussion above shows the inadequacy of this view.

While it is true that some Arminians have advocated this view, it is by no means unanimous and should not be called the Arminian view.[10] One of the chief concerns of Arminians has been to deny that infants go to Hell. Some have sought support for this denial by denying guilt before individual guilt enters the picture. Many others have believed that the guilt of Adam was imputed to the race, but was removed for all in atonement.

III. MAN AS AFFECTED BY REDEMPTION
The basic principles will be stated briefly here. A more

thorough development of the ideas will be given in connection with the doctrines of salvation.

Redemption concerns itself with restoring that which was lost in the fall. It is the design of redemption to restore the functional likeness of God in man. It is designed to make man like God in His personality. He is to be made in the likeness of God both on the conscious and subconscious levels in the way he thinks, feels, and acts.

CHAPTER EIGHT
NOTES

1. Carl F. H. Henry, "Man," *Baker's Dictionary Of Theology*, ed. by Everett F. Harrison, Grand Rapids: Baker Book House, c. 1960, pp. 340, 341.

2. *Ibid.*, p. 341.

3. A. H. Strong, *Systematic Theology*, Three volumes in one, Philadelphia: The Judson Press, c. 1907, p. 486.

4. L. Berkhof, *Systematic Theology*, Grand Rapids: Wm. B. Eerdmans Publishing Company, c. 1941, p. 321.

5. James Oliver Buswell, Jr., *A Systematic Theology Of The Christian Religion*, Vol. 1, 2 volumes, Grand Rapids: Zondervan Publishing House, c. 1962, p. 241.

6. Henry, *loc. cit.*

7. Charles C. Ryrie, "Total Depravity," *Baker's Dictionary Of Theology*, p. 164.

8. Cornelius Van Til, "Calvinism," *Baker's Dictionary Of Theology*, p. 109.

9. Strong, *op. cit.*, p. 619.

10. H. Orton Wiley, *Christian Theology*, Vol. 2, 3 volumes, Kansas City, Mo.: Beacon Hill Press, c. 1952, pp. 107-109.

The Incarnation

Christianity is Christ-centered. Jesus Christ is Creator, Redeemer, and Lord. Without Jesus Christ there would be no Christianity. We would all be hopelessly in the bondage of sin and under condemnation. We would be groping in darkness without a light to guide us. Apart from a plan to send Christ into the world, the unveiling of the nature and plan of God for man, which we refer to as special revelation, would have ended with the fall of man. All special revelation of God after the fall presupposes and is in some way related to God's plan of redemption through Christ.

The question that Jesus asked His disciples in Matthew 16:15 is a question of the greatest importance. After having asked who others thought Him to be and receiving a variety of answers, "He saith unto them, But whom say ye that I am?"

Jesus Christ is both the center and the foundation of Christianity. That fact alone tells us that it is of greatest importance that the question, "But whom say ye that I am?" be answered correctly. Our understanding of the importance of the answer does not depend upon our logical understanding alone. God reveals to us in Scripture the importance of answering this question correctly. The truth or falsity of a person's answer to this question is one of the basic tests to determine whether a person is proclaiming the gospel or heresy (1 John 2:22, 23; 4:1-3; 2 John 7-11). When we discuss some finer points of detail that may not be settled for us by exegesis of Scriptures, we cannot expect unanimous agreement. On the basics that are clearly revealed in Scripture, there must be agreement.

Our interest in the doctrine of Christ does not rest solely upon being doctrinally sound as important as that is. Jesus Christ is not simply central is a system of doctrine. He is central to us as persons. He is our Redeemer and Lord. We love Him. We worship Him. We adore Him. We want to understand Him. To understand Him is to appreciate Him more.

A knowledge of Christ satisfies both heart and mind. In a world that is marred by sin, it is He and He alone that forms the foundation for integrating the facts of reality into a pattern of life and thought that gives purpose and meaning to life. He is the only One that can rescue us from the sea of confusion and despair. He is the only Captain who can pilot our ship into the harbor of eternal happiness. It is with the highest appreciation for Him and the deepest sense of responsibility that we proceed into the study of the incarnation.

I. THE PURPOSE OF THE INCARNATION

A. That Christ Might Be Our Kinsman Redeemer

The Hebrew word for redeemer is *goel*. The word *goel* is a participle form of the verb *gaal*. Robert B. Girdlestone says, "Perhaps the original meaning of the word is 'demand back,' hence to extricate." In discussing the use of *goel* in Leviticus chapters 25 and 27, Girdlestone explains:

> The deliverance was effected in this case by payment or by exchange. In cases of poverty, where no payment was possible, the nearest of kin was made responsible for performing the work of redemption. Hence no doubt it came to pass that a kinsman came to be called by the name *Goel*, as he is in Numbers 5:8, I Kings 16:11, and throughout the Book of Ruth. Compare Jeremiah 32:7, 8.[1]

Based on the observation made by Girdlestone, we would gather that the word *goel* first meant to deliver. It came to mean a kinsman who had the right of redemption through usage growing out of the right of redemption given to a near kinsman in Leviticus 25 and 27.

In order to establish a few principles, let us make a few observations about the case of the brother who sold himself to a sojourner or stranger (Leviticus 25:47-55). It is important to observe that only a near kinsman had a right to redeem (verses 48, 49). The principle of substitution was such that it came as near as possible to being the action of the person himself. It is true that an act of a kinsman is not the act of the subject. It is, however, as near as possible to the action of the subject without it being his. When, in the chapter on atonement and justification, we look at the principle of substitution involved in atonement and justification, we will be able to see why the attempt was made to make the action as near as possible the action of the person redeemed.

The kinsman-redeemer type was used by God to prepare the way for the coming of Christ who through the incarnation became our Kinsman that He might have the right to redeem us. After having examined the use of *gaal* and *goel*, Girdlestone concludes:

> In most of the passages above enumerated redemption may be considered as synonymous with deliverance, but always with the idea more or less developed that the Redeemer enters a certain relationship with the redeemed—allies Himself in some sense with them, and so claims the right of redemption. The truth thus set forth was doubtless intended to prepare the mind of God's people for the doctrine of Incarnation.2

There could be no redemption from the curse and power of sin apart from the incarnation of deity. The payment price was greater than a mere human could have paid. The full penalty of sin could only be paid by deity. The Redeemer had to be man to have the *right* to redeem. He had to be God to be *able* to redeem.

The fact that a redeemer had to be a kinsman explains why no redemption was offered to fallen angels. They were created a company of individuals. There is no birth among them. A member of the Trinity could not identify himself with them through birth. They could have no kinsman-redeemer. Therefore, they could have no redemption.

Regardless of what the answer may be about other life in outer space, one thing is clear. It will not extend our missionary responsibility. The right of redemption through the incarnation only extends to the human race. Jesus is a kinsman only to the human race.

B. That Christ May Reveal God To Us

The image of God in man at creation embraced both a constitutional likeness and a functional likeness. In the fall, man lost the functional likeness of God. It is the design of redemption to restore the functional likeness of God in man.

The restoration of the functional likeness of God in man requires not only atonement but also a better view of what God is like. While man is still morally constituted, he is confused and his vision has become blurred concerning what God is really like. One of the purposes of the incarnation was to give us a better view of what God is like. Jesus revealed the likeness of God in terms of experiences and encounters with real life.

The writer of Hebrews speaks of Jesus as " . . . being the brightness of his [God's] glory, and the express image of his person" (Hebrews 1:3). The answer to Philip when he said, "Lord, shew us the Father, and it sufficeth us" (John 14:8) was "Have I been so long

133

time with you, and yet hast thou not known me, Philip? he that hath seen me hath seen the Father; and how sayest thou then, Shew us the Father?" (John 14:9).

A demonstration of real life in a real world offers a dimension to our understanding that far exceeds a definition. The moving examples of love as Jesus had compassion on the sick, the afflicted, the hungry, and those who were as sheep without a shepherd tell us something of the love that characterizes God that no definition could convey. The unparalleled love of Christ as shown by His death to pay the penalty of sin for those who had sinned against Him gives us a dimension of love that the wisest minds and the most gifted with words could never describe.

The example of a sinless life in spite of the cleverest designs of Satan and in spite of the provocative encounters with vile and conniving men, gives a dimension to holiness that cannot be conveyed by the lives of the most saintly among the redeemed. The staunch stand of Jesus when He pronounced judgment upon Chorazin, Bethsaida, and Capernaum; the solemn language He used when He pronounced the woes upon the Pharisees; and the determined stand against the desecration of the Temple He took when He ran the money changers out of the Temple shows a dimension of the intolerance of His holiness that doctrinal treatments cannot convey. The satisfaction of the holiness of God by the death and sufferings of the Son of God gives the highest possible revelation of God's attitude toward holiness and sin.

We needed all of the moral instruction of Scripture, but instructions alone were not enough. We needed a model that was demonstrated for us in the encounters with real life in a real world. Jesus Christ is that model. He has revealed to us and for us what it means to be in the functional likeness of God.

II. THE HUMANITY AND DEITY OF CHRIST

A. The Humanity of Christ

Since the controversy about Christ has usually focused on His deity rather than His humanity, there has been a tendency to fail to emphasize the human nature of Christ and the implications of His being human. His humanity is usually taken for granted. In view of the preceding discussion relating to Jesus being our Kinsman—Redeemer, we see that it was no less essential for Him to be human to be our Redeemer than it was for Him to be deity.

The birth of Christ attests the genuineness of His human nature (Matthew 1:18-25; Luke 2:11). It is true that He was miraculously conceived (Matthew 1:18-25; Luke 1:26-35), but at the same time it was a human birth. He possessed a human body (Hebrews 2:14; John

134

2:21; Matthew 26:12) and a human spirit (Luke 23:46). He experienced human growth and development (Luke 2:40, 52). He experienced human needs. He became hungry (Matthew 4:2; 21:18). He experienced thirst (John 19:28). He became tired (John 4:6). He slept (Matthew 8:24). He died and was buried (Mark 15:43-46).

There is never the slightest hint in the New Testament that Jesus was not human. He referred to Himself as a man (John 8:40). He is called a man by others (John 1:30; Acts 2:22; 13:38; 1 Corinthians 15:21, 47; Philippians 2:8; and others).

B. The Deity of Christ

(See the discussion on the deity of Christ in the chapter on the Trinity.)

III. ERRONEOUS VIEWS CONCERNING THE TWO NATURES AND THE PERSON OF CHRIST

In getting a clear understanding of the truth, it sometimes helps to contrast the truth with error. We will take a brief look at some of the errors in the history of the church to help us see the truth more clearly. For those who are interested in a more thorough treatment of these erroneous views than will be presented here, such a treatment can be found in most Systematic Theology books, books on the History of Doctrine, and Church History books.

A. The Ebionites

The Ebionites arose around the early part of the second century. They were a Jewish group that gave Jesus a place of importance in their beliefs, but denied that He was deity. They felt that monotheism was incompatible with attributing deity to Jesus.

B. The Gnostics

This group appeared about the same time the Ebionites did. It appears that some of the basic principles of Gnosticism can be found in the latter part of the first century as is evidenced by some of the statements of John in combating heretical views of Christ (1 John 4:1-3; 2 John 7).

The Gnostics worked on the assumption that matter is inherently evil. For this reason, they either denied the reality of Jesus' human nature or denied that there was any real incarnation.

135

Concerning the last form of Gnosticism, Dr. Alexander M. Renwick explains, "This heavenly Christ acted in the man Jesus but was never incarnate." 3

C. The Arians

Arius denied the integrity of the Divine nature of Christ. Christ was the first of created beings. Through Him the rest of creation was created. He could be called God, but not in the full sense of the word.

Arianism was condemned at the Council of Nicea in 325. Arius taught that Jesus was like substance (*homoi-ousia*) with the Father. The opposition which prevailed was led by Athanasius who taught that Jesus in His Divine nature had the same substance (*homo-ousia*) with the Father. The modern group known as Jehovah's Witnesses has a view that is similar to the Arian view.

D. The Apollinarians

While the Arians denied the integrity of the Divine nature of Christ, the Apollinarians denied the integrity of the human nature of Christ. Apollinarians held to the view that man consists of body, soul, and spirit. The human nature of Jesus had a body and soul, but not a human spirit (mind). The intelligence of Christ was supplied by His eternal Logos. This view was condemned at the Council of Constantinople in 381.

With reference to the controversy surrounding the Appollinarian error, Dr. H. D. McDonald comments:

In the fourth century Gregory of Nazianzes repudiated the abridged humanity of the Christ of Appollinarius with the observation that that which is unassumed is unhealed. If only half Adam fell, he argues, then that which Christ assumes and saves must be half also; but if the whole of his nature fell it must be united to the whole nature of Him who was begotten and so be complete as a whole. Let them not begrudge us, he concludes, our complete salvation and clothe the Saviour with bones and nerves and the portraiture of humanity.4

E. The Nestorians

There is not unanimous agreement among scholars that Nestorius was properly understood. The error for which he was

136

condemned at the Synod of Ephesus in 431 was an improper teaching regarding the union of the human and the Divine natures in Christ. What is called Nestorianism sets forth the view that the union of the human and Divine natures in Christ is somewhat analogous to the indwelling Holy Spirit in the believer. The difference is a matter of plentitude and control. The result was the existence of two persons.

F. The Eutychians

Eutyches was caught up in an overreaction against Nestorianism. He taught that the Divine and human natures combined to make a third nature. Concerning this mingling of the natures to make a third nature, Dr. A. H. Strong explains:

> Since in this case the divine must overpower the human, it follows that the human was really absorbed into or transmuted into the divine, although the divine was not in all respects the same, after the union, that it was before. Hence the Eutychians were often called Monophysites, because they virtually reduced the two natures to one.[5]

Dr. Charles Hodge raises some important questions with regard to this view:

> But what was the nature which resulted from the union of the two? The human might be exalted into the divine, or lost in it, as a drop of vinegar (to use one of the illustrations then employed) in the ocean. Then Christ ceased to be a man . . . . Where then is his redeeming work, and his bond of union or sympathy with us? Or the effect of the union might be to merge the divine into the human, so that the one nature was after all only the nature of man. Then the true divinity of Christ was denied, and we have only a human saviour. Or the effect of the union of the two natures was the production of a third, which was neither human nor divine, but theanthropic, as in chemical combinations an acid and an alkali when united produce a substance which is no longer either acid or alkaline. Then Christ instead of being God and man, is neither God nor man.[6]

Eutychianism was condemned at the Council of Chalcedon in 451. It was this same council that set forth the view that we speak of as the orthodox view.

IV. THE ORTHODOX VIEW CONCERNING THE TWO NATURES AND THE PERSON OF CHRIST

A. The Chalcedon Interpretation

The basic thrust of the decision of the Council of Chalcedon in 451 was to affirm two basic truths about Christ. (1) He had two natures—a human nature and a Divine nature. Each of these exists in its completeness and integrity. (2) Jesus Christ is one person. At the Council of Constantinople in 681 the Monothelite doctrine, which teaches that Jesus had only one will, was rejected and the doctrine of two wills and two intelligences was added to the orthodox doctrine.

B. The Union of the Two Natures

Dr. H. C. Thiessen explains:

> The person of Christ is theanthropic but not His nature. That is, we may speak of the God-man when we wish to refer to the person, but we cannot speak of the divine-human nature, but say the divine and the human nature in Christ.7

If we were to use the words "God-man" or the words "Divine-human" to refer to the natures of Christ, we would in effect be suggesting a cross between the two natures. We would be advocating Eutychianism.

We can speak of theanthropic (made up of two Greek words meaning God-man) or God-man person or personality of Christ. That He was only one person is clear. When we meet Jesus in the gospels, we get the impression that we are meeting only one person. Jesus refers to Himself as "I," not "We." He is addressed as "Thou." He is referred to as "He."

What is involved in the recognition of Jesus' person or personality as being theanthropic? We are not to think of the personality of Christ as being a cross between a Divine personality and a human personality. The personality of Christ involved all the attributes of both human and Divine personality, but was not a cross between the two.

Theologians speak about the impersonal human nature of Christ being united with the Divine nature of Christ. What is involved in this statement is the fact that while the Divine personality existed prior to the incarnation, there was not the prior existence of a human personality. The incarnation did not involve the union of a human personality and a Divine personality. In the incarnation the human nature found personal awareness in the theanthropic personality.

138

Without alteration to the Divine personality, the personality of Christ took on the attributes of human personality and became a theanthropic personality.

We might find somewhat of a parallel when we use the center of a circle that is already drawn and draw another circle using the same center. The center which was at one time the center of only one circle becomes the center then of another circle. We have one center and two circles. The two natures of Christ find personal awareness in the one personality. The Divine nature had personal awareness in this personalitybefore the incarnation when this personality took on the attributes of human personality and gave personal awareness to a human nature that had had no prior and no separate personal awareness.

The human nature of Christ is restricted to the limits of the human body. The theanthropic personality of Christ is omnipresent. The personal presence of Christ is always theanthropic at all times and at all places.

There is a mistaken idea that easily develops around the word incarnation which means *in flesh.* We are not to think, as some say, of the Divine nature being shrunk to the size of a human sperm and being placed in the womb of the virgin Mary. Following through with this idea is the idea that deity, in the incarnation, was enclosed within the confines of a human body.

With regard to these observations, let it first be said that deity will not shrink. In the incarnation, it is the union of the Divine and human natures, not the enclosure of the Divine nature within the confines of the human body.

Let us now turn our attention to a discussion of whether Christ has one or two wills. As was pointed out previously, the one will doctrine was rejected and the position of two wills in Christ was adopted at the Council of Constantinople in 681. I agree with Strong when he says: "The theory of two consciousnesses and two wills, first elaborated by John of Damascus, was an unwarranted addition to the orthodox doctrine propounded at Chalcedon."8

I think the real question is this: Is will an attribute of personality or an attribute of nature? If will is an attribute of nature, Christ had two. If will is an attribute of personality, He had one.

In deciding whether Jesus had one will or two, I think it will be helpful to see how the implications of our thinking would affect our thinking on the Trinity. In the Trinity, there are three persons and one nature. If will is related to nature, there is only one will in the Godhead. If will is related to personality, there are three wills in the Trinity.

Sometimes we have become so accustomed to thinking of will as "plan," as when we think of "God's will," that we read that meaning where it does not belong. Surely, there is one plan in the Trinity. That is not what we are talking about here. We are talking about the capacity to say, "I will." As I see it, that capacity clearly belongs to personality as distinguished from nature. If so, there are three wills in the Trinity, but only one in Christ. If will belongs to nature, there are two wills in Christ, but one in the Trinity.

What I am saying is this. The same conscious awareness that is aware of a Divine nature in Christ is aware of a human nature in Christ. The same conscious awareness of determination that directs the Divine nature also directs the human nature. In directing the Divine nature, it is consciously aware of the Divine nature and all the attributes of Divine personality. In directing the human nature of Christ, it is aware of the human nature and all the attributes of human personality.

In my estimation, to fathom the mysteries of the incarnation is more difficult, in so far as we can understand either, than it is to fathom the mysteries of the Trinity. In trying to fathom the mysteries of the incarnation, we should keep the following firmly fixed truths in mind: (1) We must adhere to two natures in Christ, the Divine and the human, both in their completeness and their integrity. (2) These two natures are in union, but are distinct and are in no way mingled one with another. (3) Christ is only one person. (4) The personality of Christ has the attributes of Divine personality and human personality, but is not a cross between Divine personality and human personality. These truths must not be denied by statement or implication. When these truths are maintained, we may err on details, but not on basic truths.

It would be helpful to show the contrast between the true view of Christ and the false views. In contrast to the Ebionites, we believe in the deity of Christ. In contrast to the Gnostics, we believe in the real humanity of Christ and in a real incarnation. In contrast to the Arians, we believe in the completeness and integrity of the deity of Christ. In contrast to the Apollinarians, we believe in the completeness and integrity of the human nature of Christ. In contrast to the Nestorians, we believe Christ is one person, not two. In contrast to the Eutychians, we reject the idea of a mingling of the natures in Christ. Each nature, the human and the Divine, maintained its completeness and integrity.

V. THE RELATIONSHIP OF THE TWO NATURES OF CHIRST IN HIS EARTHLY LIFE

A. The Problem Stated

The basic problem centers around the omniscience, omnipotence, and omnipresence which are attributes of the Divine nature. The question is: Did Jesus set aside these attributes during His life on earth? Or was some limitation placed upon their exercise? Some have

140

answered by saying yes to the first question. Others have said no to the first question, but yes to the second question.

B. An Examination of the Biblical Data

Philippians 2:7 has been a key verse in the debate over what Jesus gave up in the incarnation. The key word is the word *kenoo* which may be translated "to empty." The King James Version translates, "But made himself of no reputation." A better translation would be, "But he emptied himself."

The question is: Of what did Jesus empty Himself? There is nothing in the passage to suggest that He emptied Himself of any of His attributes. The theme of the passage is humility. Paul is challenging the readers to, "Let this mind be in you, which was also in Christ Jesus" (verse 5). He who had existed from eternity with all the glory and privileges of deity took on Himself the "form of a servant, and was made in the likeness of men: And being found in fashion as a man, he humbled himself, and became obedient unto death, even the death of the cross" (verses 7, 8).

There are two basic observations: (1) Jesus had experienced prior to coming to earth the full glory of God (John 17:5). When He came to earth, as He was viewed by men, the glory of His deity was veiled. His deity was not apparent at all except to those who believed in Him. Even they did not see the glory of His deity. (2) He was a servant. As a servant He was obedient to the Father. The passage does not elaborate the nature of this submission to the Father other than that He "became obedient unto death, even the death of the cross."

I would conclude that while the passage is very helpful in our understanding of the humility demonstrated in the incarnation that it offers no solution to the problem related to His omniscience, omnipotence, and omnipresence. The fact of submission to the Father may be of help, but how it relates to these attributes and their use must be settled by other data.

Before proceeding further, I want to comment on the problem of omnipresence. If we consider immensity to refer to the infinity of the essence of God as distinguished from omnipresence, it is impossible to think of surrendering His immensity. The immensity of the essence can in no way be subjected to voluntary limitation. If Jesus did not share the essence of God, He would not be God. The infinity of the essence is not subject to change.

Ominpresence, when distinguished from immensity, refers to personal presence. The fact of the personal presence of Christ would not be subject to limitation. Jesus declared His omnipresence during His earthly life in John 3:13. The action of the person is subject to voluntary submission to the Father, but not the fact of His omnipresence.

The question centers around omniscience and omnipotence. With regard to His omniscience, He did not always exercise it. He stated that He did not know the time of His second coming (Mark 13:32). Does this mean that He had set aside His omniscience? The evidence is to the contrary. Jesus saw Nathanael under the fig tree, though Jesus was not there. This fact when declared to Nathanael caused him to acknowledge Jesus to be the Son of God (John 1:47-50). Jesus "knew all men, And needed not that any should testify of man: for he knew what was in man" (John 2:24, 25).

As it relates to Jesus' omnipotence, He never tried to perform any act without success. His miracles attest to the fact that His Divine nature did not set aside omnipotence. It is a mistake, as some do, to have His miracles and His whole life lived out in the strength of the Holy Spirit in the same manner that the Holy Spirit works in us. If the miracles of Christ had been performed solely in the power of the Holy Spirit, they would not attest to His deity (Acts 2:22). A view that places the total success of Jesus' life on dependence upon the Holy Spirit would have a dormant Divine nature during His life on earth. The evidence is too strong to the contrary for such a view to be taken seriously. I am not denying that He had a relationship to the Holy Spirit, but I am saying that much of what He did reflected the action of His Divine nature.

There is no problem in seeing the exercise of omnipotence being subjected to the will of the Father. There is some problem with omniscience. It is diffcult to conceive of a member of the Trinity as not being in the full exercise of omniscience at all times. However, Mark 13:32 seems to clearly tell us that Jesus did not know the time of His second coming. In the face of this difficulty, some have sought other ways of explaining the verse. In spite of the problems, it seems to be best to take the obvious interpretation and conclude that there was some limitation placed on Jesus' exercise of omniscience during His earthly life. The suggestion that He did not know in His human nature, but did in His Divine nature is unsatisfactory. Jesus did not say that His human nature did not know. Rather, He said the Son did not know.

That Jesus did live His life in submission to the Father is evident. The evidence is too obvious in the gospels to require repeating here. Jesus states this truth clearly when He said, "For I came down from heaven, not to do mine own will, but the will of him that sent me" (John 6:38).

A common way of stating the voluntary limitation on the exercise of omniscience and omnipotence is: Jesus gave up an independent exercise of these attributes for a dependent exercise of these attributes. In the exercise of these attributes He was in submission to the Father's control during His life on earth. Dr. Warren Young prefers to speak of Jesus as giving up the coordinate exercise of these attributes for a subordinate exercise. He says that Jesus never made an independent use of these attributes.[9] It is probably best to speak of the coordinate and subordinate use of these attributes rather than the independent and dependent use. The same is meant of either choice of terms, but coordinate and subordinate seem to be better terms to express the ideas involved.

VI. THE PROBLEM OF THE PECCABILITY OR IMPECCABILITY OF CHRIST

A. The Problem Stated

The view of peccability is that Jesus could have sinned. The view of impeccability is that Jesus could not have sinned. There have been devout Christians who have taken each position. There is no direct teaching of Scripture that speaks to the point of the question. The Bible clearly teaches that He did not sin. That does not tell us whether He could have. I will state a case for the impeccability of Christ.

B. The Result of the Union of the Two Natures in One Person

In the union of the two natures in one person, I do not believe it is possible to impute moral guilt to His humanity without imputing it to His Divinity. When we distinguish nature and person, moral responsibility belongs to person. Nature is morally responsible only as it manifests itself in personality. Jesus had only one personality. It is clear that deity cannot sin (Titus 1:2). Moral guilt could not be experienced by theanthropic personality of Jesus without deity sinning. Since deity cannot sin, Jesus could not have sinned.

I am not saying that the human nature of Christ could not have sinned if it had not been in union with the Divine nature. Human nature in union with Divine nature cannot sin.

C. The Reality of the Temptation

Some have charged that if Jesus could not have sinned, His temptation was not real and He cannot be our sympathetic High Priest. The first point we need to clarify is that there are two sources of temptation. (1) Temptation can be from within. This is what James spoke of in James 1:14 when he said, "But every man is tempted, when he is drawn away of his own lust, and enticed." He is referring to temptation by our depraved nature. (2) Temptation can

143

be from without. This is what happens when another person tries to get us to do wrong.

Jesus was tempted in the second way mentioned. He was tempted by the devil. Jesus did not have a sinful nature. He had no inner urges to sin. The inner urge to sin is already sin. He was hungry and wanted to eat, but He did not want to eat at the expense of obeying Satan. He had not the slightest inclination to want to obey Satan. Such inclination is in and of itself sin.

The principle is well illustrated by Jesus' prayer in the garden of Gethsemane. He prayed, "O my Father, if it be possible, let this cup pass from me: nevertheless not as I will, but as thou wilt" (Matthew 26:39). Jesus dreaded drinking the cup of condemnation for our sins. He would have preferred not to do it if it were consistent with the plan of God. He shows not the slightest desire to refrain from drinking the cup in disobedience to God. It is a mistake to understand Jesus as being on the brink of disobedience and about to back out of the whole arrangement. His commitment is completely unwavering.

He felt the weight of temptation. He felt the pressures of life. He could easily sympathize with the problem of a hungry man who is struggling with the possibility of getting food in a wrong way. A person of principles and conviction in a depressed mood might not have any difficulty in refusing illegal drugs or alcohol, but he would, as a result of that experience, be able to better understand the person who does have difficulty. Jesus' encounters with life were real. His own inner needs were real, but His commitment to right never wavered. He never needed cleansing from an evil thought.

D. The Reason for the Temptation

Some say, "If Christ could not have sinned, there was no reason for the temptation." I think there was. A statement saying that Jesus could not have sinned would never have been meaningful to us as a real encounter with the devil in which the devil failed to make Him sin. A statement saying He could not have sinned would have been good for rational arguments, but it would not have met the needs of our total personality as well as actual victory in temptation.

Another purpose that was served in the temptation is that it closes the mouth of the devil. He can never say, "I did not have a chance to make Him sin. If I had I could have made Him sin."

VII. THE RESURRECTION OF CHRIST

The resurrection is treated here for two reasons: (1) It is appropriate if we want to continue our discussion of the incarnation

144

to make observations about the incarnation of Christ as He is now. (2) The discussion of atonement, as will be made in the next chapter, should be followed by a study of the application of salvation without interrupting the thought to study the resurrection.

A. A Bodily Resurrection

To the naturalist who does not believe in God and the person who believes in a god, but restricts his activities to the framework of natural law, there can be no resurrection of Christ from the dead by God. He has ruled out such a conclusion before he examines the data. Even if he were convinced that Jesus became alive after being killed, he would not believe that God raised Him from the dead. His system has no room for such. He will not believe that God raised Jesus from the dead until he rejects naturalism and believes in Divine revelation. The issue with the rationalist must be God and God's revelation, not a list of proofs of the resurrection. We declare the fact of the resurrection to unbelievers with hopes that God may use His Word to bring repentance. We do not try to argue with them for the sake of winning an argument.

For those who believe in God and the Biblical revelation, there is proof. The tomb was empty. Only a bodily resurrection needs an empty tomb. Jesus had prophesied that His body would be raised (John 2:19-22; Matthew 27:62-66). He showed His body to Thomas (John 20:26-28). He declared to His disciples that He had a body of flesh and bones (Luke 24:39).

The question is frequently raised: Was Jesus' resurrection body a physical, material body? There is certainly no Biblical evidence to the contrary. The fact that it went through closed doors shows that it is not subject to the same laws that it was formerly, but that is not an argument against a physical body. When Jesus fed the 5,000, the fish and loaves were multiplied by a process other than a natural process, but that is no reason to deny that what Jesus fed them with was real material food. The burden of proof that Jesus' body was not material rests with those who make the claim. Unless we labor under some influence of the Gnostic view that matter is inherently evil, there is no reason for denying that Jesus' resurrection body was material. Matter is not inherently evil.

Once our system of thought allows the possibility of the resurrection of Christ, we have a right to appeal to the Divine revelation and to the witnesses mentioned therein. For those of us who accept the possibility of resurrection, there is as much reason to believe in the historicity of the resurrection as there are a number of other historical events. Witnesses attest to the bodily resurrection of Christ, but the fact that "God hath raised him from the dead" comes only by revelation. Those who received the revelation have passed it on to us in theBible (Romans 10:9).

B. Differences and Likenesses as Compared with His Body Prior to the Crucifixion

The resurrection body was a body of flesh and bone. We would judge from 1 Corinthians 15:50 that it did not possess blood. His body bore the marks of the crucifixion (John 20:24-28). It was not bound by the same limitations as before (John 20:19, 26). It is no longer subject to death (Romans 6:9; Revelation 1:18).

C. The Significance of Christ's Resurrection

Without the resurrection of Christ, the whole system of Christian truth would crumble. The resurrection assures us of the truth of Jesus' Divine claims (Romans 1:4). It assures us of our justification (Romans 4:25). The atonement wrought at the cross could not have been applied by a dead Christ. Only a living Christ can bestow the benefits of His death. The bodily resurrection of Christ assures us of our own bodily resurrection (1 Corinthians 15:13-23; 1 Thessalonians 4:14). His resurrection is the ground of victorious living for us (Romans 6: 4, 5, 8).

VII. THE ASCENSION AND EXALTATION OF CHRIST

A. The Continuity of the Natures of Christ

Jesus will forever remain the incarnate Son of God. He will forever be fully human and fully God. His body is now a resurrected and glorified body, but it is still a body. Dr. Buswell explains:

> Our Lord Jesus Christ continues to be a man and ever will be a member of our race. This, of course, does not mean that He is subject to the material limitations which characterize our life upon this earth, but it does mean that He has a bodily tangible form such as was manifested to His disciples after His resurrection, and such as will appear to us all in His glorious second coming. 10

We are told in Acts 1:11, " . . . This same Jesus, which is taken up from you into heaven, shall so come in like manner as ye have seen him go into heaven."

B. The Exaltation of Christ

Paul tells us: "Wherefore God also hath highly exalted him, and given him a name which is above every name: That at the name of

Jesus every knee should bow, of things in heaven, and things in earth, and things under the earth; And that every tongue should confess that Jesus Christ is Lord, to the glory of God the Father" (Philippians 2:9-11).

Jesus will never die again. He will never be spit upon and jeered again. He is King of Kings and Lord of Lords. He sits in glory at the right hand of the Father (Hebrews 10:12). He is coming again in triumphant power (Revelation 19:11-16).

CHAPTER NINE
NOTES

1. Robert Baker Girdlestone, *Synonyms of The Old Testament*, Grand Rapids: William B. Eerdmans Publishing Company, reproduction of the second edition which appeared in 1897, pp. 117, 118.

2. *Ibid.*, p. 119.

3. Alexander M. Renwick, "Gnosticism," *Baker's Dictionary of Theology*, ed. by Everett F. Harrison, Grand Rapids: Baker Book House, c. 1960, p. 238.

4. H. D. McDonald, *Jesus—Human and Divine*, Grand Rapids: Zondervan Publishing House, c. 1968 by H. D. McDonald. Published by special arrangement with Pickering and Inglis Ltd., London, p. 20.

5. Augustus Hopkins Strong, *Systematic Theology*, three volumes in one, Philadelphia: The Judson Press, c. 1907, p. 672.

6. Charles Hodge, *Systematic Theology*, Volume II, 3 Volumes, Grand Rapids: William B. Eerdmans Publishing Company, 1952, originally published in 1871, p. 408.

7. Henry Clarence Thiessen, *Introductory Lectures in Systematic Theology*, Grand Rapids: William B. Eerdmans Publishing Company, c. 1949, p. 305.

8. Strong, *op. cit.*, p. 695.

9. Taken from a lecture in Systematic Theology taught by Dr. Warren C. Young at Northern Baptist Theological Seminary, 1962.

10. James Oliver Buswell, Jr., *A Systematic Theology of the Christian Religion*, Volume II, 2 volumes, Grand Rapids: Zondervan Publishing House, c. 1962, p. 69.

Atonement
and Justification

Of all the events in the experience of Christ, His birth, His life, His death, His resurrection, and His return, His death stands central. As important as the other events are both in themselves and in relation to His death, the death of Christ remains central because apart from atonement there would be no forgiveness of sins. Christianity would be non-existent. It is the birth that makes the death of Christ possible, but it is the death that makes the birth important. It is the resurrection that makes possible the application of the benefits of His death. It is the death that makes His resurrection important and makes the one who has been restored to life the Redeemer.

It is of utmost importance that we maintain a sound doctrine of atonement. The study of atonement must be done with the whole personality, not just the rational mind. While a study of atonement is fascinating in its logical consistency, it must go much deeper than that to be comprehended. It must grip the heart also. There is nothing that sheds light on the seriousness of holiness and sin like the atonement that God provided to bring forgiveness of sin. A proper view of atonement puts seriousness into the whole study of theology. Any system of ethics that does not read from atonement the seriousness of sin and the understanding of God's holiness and God's love that is seen in atonement will be grossly inadequate. Any view of grace that is not grounded in the understanding of sin, holiness, and the high regard for law that is manifested in atonement will be empty, shallow, and shot through with the tendencies of antinomianism.

It is not enough to proclaim the statement: "Jesus died to save sinners." That statement must be grasped, at least in its essential meaning, before it is the gospel. That statement could be made by either a liberal or a fundamentalist, but with drastically different

149

interpretations growing out of drastically different views of the authority of Scripture. It is with a realization that our task is serious that we enter our study of atonement and its application in justification.

I. THE SATISFACTION VIEW OF ATONEMENT

A. Basic Assumptions

There are five basic assumptions upon which the satisfaction view of atonement rests: (1) God is sovereign. (2) God is holy. (3) Man is sinful. (4) God is loving. (5) God is wise. It is from a development of the inherent principles that are in these basic assumptions that we see the necessity, the provision, and the nature of atonement.

Lest we fall into the trap of mechanical versus personal reasonings, it is important for us to remind ourselves that atonement is designed to settle a conflict between persons—God and man. We must see sovereignty as personally administered by one who thinks, feels, and acts. God is capable of feeling joy, satisfaction, sorrow, and holy wrath. To deny God the ability to feel is to deny the integrity of His personality. Dr. H. C. Thiessen explains:

> Philosophers frequently deny feeling to God, saying that feeling implies passivity and susceptibility of impression from without, and that such a possibility is incompatible with the idea of the immutability of God. But immutability does not mean immobility. True love necessarily involves feeling, and if there be no feeling in God, then there is no love of God.[1]

Holiness is not an abstract principle, but an attribute of personality. It is not simply an attribute. It is an experience of the Divine personality. It involves the principles and attitudes by which the Divine personality operates. The same observations that have been made of holiness can also be applied to love and wisdom. These are experiences of the Divine personality.

Man is personal. Sin is an experience of the human personality in conflict with a personal God. Atonement is designed to resolve this conflict and to form the foundation for restoring holiness as the experience of the human personality.

B. Why Atonement Was Necessary

The necessity of atonement draws upon the first three of the previously given basic assumptions. God as Sovereign is both Lawgiver and Judge of the universe. This places man in a position of accountability before God. God cannot lay aside His responsibility as Judge, and man cannot escape his accountability before God—the Supreme Judge of the universe.

If there were no responsibility on God's part and no accountability on man's part, there would be no need of atonement, but this relationship is inescapably bound up in the nature of the case. Having established this responsibility—accountability relationship, there is still no necessity of atonement except as that necessity grows out of the holy nature of God. It is the holy nature of the One who is Sovereign, Lawgiver, and Judge that makes atonement necessary to resolve the conflict between man and God who has placed man under condemnation.

From the forewarned judgment against sin in Genesis 2:17 to the Great White Throne Judgment in Revelation 20:11-15, the Bible repeatedly warns us of God's attitude toward sin. The culmination of God's attitude toward sin is seen in the eternal condemnation of the wicked (Matthew 25:45; Mark 9:43-48; Romans 6:23; Revelation 21:8).

Why is there such a dreadful penalty against sin? No principle of expediency for Divine government could ever justify taking such a strong measure against sin apart from absolute necessity. Our whole being abhors the idea of taking such a drastic step as eternal punishment apart from an absolute necessity in the nature of God. Our confidence in God tells us that He would not have taken such a step if it had not been a necessity.

God's law issues from and is an expression of His holy nature. For holiness to be holiness, it not only differs from sin, but it is intolerant of sin. This intolerance manifests itself in a penalty against the violation of the moral law of God. As Dr. Buswell remarks:

> The punishment of all that violates, or is contrary to the holy character of God is a logical implication and a necessary consequence of God's holiness. If God is holy, it must follow that He will vindicate His holiness as against all sin and corruption which is contrary thereto.[2]

The holy law of God pronounces a penalty upon the person who violates that law. It is the work of Divine justice to execute the penalty of the law and thus protect the holiness of God. The justice of God will not tolerate any attempt to set aside or diminish the penalty of the broken law of God. There can be no forgiveness of sin without a full satisfaction of the justice of God in the payment of the penalty.

Romans 3:23 declares that the design of propitiation was to

make it possible for God to maintain His justice while at the same time He justifies the sinner who comes to God believing in Jesus. The implication is that to justify without atonement would compromise the justice of God, which of course could not be. It is clear that in this passage Paul is telling us that justice required atonement before there could be forgiveness.

Our view of both the necessity and the nature of atonement arises out of the absolute necessity of the punishment of sin. This necessity comes from His holiness.

C. The Nature of Atonement

Sinful man is in a predicament for which he has no remedy of his own. He is under the condemnation of eternal death. The justice of God requires that the penalty be paid. Nothing less will be accepted.

I am not suggesting that an actual council, as described, took place, but I am saying that what follows illustrates the principles involved. The justice of God demanded that the penalty of sin be paid. The love of God was interested in saving man but had to submit to the justice of God. The wisdom of God came forth with a plan that would satisfy both holiness and love. Through the incarnation of Christ and the substitutionary death of Christ, love could fulfill its desire to save and holiness could hold to its insistence that sin be punished.

There are two aspects of atonement: (1) Passive obedience, and (2) Active obedience. The passive obedience refers to the death of Christ. He submitted to the wrath of God for our sins. Most of the discussion centers around the passive obedience because it involved the payment of the penalty for our sins. A complete accounting of atonement also embraces the righteous life Christ lived on our behalf which was His active obedience.

What happened in the passive obedience of Christ? The Bible is quite clear on the basic principles involved. Isaiah 53:6 tells us, "The LORD hath laid on him the iniquity of us all." First Peter 2:24 reads, "Who his own self bare our sins in his own body on the tree." Galatians 3:13 tells us, "Christ hath redeemed us from the curse of the law, being made a curse for us." Second Corinthians 5:21 says, "For he hath made him to be sin for us, who knew no sin."

When Jesus Christ went to the cross, all the sins of all the world that ever had been committed, were being committed, and ever would be committed were laid on Him. With our sins upon Him, God poured out His wrath upon Him as if He had committed every one of them. We read in Isaiah 53:10, "Yet it pleased the LORD to bruise him; he hath put him to grief."

It is a mistake to restrict the sufferings of Jesus Christ to that

152

which was inflicted upon Him by the Roman soldiers. He took the sinners' place before God and drank the cup of wrath that was due sinners. He suffered as much on the cross as sinners will suffer in an eternal Hell. He experienced separation from the Father. He who had enjoyed unbroken fellowship with the Father in eternity past uttered the words on the cross, "My God, my God, why hast thou forsaken me?" (Matthew 27:46). This cry was probably a cry of agony rather than a cry from lack of understanding.

When Jesus finished suffering for the sins of the world, He said, "It is finished" (John 19:30). The same one who had a short time before uttered the words, "My God, my God, why hast thou forsaken me?" was now able to say, "Father, into thy hands I commend my spirit" (Luke 23:46).

When Jesus uttered the words, "Father, into thy hands I commend my spirit," this was the greatest reunion the universe has ever known. The one whose fellowship with God had been interrupted by having our sins placed upon Him had paid the penalty and removed the obstacle that separated Him from the Father. The way for His reunion was open. In opening it for Himself, He opened it for us. He identified Himself with our broken fellowship that we might be identified with His fellowship. He identified Himself with our sin that we might be identified with His righteousness.

Payment of the penalty through a qualified substitute was the only way God could save man. As Dr. William G. T. Shedd explains:

> The eternal Judge may or may not exercise mercy, but he must exercise justice. He can neither waive the claims of the law in part, nor abolish them altogether. The only possible mode, consequently, of delivering a creature who is obnoxious to the demands of retributive justice, is to satisfy them for him. The claims themselves must be met and extinguished, either personally, or by substitution . . . . And this necessity of an atonement is absolute not relative. It is not made necessary by divine decision, in the sense that the divine decision might have been otherwise. It is not correct to say, that God might have saved man without a vicarious atonement had he been pleased to do so. For this is equivalent to saying, that God might have abolished the claims of law and justice had he been pleased to do so.3

How was Christ able to pay the full penalty of our sins in a short time on the Cross? It will help to elaborate on the penalty of sin. As the penalty of sin is related to man, it is called eternal death. The sinner will be paying it forever. Why is this so? I will suggest the following explanation. The penalty for sinning against a holy and infinite Person is an infinite penalty. Man is infinite in only one dimension of his being, i. e., his duration. Man will exist forever. The only way a man can pay an infinite penalty is to pay it forever. Therefore, Hell is eternal.

As this relates to Christ, because of His Divine nature He is infinite in capacity. He can suffer an infinite penalty without it going into infinite time. Apart from this fact, there could have been no salvation. The only qualified redeemer is one who is the incarnation of deity. He had to be man to have the right to redeem. He had to be God to be able to redeem.

I am not saying that Jesus suffered the identical penalty that man would have suffered. I am saying that He suffered an equivalent. If we say that Jesus went to Hell for us when He paid our penalty, we are not meaning that He went to the lake of fire. We are meaning that He was subjected to equivalent punishment.

Now let us turn our attention to the active obedience of Christ. The word "propitiation" is the most inclusive term in the New Testament denoting atonement. The key passage for understanding propitiation is Romans 3:25, 26. It is not necessary to become involved in all the controversies about how to translate the word. Personally, I think propitiation or propitiatory sacrifice translates the word properly. For those interested in a discussion on this problem, I would suggest that they read "Propitiation" in Baker's *Dictionary of Theology* by Leon Morris, pp. 424-425.

The word propitiation means, in the Biblical setting, to turn away the wrath of God and restore a person to favor with God. The word for propitiation is translated "mercyseat" in Hebrews 9:5 where it refers to the lid on the Ark of the Covenant. The lid on the Ark of the Covenant was the place of propitiation in the Old Testament Tabernacle. An understanding of what happened at the place of propitiation in the Tabernacle will help at this point.

The Ark of the Covenant was located in the Holy of Holies where the High Priest went only once a year on the day of atonement. The Ark of the Covenant had within it the tables of the law. The law represented the demands of the law which were righteousness and a penalty against sin in case of disobedience. When the High Priest slew the goat that was slain on the day of atonement and took his blood into the Holy of Holies and sprinkled it on the mercyseat, it was as if he were saying to the law, "This symbolizes the meeting of the demands that you have made from sinners."

The fact that the animal was without spot and blemish symbolized righteousness. The fact that the animal was slain symbolized the payment of a penalty through a substitute. The satisfaction of the law was symbolized. This satisfaction included both the payment of the penalty and the provision of righteousness.

From the above discussion, we would observe that at the place of propitiation the law is satisfied. This, of course, tells us what the

154

design of propitiation was. It was designed to satisfy the penal demands of the law, thus making it so that God can turn away His wrath from the sinner who believes in Christ, and at the same time maintain His justice. It was designed to satisfy the demand for righteousness, thus giving positive grounds for God to view favorably the sinner who believes in Jesus and at the same time maintain His justice.

What the Old Testament sacrifice did in symbol on the day of atonement, Jesus Christ did in reality. He lived a completely holy life, thus fulfilling the demand for righteousness. He paid the full penalty for sin, thus fulfilling the demand for a penalty. Propitiation, to sum it up, is the full satisfaction of the demands of the law, for righteousness and the payment of a penalty, by Jesus Christ, thus making it possible for God to turn His wrath from the sinner who believes in Jesus, and to view him with favor, and at the same time remain a God of justice.

In the atoning work of Jesus Christ, we have the highest revelation of God's holiness and God's love. The holiness of God is seen in its refusal to approve a way of forgiveness that did not meet every demand of the moral law of God. The highest honor ever paid to God's holiness was paid by the Son of God, when He fully satisfied the demands of the law to make possible our salvation. The highest possible regard for God's holiness is manifested in the atonement.

The love manifested at the Cross is the highest possible manifestation of love. It will forever remain the unparalleled example of love. The sinless Son of God, on behalf of those who had sinned against Him, suffered the full wrath of God for their sins that they might be forgiven of them. The cross as no other point in history or in the future demonstrates the supremacy of holiness and the submission of love to holiness. While the Cross is the foundation of grace, it is also the foundation of the highest interest in holiness on our part.

II. JUSTIFICATION ACCORDING TO THE SATISFACTION VIEW OF ATONEMENT

The full view of atonement cannot be developed without also embracing the doctrine of justification. It is for this reason that I am treating justification here rather than in a later chapter.

A. The Nature of Justification

There are two aspects in justification. There is the negative aspect which deals with the remission of the penalty for sin. There is the positive aspect which deals with restoration to favor with God.

B. The Ground of Justification

Our justification is based on the imputation of the atoning work of Christ to our account. The chart below will help see what takes place in justification.

Debits	The Sinner	Credits
Absolute Righteousness		Unpaid
Eternal Death		Unpaid

Debits	The Believer	Credits
Absolute Righteousness		Christ's Righteousness
Eternal Death		Christ's Death
	Paid in Full or Justified	

We have already looked at how atonement was accomplished. Now the question, how does the death and righteousness of Christ come to be placed on our account? The condition for having the death and righteousness of Christ placed on our account is faith in Christ (Romans 3:28; 4:1-25; Galatians 2:16; 3:1-18). Since there will be an elaboration on faith as the condition of salvation in a later chapter, I will not elaborate further at this time.

While faith in Christ is all that is involved on our part for us to receive the death and righteousness of Christ, there is more involved in the imputation of the death and righteousness of Christ to our account. The ground of the imputation of Christ's death and righteousness to Christ is the union of Christ and the believer. The substitutionary work of Christ for us was not substitution pure and simple. It was a substitution of the kind that in its application made it so that the believer can say, "I am" or "I [have been] crucified with Christ" (Galatians 2:20).

The scriptural evidence is clear that it is through union with Christ that the benefits of Christ's atonement, by which we are justified, are applied to us. Paul tells us: "Likewise reckon ye also yourselves to be dead indeed unto sin, but alive unto God through [The Greek preposition is *en* and should be translated 'in'] Jesus Christ our Lord" (Romans 6:11). It is "in Jesus Christ our Lord" that we are to reckon ourselves to be dead to sin and alive to God. Again Paul says, "There is therefore now no condemnation to them which are in Christ Jesus . . . " (Romans 8:1). The grounds for there being no condemnation is being "in Christ Jesus."

156

In Romans 6:3, 4 and Galatians 3:27, baptism is used as a metonymy. A metonymy is a figure of speech in which one word is used for another which it suggests such as the cause may be given for the effect or the effect for the cause. An example of this is, "For he [Christ] is our peace . . . " (Ephesians 2:14). The meaning is that Christ is the cause or source of our peace. The container may be given for that which is contained. An example of this is referring to the contents of the cup as the cup in the Lord's Supper (1 Corinthians 11:25). The symbol is given for the thing symbolized. I believe an example of this is baptism in the verses under study.

In Romans 6:3, Paul says, "Know ye not, that so many of us as were baptized into Jesus Christ were baptized into his death?" This verse is designed to tell us how the believer's death to sin referred to in verse 2 was accomplished. By being baptized into Jesus Christ, we were baptized into His death. It was in this manner that His death became our death. It also tells us what kind of death is referred to. It is Jesus' death. The only kind of death that He died to sin was a penal death.

In saying that baptism is a metonymy in this passage, we are saying that the wording credits baptism with what actually belongs to the thing symbolized. Water baptism does not baptize a person into Christ. It only symbolizes baptism into Christ. It is baptism by the Holy Spirit (1 Corinthians 12:13) that baptizes into Christ. In this baptism we are united to Christ. In this union, His death becomes our death.

That Paul is saying that a union with Christ is accomplished by this baptism into Christ is made clear in verse 5. The word *sumphutos* which is translated "planted together" is better translated "grown together." It speaks of an intimate union. The idea of union is frequently expressed in translations. The meaning is that by union with Christ we have the likeness of His death. As a rule it is simply said that we died with or in Him. In this case likeness is used to stress the fact that we have the credit for His death but did not experience the pain and agony of it.

That we received Jesus' death as our death in this union is further developed in this passage. In verse 6 which is given to explain verse 5, we are told, " . . . Our old man is [or 'was' based on the Greek] crucified with him." Our old man here is our pre-salvation self or person, not our sinful nature. When we became a new man in conversion, what we were before that time became our old man because we are now a new man.

That the crucifixion of our old man was the penal death we died with Christ is clear from verse 7 where this death results in justification. The word that is translated "freed" is *dikaioo* and should be translated justified. Only a penal death justifies. The only penal death that can justify us is the death of Christ.

Death by identification is further developed in verse 8, "Now if

157

we be dead [or 'died' based on the Greek] with Christ." If there has been any lack of clarity on the part of anybody's mind about having died by our union with Christ before reaching verse 11, verse 11 should remove all doubt. Paul plainly tells us that we are to reckon ourselves to be dead to sin and alive unto God "in Christ Jesus our Lord" (see note given earlier on the translation "in" in this verse).

Three things are very clear in this passage: (1) Paul talks about union with Christ. (2) This union identifies us with Christ's death. (3) This death is a penal death.

I am aware of the fact that most people understand the death to sin in this passage to be ethical rather than penal. In research for a thesis dealing with the believer's death to sin I became firmly convinced that Paul was referring to a penal death. Support for this position was found in commentaries on Romans by David Brown, Thomas Chalmers, Robert Huldane, James Morrison, H. C. G. Moule, and William G. T. Shedd.[4] Some would insist on the ethical interpretation since Romans 6 deals with sanctification. I will show how the penal death relates to sanctification in the chapter on sanctification.

We are not dependent upon this passage alone. The penal death interpretation fits the context of Galatians 2:20. With reference to Galatians 2:19, 20, Dr. William G. T. Shedd quotes Ellicot:

> The meaning is: 'I died not only as concerns the law, but as the law required.' The whole clause, then, may be thus paraphrased: 'I, through the law, owing to sin, was brought under its curse; but having undergone this curse, with, and in the person of, Christ, I died to the law, in the fullest and deepest sense: being both free from its claims, and having satisfied its course.'

Shedd in making his own comment on the passage explains:

> Some commentators explain St. Paul's crucifixion with Christ, to be his own personal sufferings in the cause of Christ. But St. Paul's own sufferings would not be the reason he is 'dead to the law.' Christ's atoning suffering is the reason for this.

After referring to 2 Corinthians 5:15, 16 and 2 Timothy 2:11, Shedd concludes:

> These passages abundantly prove that the doctrine of the believer's unity with Christ in his vicarious death for sin is familiar to St. Paul, and is strongly emphasized by him.[5]

Shedd calls the union between Christ and the believer a spiritual union. In speaking about this union, he explains:

Upon this spiritual and mystical union, rests the federal and legal union between Christ and his people. Because they are spiritually, vitally, eternally, and mystically one with him, his merit is imputable to them, and their demerit is imputable to him. The imputation of Christ's righteousness supposes a union with him. It could not be imputed to an unbeliever, because he is not united with Christ by faith.6

Dr. John F. Walvoord says concerning the union of Christ and the believer:

Important theological truths are related to the doctrine of identification [he explained elsewhere in the article that union is commonly taken as a synonym for identification] in Scripture. The believer is identified with Christ in his death (Romans 6:1-11); his burial (Romans 6:4); his resurrection (Colossians 3:1); his ascension (Ephesians 2:6); his reign (2 Timothy 2:12); and his glory (Romans 8:17). Identification with Christ has its limitation, however. Christ is identified with the human race in incarnation, but only true believers are identified with Christ. The identification of a believer with Christ results in certain aspects of the person and work of Christ being attributed to the believer, but this does not extend to possession of the attributes of the Second Person, nor are the personal distinctions between Christ and the believer erased. Taken as a whole, however, identification with Christ is a most important doctrine and is essential to the entire program of grace.7

Identification by union makes that which was not actually a part of a person's experience his by identification. For example, prior to the time that Hawaii became a part of the United States, a citizen of Hawaii could not have said, "We celebrate our day of Independence on July 4." Immediately upon their becoming a state, the same person who formerly could not make the statement could say, "We celebrate our day of Independence on July 4." What happened on July 4, 1776, became a part of their history. The history of the United States became the history of Hawaii, and the history of Hawaii became the history of the United States.

Prior to the union of Christ on the condition of faith, a person could not say, "I died with Christ." Immediately, upon union with Christ a person can say, "I died with Christ." The history of the cross became his history, not in the actual sense, but by identification so that he received full credit for that death. At the same time, the history of our sins became Jesus' history, not in the sense that His character was affected, but so that they would come in contact with the penalty He had already paid for them. He took the responsibility for them, but it was a responsibility that He had already assumed on the cross. It is this side of the truth that Shedd was addressing in the quotation listed earlier when he said, " . . . And their [believers'] demerit is imputable to him. "

Attention has been given thus far to the imputation of the death of Christ to the believer; let us now turn our attention to the imputation of Christ's righteousness. By the righteousness of Christ, we mean the active obedience of Christ in which He lived a completely holy life. It may be that we should understand righteousness to mean "that which is required to make one right or righteous before God" and make it include both the penal death and the righteous life of Christ. At any rate, it would definitely include the righteous life of Christ.

Paul says in 2 Corinthians 5:21, " . . . That we might be made the righteousness of God in him." In Philippians 3:9, Paul says, "And be found in him, not having mine own righteousness, which is of the law, but that which is through the faith of Christ, the righteousness which is of [from] God by faith." In these verses, righteousness is ours "in Christ." Philippians 3:9 makes it clear that Paul is talking about a righteousness that is not his own in the sense of having personally produced it, but a righteousness that is from God.

In Romans 1:18—3:20, Paul had talked about the fact that man needed righteousness, but in and of himself did not and could not have righteousness. In Romans 3:21, Paul came through with a message of hope for those who were helpless. He spoke in 3:21 of a God-provided righteousness which was apart from personal law-keeping. It was provided by God on the condition of faith (3:22). In Romans 4:6, Paul spoke about the imputation of righteousness without works. In Romans 5:17, he spoke of the gift of right-eousness. In Romans 10:3, he spoke of a righteousness that is not established by our own efforts but is submitted to. By taking all of this evidence together, we conclude that the righteousness which justifies is the righteousness of Christ placed on our account as a gift on the condition of faith.

On the condition of faith, we are placed in union with Christ. Based on that union we receive His death and righteousness. Based on the fact that Christ's death and righteousness became our death and righteousness, God as Judge declares us righteous.

C. Justification Based on Real Righteousness, Not Simply Declared Righteous

Some give great stress to the word "declare." They say that we are declared righteous, but we are not righteous. I beg to differ.

Based on the death and righteousness of Christ becoming ours, we are righteous. The righteousness upon which this declaration is made is a real righteousness. It is true that in our own persons we are not absolutely righteous, but we are not declared to be righteous in our own persons. We are declared to be righteous on the basis of a real righteousness, the righteousness of Christ. As will be seen later, the stress on the word "declared" belongs not to the satisfaction view but the governmental view.

D. Justification, The Work of God as Judge

It is important to observe that justification is the work of God as judge. God, as judge, will not justify us in any way other than that which protects His own holiness and shows an interest in our holiness. The moral concerns of God are fully protected and are clearly manifested in God's provision of atonement and justification.

A shallow look at an account balanced by a gift of the death and righteousness of Christ leads to a cheap view of grace and has serious moral consequences. It has traces of antinomianism which lacks appreciation for the moral responsibility of the believer.

It is true that justification is by grace which is an unmerited favor. That fact must never be compromised. It must never be corrupted. There is a right way and a wrong way to approach grace. Grace must be understood in the context of moral law, not moral law in the context of grace. By this I mean that we start with law, and grace conforms to the requirements and interests of law. We do not begin with grace and make law conform to grace.

In Romans 3:31, Paul says, "Do we then make void the law through faith? God forbid: Yea, we establish the law." The provision of grace operates within the framework of the highest regard for law. Man was condemned by the holy law of God because of his own sin. The holiness of God would not tolerate a plan of redemption that did not pay full respect to the law of God. The only plan of atonement that God would approve was one that gave full satisfaction to the holiness of God by meeting all the demands of the law. Justification must be the work of God as Judge. As Judge He sees to it that the fullest interest of the law is maintained. No person is justified apart from the complete satisfaction of the law. Nothing could be clearer than that the full protection and the clear manifestation of God's moral concern is seen in the way God provided atonement and justification. For God to be so determined to protect the interest of His holiness in atonement and then, by justification, to open the way for a Christian experience in which holiness is something we can take or leave would be absurd.

When we begin with grace or try to build grace on a weak moral foundation, we corrupt both grace and law. The hasty conclusions that are drawn in such a manner are both false and dangerous. It is reasoned that while moral responsibility might be good, it is optional. Since Jesus satisfied the demands of the law and the only condition of salvation is faith, it is felt by some that it is conceivable that a person can be a Christian and at the same time live in most any degree of sin. We need to be careful in combating this error lest we corrupt grace; at the same time we must combat it lest we corrupt both law and grace. We combat it not by changing the nature of atonement and justification, but by having a view of sanctification that is an appropriate accompaniment of justification. This we will propose to do in the chapter on sanctification.

E. Reconciliation The Result

Atonement and justification were designed to resolve a conflict between God and man. The guilt of man closed the door of fellowship with man from God's side. Justification opened that door. It prepares the way for reunion and fellowship with God.

Full reconciliation involves reconciliation on our part. This involves repentance and regeneration which will be discussed later. As a result of all of this we are restored to fellowship with God. The functioning personal relationship that we so drastically need becomes a reality in salvation. The foundation for it all rests upon atonement and justification. The logical consistency and adequacy of atonement and justification meet the needs of our mind. The forgiveness of sins and restoration to favor and fellowship with God meet the needs of our hearts.

III. THE GOVERNMENTAL VIEW OF ATONEMENT

The majority of conservative theologians have adhered to the basic ideas of the satisfaction view of atonement. There have been some who have held to the governmental view. This view was first introduced by Hugo Grotius (1583—1645). Adherents of this view since Grotius have included John Miley, Charles Finney, James H. Fairchild, and H. Orton Wiley. In order to avoid some of the criticisms that have been given to this view, some have modified it but have still held to most of the essentials.

A. Basic Assumptions

The basic assumptions are: (1) God is sovereign. (2) Man is sinful. (3) God is loving. (4) The end of God's sovereignty is the happiness of man.

B. Why Atonement Was Necessary

One of the basic principles of the governmental theory is the rejection of the absolute necessity that sin be punished. Dr. John Miley says:

> While thus asserting the intrinsic evil of sin, Grotius denies an absolute necessity arising therefrom for its punishment. The punishment of sin is just, but not in itself an obligation.8

Sin requires punishment only as it is necessary to secure the ends of God's government. James H. Fairchild explains the interpretation of the end of government as it is perceived by those who advocate the governmental theory:

> And when we speak of detriment to God's government, we should mean harm to the great interests of his rational and dependent universe. We sometimes speak of the necessity of protecting God's honor as a ruler, or of magnifying the law of God, and or meeting the claims of justice. These terms have a limited significance; but all essential facts implied are summed up in the comprehensive idea of securing the well-being of God's rational creatures, the subject of his government. This is the sole end of government; and when this is secured the honor of God, and of the law, and of justice, will all be safe. Atonement is adopted to secure these ends.9

Since it is not an absolute necessity that sin be punished, the penalty can be set aside and never be paid either by the person or a substitute as long as another means can be provided which will protect the interests of government. It is concluded that atonement is necessary to protect the interests of government since forgiveness too easily granted would present problems. Miley explains concerning Grotius' view:

> Forgiveness too freely granted or too often repeated, and especially on slight grounds, would annul the authority of the law, or render it powerless for its great and imperative ends. Thus he finds the necessity for an atonement—for some vicarious provision—which, on remission of penalty, may conserve these ends.10

The necessity of atonement rests in the need of a means by which sin can be forgiven without loss of respect for government.

163

When this is achieved the penalty can be set aside and sins can be forgiven.

C. The Nature of Atonement

In the governmental view of atonement, public justice, not retributive justice, is satisfied. It is not the holy nature of God that is satisfied, but the public good. Charles G. Finney explains:

> Public justice, in its exercise, consists in the promotion and protection of the public interests, by such legislation and such an administration of law, as is demanded by the highest good of the public. It implies the execution of the penalties of the law where the precept is violated, unless something else is done that will as effectually serve the public interests. When this is done, public justice demands, that the execution of the penalty shall be dispensed with, by extending pardon to the criminal. Retributive justice makes no exceptions, but punishes without mercy in every instance of crime. Public justice makes exceptions, as often as this is permitted or required by the public good. 11

In serving the need of public justice a penalty is a moral force to discourage disobedience. The death of Jesus Christ is not a penalty for sin. Occasionally some who hold to the governmental view use penalty in a loose sense but never in a technical sense. The death of Jesus Christ is a substitute for a penalty. It takes the place of a penalty and serves the same purpose as a penalty.

According to Miley, Grotius viewed the death of Christ as a penal example.

> And he makes a very free use of the term penal substitution. Yet he does not seem to regard the sufferings of Christ as penal in any very strict sense—certainly not as a substitutional punishment of sin in the satisfaction of a purely retributive justice. 12

Fairchild explains concerning the governmental view of the death of Christ:

> The theory presented does not present that Christ suffered the penalty of the law . . . . In a very proper sense the death of Christ takes the place of the penitent sinner's punishment, as a moral force in the government of God; and thus it is that the Scriptures represent that Christ died for us; that 'he bore our sins in his own body on the tree.'

The suffering of Christ made the punishment of the penitent unnecessary. 13

It may be asked what is it that constitutes this moral force in the death of Christ. Fairchild explains:

> ... It is an exhibition of God's estimate of sin, in that no arrangement less significant than the coming of the Emmanuel, and his patience and obedience unto death, could be devised, to counteract the mischief of sin, and deliver men from ruin . . . .
>
>   Again, it is to be observed that in the death of Christ sin has made an exhibition of itself . . . . Sin never so displayed its malignity and hatefulness, as in that infamous deed; and the sight of the cross from that day to this, has tended powerfully to make the world ashamed of sin . . . .
>
>   ... It exhibits the beauty of holiness, even more impressively than the odiousness of sin. The character and consecration of the Savior is the highest exhibition of goodness and unselfish devotion that the world has seen . . . .
>
>   Again, the cross is an exhibition of the love of God, in the sense of sympathy and compassion for sinners . . . . The goodness and the severity of God are united in the great lesson of the cross.14

The value of Christ's death in the governmental view is *revelational.* It reveals God's attitude toward sin, that sin is odious, the beauty of holiness, and the love of God.

IV. JUSTIFICATION ACCORDING TO THE GOVERNMENTAL VIEW OF ATONEMENT

A. No Imputation of Either the Death or the Righteousness of Christ to the Believer

Fairchild comments:

> Theologians who hold to the imputation of our sin to Christ, and of his righteousness to us, treat Justification as a judicial act, a pronouncing of the sinner just before the law . . . . The simpler and more reasonable view is, that there can be no transfer, or imputation, either of guilt or of righteousness. 15

B. Faith Imputed for Righteousness

In the governmental view the penalty is set aside in the light of atonement when the sinner exercises faith in Christ. The chart below will help us see what takes place in justification according to this view.

Debits	The Sinner	Credits
Absolute Righteousness		Unpaid
Eternal Death		Unpaid

Debits	The Believer	Credits
Absolute Righteousness		Faith
Eternal Death		Canceled
		Justified

Absolute Righteousness is what God required of the sinner, and eternal death is the penalty for disobedience. In view of faith in Christ, God sets the penalty aside and the same consideration that would have been given to absolute righteousness is given for faith. Faith is not absolute righteousness, but it is counted "for" or "as" righteousness. Fairchild says, "Faith is another word for the righteousness which the law requires." 16 The exact meaning of "faith counted for righteousness" is understood with some variations among governmentalists, but all concur in denying that there is any imputation of the death or righteousness of Christ to the believer. These variations do not have any essential effect on the view.

Since justification, in the governmental view, declares the person to be righteous without this declaration being based on an absolute righteousness, it can be seen that it is appropriate to give stress to the word "declare." The believer is declared to be righteous, but he is not righteous. This is supposed to be the way grace works. The satisfaction view does not require this interpretation of "declare." The believer is declared righteous because the righteousness of Christ, which is a real righteousness, is his.

C. Justification, The Work of God as Sovereign

The judge must go by the law and uphold the law. He can declare a person righteous only as he is righteous by the standard of the law. A ruler has more latitude. This can be seen in the right of a governor to pardon.

In the governmental view, God as Ruler declares the believer righteous not by the strict standard of law but in a manner that is designed to protect the public good. This is what allows Him to set

166

the penalty aside. The justice administered is not retributive justice but public justice.

Finney explains:

> Courts never pardon, or set aside the execution of penalties. This does not belong to them, but either to the executive or to the lawmaking department. Oftentimes, this power in human governments is lodged in the head of the executive department, who is generally at least, a branch of the legislative power of government. But never is the power of pardon exercised in the judicial department . . . .
> It consists not in the law pronouncing the sinner just, but in his being ultimately governmentally treated as if he were just; that is, it consists in a governmental decree of pardon or amnesty—in arresting and setting aside the execution of the incurred penalty of law— . . . . [17]

V. CRITICISM OF THE GOVERNMENTAL VIEW OF ATONEMENT AND JUSTIFICATION

While the governmental view has many important differences that distinguish it from the moral influence theory of liberalism, it has some dangerously close parallels. (1) Both views deny that there is any principle in the Divine nature that requires satisfaction in atonement. (2) Both deny that it is absolutely necessary to inflict a penalty on sin. (3) Both views consider the value of Christ's death to be revelational.

The governmental view does believe in the doctrine of Hell for those who do not receive Christ by faith. Liberalism believes in universalism. There is no penalty against sin in the strict sense of the word. In liberalism, the emphasis in the revelational value of the death of Christ stresses the love of Christ. It is God's love on the one hand assuring the sinner that there is no obstacle to his return. On the other hand, God's love is a moral force to bring about moral transformation in the sinner. The great love of God manifested in sending Jesus to die to show us that God loves us is a heart-moving revelation and is designed to bring about moral change. In the governmental view the death of Christ reveals the holiness of God, the seriousness of sin, the love of God, and God's interest in maintaining His government.

In the discussion of the satisfaction view, I set forth the reason for believing that it is an absolute necessity for sin to be punished. God's holy nature requires it. If the holy nature of God does require that sin be punished, it is very serious to deny that truth. The governmental view proposes to emphasize the importance of holiness and the seriousness of sin. As weighed against the importance of God's holiness and the seriousness of sin in the satisfaction view, the governmental view falls far short. In the satisfaction view, holiness is so important and sin is so serious that nothing short of full satisfaction to God's law, so as to permit God in His capacity as Judge to declare one righteous, is necessary for salvation. In the governmental view, God in His capacity as Ruler can set aside the penalty of sin and declare one to be righteous, who is in fact not righteous.

All of the valid principles that the governmental view proposes to uphold are done better by the satisfaction view. The satisfaction view more successfully shows the importance of holiness and the seriousness of sin. It gives a much higher view of the love of God. It creates a more solid foundation for respect for God's government.

It should be pointed out that while the satisfaction view does reveal the importance of holiness, the seriousness of sin, and the wonder of God's love, what it reveals is not what makes atonement. Atonement is based on full satisfaction of the demands of the law. God uses atonement as an instrument of revelation, but revelation is not a means of atonement. This revelation of God is used by God to bring people to Christ and promote holiness and love among believers.

While important differences can be pointed out in the revelation principle in the governmental view and the liberal view, I do not believe that these differences are adequate to give the needed protection against liberal influence. I am inclined to believe, though I have not researched the subject to see, that history would show that there had been a loss among governmentalists in this direction.

The most important thing that can be said for the governmental view is that its advocates have held to a serious view of Scripture. They have proposed their view to be the scriptural view. The advocates of the moral influence view have had a low view of Scripture. Whatever protection the governmentalists have from taking up the liberal view rests far more upon their respect for Scripture than upon logical arguments to maintain the govermental view as opposed to the moral influence view.

One of the important distinctions between the satisfaction view and the governmental view is the ends they propose to serve. The governmental view is man-centered. It seeks to protect the welfare of mankind. The satisfaction view is God-centered. It seeks to vindicate the Divine nature.

In my opinion, the governmental view is seriously inadequate. It is dangerously close to liberalism's view. Once a person denies the absolute necessity of the punishment of sin, there is no logical barrier which prohibits the slide into the moral influence theory. Whatever safety there is lies in the commitment to Scripture rather than a

168

safety in the logic of the case.

VI. OBJECTIONS TO THE SATISFACTION VIEW AS RAISED
BY THE GOVERNMENTAL VIEW

A. Penal Satisfaction Not Necessary

Since I have already dealt with this problem when setting forth the satisfaction view, I will not deal with it here. I mention the objection here to make the list of objections complete.

B. Penal Satisfaction Through a Substitute Not Possible

There are two types of punishments meted out by the judicial system—pecuniary punishment and penal punishment. Pecuniary punishment is the punishment that takes the form of a fine. It is possible for a substitute to pay a fine for a person. Penal punishment involves a punishment of the person. The person goes to jail, to prison, or is put to death. In our judicial system there is no substitution in the area of penal punishment. The punishment of sin is not pecuniary, but penal. Therefore, it is argued that there can be no substitution for us.

This objection does bring up a valid point. Substitution pure and simple whereby one person does something for or in the place of another would be invalid in atonement.

The answer to this objection is found in the union of Christ and the believer as was discussed in connection with the satisfaction view. By identification with Christ the believer can say, "I died with Christ." The action can be considered to be his, not simply an action that was performed for him.

In our judicial system, we cannot have penal substitution because there is no way it can be said that a person went to jail without actually going. In Christ, we can say we died with Him without actually going through this experience. Therefore, penal substitution is possible.

C. Universal Salvation or Limited Atonement a Necessary Result

It is argued that all for whom Christ died must of necessity be saved since His death settles their account and therefore forms the necessary basis for their forgiveness. Either Christ died for everybody and everybody would be saved, or He died only for the elect and only the elect will be saved, the objection states.

169

Again the answer is found in the kind of substitution involved. Christ died for the whole world in a provisionary sense. He suffered the penal wrath of God for sin, but that fact alone does not place His death on everybody's account. It can be effective only as it is placed on a person's account. It can be placed on a person's account only as a result of a union with Christ. Union with Christ is conditioned on faith. Provisionary atonement was made for all people (1 John 2:2). It is applied to whosoever will meet the condition of faith (John 3:16; Romans 10:13; Revelation 22:17).

The Calvinist may want to insist that the objection is valid and that Christ died only for the elect. The only way this argument could have any validity would be to deny the possibility of provisionary atonement. If there can be no provisionary atonement, it does follow that if Christ died for a person his justification is never provisionary but always real.

I do not think the Calvinist wants to deny the provisionary principle in atonement. To deny it means that the elect were justified before they experienced faith. The Calvinist teaches that the person for whom Christ died will surely be justified, but they do not consider a person justified until he experiences faith as the condition of justification. The only way to deny the provisionary nature of atonement is to consider all people for whom Christ died to be justified before they experience faith.

Once it is accepted that atonement is provisionary, the objection which states that penal satisfaction leads to either universalism or limited atonement is seen to be invalid. Provisionary atonement that is applied on the condition of faith and on the grounds of a union with Christ answers this objection and sustains the penal satisfaction view.

D. Double Payment With Regard to Sinners Who Go to Hell

The discussion above about provisionary atonement and union with Christ forms the basis for answering this objection. The death of Christ is not on the sinner's account who goes to Hell. His account does not show a double payment. It is true that his sins were paid for provisionally, but there is no problem with justice which forbids collection of double payment as long as there is no double entry on the person's account.

E. Antinomianism The Logical Result

It is argued that if we receive the death of Christ and the righteousness of Christ, the way is open for license to sin. If the account was completely settled by Christ, it is argued that a person can live as he pleases.

170

If we think of justification apart from sanctification, we have antinomianism. However, when we understand that justification is always accompanied by sanctification, we see that the antinomian charge is invalid. It is the nature of sanctification that disallows antinomianism. The evidence that sanctification nullifies the charge of antinomianism will be seen in the development of the doctrine of sanctification in the next chapter.

We should not be surprised when our doctrine of atonement and justification causes us to be accused of giving license to sin. Paul was accused of the same thing (Romans 3:8; 6:1). We should be concerned if we cannot answer the charge. We do not answer the charge by tampering with the doctrine of justification, but by setting forth the doctrine of sanctification.

F. Necessarily Leads to the Conclusion: Once Saved Always Saved

It is not hard to see why this objection would be raised, but it is easily answered. If we had actually experienced what Jesus did on the Cross, it would follow that we could never be called upon to pay the same price again. It is true that as long as we have the death and righteousness of Christ we are saved.

What makes it possible for us to lose our salvation and be lost again? The death and righteousness of Christ are ours by identification. They remain ours only as we remain identified with Him. The identification with Christ is ours as long as we remain in union with Him. The union is ours conditionally. It is conditioned on faith in Christ. If we make shipwreck of our faith, the union will be broken. We will lose our identification with Christ. His death and righteousness will no longer be ours.

John 15:2 teaches that we can be taken out of Christ. It is the branch "in me" that "he taketh away." I will give further discussion of this subject in the chapter on perseverance. It was mentioned here only to answer the objection raised against the satisfaction view.

VII. INFANT SALVATION

A. Scriptural Grounds for Believing in Infant Salvation

The Bible does not address the subject of infant salvation directly. We go on the basis of implications. When the young son of David died, in explaining to his servants why he ceased to fast after the child died, David said, "But now he is dead, wherefore should I fast? Can I bring him back again? I shall go to him, but he shall not return to me" (2 Samuel 12:23). It is inferred that David and the

171

child would meet each other after death. The implication is that the child will be with God in eternity.

In Matthew 18:10, Jesus said, "Take heed that ye despise not one of these little ones; for I say unto you, That in heaven their angels do always behold the face of my Father which is in heaven." The reference to "their angels" implies that they are in a favorable relationship with God. To me the implications involved in these passages give a solid foundation for rejecting the idea that infants will go to Hell.

B. Suggested Explanation of How Infants are Saved

It should be restated here that the position I am taking is infant salvation. I disagree with those who base the safety of the infant on the innocence of infants. According to such a view, infants are "safe," not "saved."

The reason for there being a problem is that faith is the condition of salvation. Infants are not capable of exercising faith. If they cannot exercise faith, how can they be saved?

The requirement of the condition of faith is God's way of dealing with us as persons—those who have wills. God will not transgress our personality or our will. In requiring faith, God treats us as persons and requires a response from us. Failure to require a response in which we choose Christ would be a failure to treat us as persons. This problem does not exist with the infant. He is a person but is not fully developed so he can exercise all the rights and privileges and assume all the responsibilities of being a person. There is no transgression of his personality or will if God should remove from him his racial guilt since he is not capable of saying either yes or no. This approach may be all that needs to be said, but I will give more thoughts on the subject following.

Racial guilt belongs to us simply by being a member of the human race—a descendant of Adam. Personal guilt is ours because of our own personal sins. It should not seem strange if the application of atonement be approached somewhat differently for forgiveness of racial guilt than from forgiveness of personal guilt.

Our personal sins were laid on Jesus on the cross. We receive forgiveness for them when we exercise faith in Christ and are placed in union with Him on an individual basis.

When Jesus Christ became incarnate, He became a member of the race. He identified Himself with a race that was under racial condemnation because of Adam's sin. This identification with the race made it possible for Him to automatically pay the penalty for racial guilt. This could be done because He was identified with the race. Personal guilt could not be taken care of automatically because the incarnation, as such, did not identify Him with our personal

172

guilt. The actual transfer of guilt to Christ and the transfer of His death and righteousness for personal guilt requires a union between Christ and the individual person.

Certain points need to be made clear. (1) Jesus did not have a depraved nature. This was taken care of by miraculous, immaculate conception. (2) Jesus did not *actually* sin in Adam. He simply became identified with Adam's sin. It did not change His character any more than it did when our personal sins were laid on Him. He no more actually sinned in Adam than we actually died in Christ. (3) The identification of Christ with the race, while not changing His character, did place Him in a position that He could assume the responsibility for racial sin and pay the penalty for it. (4) The identification to which I am referring cannot be labeled pantheism because it involves no different identification than what is based on the incarnation itself.

If we accept this view, we believe that guilt and condemnation passed on the race from Adam. If it had not been for Christ, the whole human race would have been lost, including infants. Because of the atoning work of Christ, racial guilt has been lifted from everyone. If a person goes to Hell, he will go because of his own personal sins.

This does not open the way for a person reaching the age of accountability and then living a righteous life and not need to be saved. Depravity assures us that every person will sin (Romans 8:7, 8).

CHAP7ER TEN
NOTES

1. Henry Clarence Thiessen, *Introductory Lectures in Systematic Theology*, Grand Rapids: William B. Eerdmans Publishing Company, c. 1949, p. 131.

2. James Oliver Buswell, Jr., *A Systematic Theology of the Christian Religion*, Volume II, 2 volumes, Grand Rapids: Zondervan Publishing House, c. 1962, p. 114.

3. William G. T. Shedd, *Dogmatic Theology*, Grand Rapids: Zondervan Publishing House, Classic Reprint Edition, pp. 436, 437.

4. Leroy Forlines, *A Study of Paul's Teachings on the Believer's Death to Sin and Its Relationship to a New Life*, an unpublished thesis submitted in partial fulfillment of the requirements for the Master of Arts degree, Winona Lake School of Theology, 1959.

5. William G. T. Shedd, *A Critical and Doctrinal Commentary on the Epistle of St. Paul to the Romans*, Grand Rapids: Zondervan Publishing House, reprinted from the 1879 edition, pp. 148, 149.

6. William G. T. Shedd, *Dogmatic Theology*, Volume II, 2 volumes, Grand Rapids: Zondervan Publishing House, Classic reprint edition, p. 534.

7. John F. Walvoord, "Identification with Christ," *Baker's Dictionary of Theology*, edited by Everett F. Harrison, Grand Rapids: Baker Book House, c. 1960, p. 276.

8. John Miley, *Systematic Theology*, Volume II, 2 volumes, New York: Hunt and Eaton, c. 1894, p. 162.

9. James H. Fairchild, *Elements of Theology*, Oberlin, Ohio: Pearce and Randolf Printers, c. 1892, p. 224.

10. Miley, *op. cit.*, p. 163.

11. Charles G. Finney, *Finney's Lectures on Systematic Theology*, edited by J. H. Fairchild, Grand Rapids: William B. Eerdmans Publishing Company, reprint of 1878 revised edition, p. 259.

12. Miley, *loc. cit.*

13. Fairchild, *op. cit.* p. 229.

14. *Ibid.*, pp. 227, 228.

15. *Ibid.*, p. 277.

16. *Ibid.*, p. 278.

17. Finney, *op. cit.*, pp. 383, 384.

11

Sanctification

There are two aspects of sin: guilt and depravity. Sin as guilt makes a person liable to punishment. Sin as depravity is a power in a person's life that causes him to commit sin.

There are two aspects of salvation that are designed to deal with the two aspects of sin: justification and sanctification. Justification settles the problem of guilt. It changes our standing before God. Sanctification deals with the problem created by depravity. It changes our experience with God and with sin.

It is very helpful in understanding the doctrine of salvation to get a clear understanding of the difference between justification and sanctification and the relationship between the two.

I. CONTRAST BETWEEN JUSTIFICATION AND SANCTIFICATION

Justification	Sanctification
1. Positional (Standing)	1. Experiential (State)
2. Objective	2. Subjective
3. Rightstanding with God	3. Conformity to the Image of Christ
4. Always Full and Complete	4. Moving Toward Completion
5. Christ's Righteousness	5. Personal Righteousness
6. Absolute Righteousness	6. Relative Righteousness Now— Absolute in the Life to Come

175

A review of this chart after studying this chapter will make it more meaningful. Presenting it here puts the mind on the alert so we can avoid confusing justification and sanctification. Let it be said here that while there are clear distinctions between justification and sanctification, the Bible knows of no separation of the two. We cannot receive justification without also receiving sanctification.

II. THE RELATIONSHIP BETWEEN JUSTIFICATION AND SANCTIFICATION

At conversion, we receive justification and sanctification simultaneously. While both are received at the same time, logically justification is prior to sanctification and makes sanctification possible. Sanctification is dependent upon justification. Justification is not dependent upon sanctification. Justification is dependent upon the death and righteousness of Christ.

Charles Finney's view, on this point, is an illustration of the errors that can grow out of the governmental view of atonement and justification. He remarks:

> Present sanctification, in the sense of present full consecration to God, is made another condition, not ground of justification. Some theologians have made justification a condition of sanctification, instead of making sanctification a condition of justification. But this we shall see is an erroneous view of the subject . .
> . . Sanctification is sometimes used to express a permanent state of obedience to God, or of consecration. In this sense it is not a condition of present justification, or of pardon and acceptance. But it is a condition of continued and permanent acceptance with God. It certainly cannot be true, that God accepts and justifies a person in his sins. The Bible everywhere represents justified persons as sanctified, and always expressly, or impliedly, conditionates justification upon sanctification, in the sense of present obedience to God.1

I can appreciate Finney's concern for not separating justification and sanctification and thus allowing a person to be justified who is not sanctified. However, his approach confuses the doctrine of justification and places it in jeopardy.

Sanctification is always an accompaniment of justification, but it is not a condition or ground of justification. It is simply that the salvation "package" includes both, and the package cannot be broken to separate the two. We can no more have justification without sanctification than we can sanctification without justification.

The ultimate concern of God in redemption is to restore fallen men to favor and a functional relationship with God. Justification is an absolutely essential step in the process of redemption. To bypass justification or to ground it on anything other than the death and righteousness of Christ is to do violence to the holiness of God. To break the package and allow justification without sanctification is to commit the following errors: (1) It is to misunderstand the Scripture as we shall see later.

(2) It is to ground the satisfaction of the holiness of God in atonement and justification in a technical necessity in God rather than a personal necessity in God. If the satisfaction of holiness is a technical necessity, that interest can be set aside when the technicality is settled. It would be a formality required to uphold the letter of the law. If the satisfaction of holiness is grounded in God's personal experience of holiness and His attitude toward sin, that interest is just as strong once a person is justified as it was before. Justification is a step in the process of redemption that makes sanctification possible. A holy God will most definitely pursue His interest in holiness with the believer.

(3) It opens the door to antinomianism. Any time that holiness is made an optional accessory to salvation rather than a necessary result, even when the acceptance of the accessory is urged, the influence of antinomianism is present.

(4) It opens the door to cheap easy-believism which promises justification without sanctification—forgiveness without change. Such a view is not the gospel. It is another gospel. For years we have operated on the assumption that we could so corrupt grace through a wrong involvement of law that it would in effect become another gospel; but the reverse danger received, in most cases, no attention. It is true that a wrong involvement of law can corrupt grace so that we would be preaching another gospel. This is what Paul taught in Galatians (Galatians 1:8, 9). It is also true that we can so abuse grace and void its interest in law that we would be preaching another gospel. This is what Paul was warning against in 1 Corinthians 6:9-11; Galatians 5:19-21; and Ephesians 5:3-7. The Book of James exposes this error. Particular interest is given to it in James 2:14-26. First John gives a clear warning against this error (1 John 1:6; 2:3, 4, 9-11; 3:3-10, 14, 15; 4:20). The correction of this error does not change the nature of the doctrine of justification, but the correction must insist that justification is always accompanied by sanctification. Forgiveness and change always go together.

A corruption of the Calvinistic doctrine of perseverance has been largely responsible for the spread of cheap easy-believism. It has talked about people being eternally secure who show no evidence of sanctification. This is a corruption of Calvinism. Historic Calvinism has taught the perseverance of the saints, not eternal security whether they persevere or not.

177

Dr. Buswell, who is a Calvinist, calls this corruption of Calvinism pseudo-Calvinism. He explains:

> I have heard several pseudo-Calvinistic speakers in Christian college chapel exercises say, 'Dear young people, there are two ways to go to heaven: The spiritual way and the carnal way. It is so much better to take the spiritual way!'
>
> I knew a certain young person who believed this false doctrine and said to the Dean, 'I am a Christian, but I do not mind sitting in the bleachers. I choose to go to heaven the carnal way!'
>
> No! The carnal way is the way to eternal punishment. 'Those who practice things of this kind are not going to inherit the kingdom of God' (Galatians 5:21).[2]

As has already been observed in earlier chapters, I am not a Calvinist, but I do think it is important that both non-Calvinists and Calvinists be aware of the difference between historic Calvinism and the corruption of Calvinism by pseudo-Calvinists. The pseudo-Calvinist reminds me of Ahimaaz. When Absalom was killed, he prevailed upon Joab to let him go and tell David. At first Joab denied the request and sent Cushi. Ahimaaz again prevailed upon Joab to let him go. With reluctance, Joab consented. With great zeal, Ahimaaz overtook Cushi and was the first to get to David. When Ahimaaz gave his report, he said, "I saw a great tumult, but I knew not what it was" (2 Samuel 18:29).

The pseudo-Calvinist has heard that salvation is free. It is a gift. It is by grace. Without thinking things through and getting things in perspective, he concluded that it meant that sanctification was optional. Off he goes with his half-truth. It is true that salvation is free, but it is not true that sanctification is optional. He goes off half-cocked having misunderstanding of both Calvinism and Scripture. The harm that this has done to the Church of Jesus Christ is beyond estimate. A morally drained society is being confronted by a morally anemic church.

It would be unfair to lay the spread of cheap easy-believism altogether at the feet of the pseudo-Calvinist. Many non-Calvinists have picked up the chant of cheap easy-believism with no significant modifications and have preached it. Cheap easy-believism is inherent in all weakening of the moral thrust of Christianity.

The tragedy of cheap easy-believism is that it leads to many false professions. It offers assurance to people who have never been saved. It is not the gospel. It is another gospel. It is as much heresy as the corruption of the gospel by a wrong emphasis on law is. There is less hope of leading people out of cheap easy-believism than there is from a corruption of the gospel by a wrong emphasis on law. The

178

wrong emphasis on law corrupts grace but does not corrupt law. Cheap easy-believism corrupts both law and grace. In neither understanding law nor grace, it has weakened all points of appeal that could be used to bring about correction.

It is not easy to correct the view that corrupts grace through a wrong emphasis on law, but there is a possibility. By leaving law intact and in good shape, law can be used as a starting point from which to show a person that a proper understanding of grace satisfies, honors, and upholds the law.

We need to elaborate now on how justification contributes to sanctification. On the negative side, the power of sin is broken. Paul says, "For sin shall not have dominion over you: for ye are not under the law, but under grace" (Romans 6:14). As we observed in the previous chapter, Romans 6:7 should be translated, "For he that died is justified from sin." The death referred to is the penal death of Christ which belongs to the believer by union with Christ. Justification based on the identification of the believer with the penal death of Christ is given by Paul as the grounds for " . . . that henceforth we should not serve sin" (verse 6).

How does the penal death of Christ received in justification break the power of sin? David Brown explains:

> As death dissolves all claims, so the whole claims of sin, not only to 'reign unto death,' but to keep its victim in sinful bondage, has been discharged once for all, by the believer's penal death in the death of Christ; so that he is no longer a 'debtor to the flesh, to live after the flesh' (chapter 8:12).3

Before the guilt problem is solved by the death of Christ, there is nothing to check the power of sin. Sin reigns unchecked. When the believer has the guilt problem settled by the death of Christ, the power of sin is broken. The believer is delivered from the sphere where sin reigned into the sphere of grace "That as sin hath reigned unto death, even so might grace reign through righteousness unto eternal life by Jesus Christ our Lord" (Romans 5:21).

On the positive side, the penal death of Christ received in justification opens the way for the entrance of God's sanctifying grace. Paul says, "For if we have been planted together [grown together or united] in the likeness of his death, we shall be also in the likeness of his resurrection" (Romans 6:5). To be in the likeness of Christ's death is to have His death become our death so we receive the benefits of it. This involves justification.

To be in likeness of Christ's resurrection is to live a life of triumphant power over sin. In verse 4, Paul explains "like as Christ was raised up from the dead" to involve the "walk in newness of life." The likeness of Christ's resurrection manifests itself in newness of life. This involves sanctification. The likeness of Christ's death (justification) opens the way for likeness of Christ's resurrection (sanctification).

Our guilt stood as a barrier between the sanctifying power of God and us. God's holiness would not allow Him to enter into a personal relationship with us as long as our guilt was still upon us. When the guilt was removed by the justifying grace of God, the way was open for the entrance of God's sanctifying grace. As Robert Haldane explains:

> So long as the sinner is under the guilt of sin God can have no friendly intercourse with him; for what communion hath light with darkness? But Christ having cancelled his people's guilt, having redeemed them from the curse of the law, and invested them with the robe of his righteousness, there is no longer any obstacle to their communion with God, or any barrier to the free ingress of sanctifying grace.4

As the justifying grace of God is effective in forgiving our sins and restoring us to favor with God, so the sanctifying grace of God is effective in changing our experience with God and sin. It guarantees a change in our lives.

It can be seen that justification is foundational for sanctification. To interpret sanctification on the one hand to be a condition or ground of justification, or on the other hand to interpret justification as contributing to a weak view of sanctification, is to grossly misunderstand the Biblical teaching on salvation.

In interpreting principles that apply to persons and to personal relationships, we tend to become mechanical. We cannot totally avoid the treatment of principles this way at times. We can and must offset the influence of this tendency by constantly putting things in perspective by reconstructing the context in terms of persons and personal relationships. The concerns of holiness in atonement is God's personal concern for holiness. He is not simply protecting the letter of the law or some legal technicality. When the demands of holiness are put into the context of personal concern for holiness, that concern can neither be stopped nor depreciated by the satisfaction of the law involved in justification. It will manifest itself in a concern for sanctification that is consistent with the holy nature of God. The redemptive process is designed to restore us to favor with God and to restore the holiness that was lost in the fall. Justification is a step in that process by a personal God who is intensely interested in holiness. That interest will never be diminished.

III. THE NATURE OF SANCTIFICATION

A. The Meaning of the Word

To sanctify is to make holy. Holiness is more than a moral term. It also speaks of a relationship with God. There can be a measure of morality without dedication to God, but there can be no holiness without dedication to God. The person whom we refer to as a 'good moral' person, who is not dedicated to God, is unholy. Holiness embraces godliness (reverential living before God) and righteousness (conformity to God's moral standard).

The primary meaning of holiness is dedication to God, but we cannot think of the primary meaning as existing apart from the secondary meaning which is separation from sin. To move toward God is to move from sin as surely as to go north means to go away from south.

B. Positional Sanctification

Positional sanctification means to be positionally set apart for God. Positional sanctification is with a view to experiential sanctification.The thought here is similar to that of electing a person to be president of an organization. He is elected to serve. At the moment the former president's term expires, he is president positionally on the basis of being elected. He is president in experience only as he functions in the capacity for which he was elected. We are positionally set apart by God at conversion. We are experientially sanctified only as we practice holiness.

We can distinguish in fact between positional sanctification and experiential sanctification so far as meaning is concerned, but we are not to think of the believer being positionally sanctified without being experientially sanctified. Almost all the use of the term sanctification will be referring to experiential sanctification. The only reason for mentioning positional sanctification is for clarification. From now on all use of the word sanctification will refer to experiential sanctification unless otherwise indicated.

C. Experiential Sanctification

We not only study the subject of sanctification where the word and related words are found, we also study it anywhere the concept is found whether the word or related words appear or not.

Sanctification begins with conversion (2 Corinthians 5:17). It is at that very moment that a person begins to experience holiness. A changed life is essential fruit of conversion.

Sanctification continues to progress in this life by the process of growth (2 Peter 3:18). Every challenge to dedication or separation from sin that is addressed to Christians is evidence of the fact that the New Testament treats sanctification as being progressive and involving growth.

Sanctification will be complete at the resurrection. The spirit will be completely sanctified at death. At the resurrection, sanctification will be complete so far as the body is concerned. After death, we will be completely holy. We will never again have anything in our personality that will not be compatible with God and acceptable to God.

D. The Goal of Sanctification

This brings up again the subject of the image of God in man. As was observed earlier, at creation the image of God embraced constitutional likeness which embraced personhood and functional likeness which embraced personality. All of the constituent parts of personality remained after the fall, though they suffered damage. The damage reflects itself in man's personality. Man lost his functional likeness of God in the fall. He no longer thinks, feels, and acts in the likeness of God. It is the design of redemption to restore the functional likeness of God to man's personality. As Paul tells us in Romans 8:29, we are to be "conformed to the image of his Son [Christ]."

It is very important that our concept of the Christian life take into account the fact that man is a person. God has made us persons who think, feel, and act. We are never more personal than when we are the closest to God and when our personality is more closely conformed to His likeness.

Mechanical terms and expressions can be used to illustrate as long as we do not take them too far. The control of a machine, the use of an instrument, the filling of a vessel, the molding of clay, and the control of a puppet may all be used to illustrate our dependence upon God. However, we should recognize the limitations of these illustrations. There is one drastic difference. A person is one who thinks, feels, and makes choices. If this observation is not taken into account the error can be serious. A puppet cannot refuse to obey the directions of its master; a person can. The actions of a person must reflect his own basic nature before they are his in the truest sense of what it means to be a person. If the actions of a being are not in some sense his own, he is not a person. The old arguments of freedom of will versus no freedom of will must take on the form of personal versus sub-personal.

We need to say again that we must not interpret the relationship between persons in terms of mechanical cause and effect. Influence and response are more appropriate terms. Also, the choice is not to be made between being either active or passive. Such a choice fits mechanical relationships but not personal relationships. In many decisions we are both active and acted upon. We are dependent, independent, and interdependent in our personal relationships.

If we are to truly be in the likeness of Christ, we must be in His likeness both on the conscious and subconscious level of our personality. Thoughts, words, and actions take place on the conscious level but are expressions of our inner basic nature which exists on the sub-conscious level.

It is the design of sanctification to change our thoughts, words, and actions into the likeness of Christ and to so change our basic inner nature that these thoughts, words, and actions represent a real attitude of heart. Anything less than this fails to recognize the implications involved in the fact that man is personal.

The view of redemption that makes man, in his highest dedication, a surrendered instrument or machine to be controlled by God, to the point that a Christian's decisions are in no real sense his own, fails to understand what is meant to be changed into the image of Christ. Such a view fails to reckon fully with the fact that man is a personal being.

The church has always been plagued with the idea that there is no real redemption of the personality in this life. Man is pictured by some as being so totally wrecked by sin that he is beyond repair in this life, even by God. Salvation becomes a Divine towing service for the wrecked human being. Nothing can be done to restore him in this life. Everything will be made all right when we are finally towed into the heavenly garage, but that will be in the next life.

The best thing, according to this view, is for a person to dwell on the idea of his own nothingness and worthlessness. He is to believe that he is doing nothing and cannot do anything worthwhile. God is doing everything. The best he can do is to keep from being a hindrance while God is towing His wrecked humanity into the heavenly garage. To despise himself is about his highest virtue. To respect himself or to have anything like self-confidence is a sin.

I appreciate the problems that many sincere Christians have that move them, to whatever extent, along the line of thought described above. However, I think that the Bible clearly teaches that there is a basic change in the personality of redeemed people both on the conscious and sub-conscious level that makes our actions in a real sense our own and a reflection of our inner nature.

In Romans 8:29, the word for "conformed" is the Greek word *summorphos*. Sanday and Headlam explain that this word " ... denotes inward and thorough and not merely superficial likeness."[5]

In 2 Corinthians 3:18, when Paul speaks about the process of change into the image of the glory of the Lord, he uses a very interesting word. He uses a verb that is kin to the word used in

Romans 8:29. It is the word *metamorphoo*. The word is made up of two words meaning "after" and "to form." The noun which comes from the same root is the word *morphe*. There is another word with which this word is interestingly contrasted. It is the word *schema*. According to R. C. Trench, *morphe* " . . . signifies the form as it is the utterance of the inner life . . . "6 *Schema* refers to outward appearance or fashion and can be superficial.7 *Suschematidzo* is a verb which is made up of two words "with or together" and the verb form from the same root as *schema* which means " to fashion." *Metamorphoo* refers to an internal change rather than a mere external change. *Suschematidzo* refers to an outward, superficial change.8

The choice of the word *metamorphoo* in 2 Corinthians 3:18 shows us that when Paul speaks of being changed into the image of the Lord, he is speaking about a deep, basic change in the inner nature of the Christian. It is a change of our personality on the subconscious level that manifests itself in conscious actions that are true reflections of the person.

In Romans 12:2, Paul says: "And be not conformed to this world: but be ye transformed by the renewing of your mind."

The Greek word for conformed is *suschematidzo*. The Greek word for transformed is *metamorphoo*. Trench explains:

'Do not fall in,' says the apostle, 'with the fleeting fashions of this world, nor be yourselves fashioned to them *(me suschematidzesthe)*, but undergo a deep abiding change *(alla metamorphousthe)* by the renewing of your mind, such as the spirit of God alone can work in you' (cf. 2 Corinthians iii.18).9

It is clear from the words used in Romans 8:29; 12:2; and 2 Corinthians 3:18 that Paul is referring to the fact that as Christians we experience a deep, basic, inner change. The life is brought into the likeness of the life of Christ. The life is to be a manifestation of an inner reality.

The New Testament teaches that conformity to the image of Christ extends to each area of the personality. It affects the way we think, feel, and act. Romans 12:2 proves to be very interesting at this point. Paul speaks about a bisic, inner change taking place "by the renewing of your mind."

As I understand it, the renewing of the mind is not a process that stands outside the basic inner change that brings it about. Rather, it is involved in the change. The renewing of the mind is involved in the basic inner change.

The important question here is: What is the mind? In the English language, the word "mind" means: (1) that with which we think and reason, (2) the mind (in the limited sense just referred to) plus the heart and the will. It is this use of the word mind that is reflected in the statement: "I have made up my mind to serve the Lord." We mean by this that our whole being—mind, heart, and will—is involved in the decision.

I believe the Greek word *nous* as Paul is using it embraces mind, heart, and will. Concerning the meaning of *nous*, J. H. Thayer gives as one of its meanings: "*The mind, comprising* alike *the faculties of perceiving and understanding* and those of *feeling, judging, determining* . . . . " 10 This use of the word mind is closely related to person or personality. We would be correct in saying that in Romans 12:2 when Paul speaks of a change in our basic inner nature by the renewing of our mind that he was referring to a basic inner change in our personality.

We are told in Scripture that God said with reference to the New Covenant, " . . . I will put my laws into their mind . . . " (Hebrews 8:10). The evidence that we have examined up to this point, along with the fact that we are challenged to use our mind and our heart in our relationship with God and the challenges that are made to our will, leaves no doubt that in a very real sense as Christians our actions are to spring from the inner realities of our personality.

It is a misunderstanding of Scripture for us to reduce ourselves to instruments for God to use or channels for God to work through. These metaphors are all right if we do not press them too far. When we press them to the point that we are to passively yield ourselves to God with the idea that we are to do nothing and let God use us like a puppet, we are overlooking the fact that God has made us as persons and treats us accordingly in His dealings with us.

In our relationship with God, we are both dependent and independent. We are dependent in the sense that we need His help and cannot be what we should be without His help. We are independent in the sense that even though we cannot be what we should be without God's help, in a real sense, our actions are our own. God does not treat us like puppets. We have latitude for obedience and disobedience.

Let me illustrate by applying the basic principles of our discussion to the fruit of the Spirit in Galatians 5:22, 23. Dependence is seen in the fact that the various virtues listed are called the fruit of the Spirit. But when we talk about love, joy, peace, longsuffering, etc., we are not simply talking about Divine activity in which we are used as channels. It may sound good to talk about God loving through us, but what about God having joy through us, or God having peace through us, and so on down the line through the list? The Holy Spirit is making us the kind of person who loves, experiences joy, peace, longsuffering, etc. As the Holy Spirit produces fruit in us, these virtues begin to characterize us and express our inner nature.

I am not suggesting that our inner being is completely transformed in this life. I am not suggesting that there are no inner conflicts. I am, however, suggesting that though there be inner conflicts there are also inner realities.

A proper view of redeemed man gives a foundation for a sense of self-worth, self-respect, and a good self-image. We were created in God's image. This gives a sense of self-worth. Sin made us unworthy, but it did not destroy all sense of worth. We are now sons of God. We belong to the family of God. This gives a sense of self-worth. We are being transformed into the image of God in our personality. This runs counter to the idea of downgrading ourselves. We dare not downgrade the redemptive work of God in our lives.

It is no compliment to God for a Christian to grind himself into the dust of nothingness so he can claim no credit for what he is and so he can give all the glory to God. It is no compliment to God for us to thank Him for making us "nothing." I think it brings far more glory to God for us to recognize the positive good He has done for us, to us, and in us and to thank Him for it and to give Him the glory for it.

Along the same line of thought there seems to be a widespread confusion about "self." I can appreciate the difficulty of being exact and precise. Frequently, wrong terminology may be used for the right meaning, but to speak of crucifying self and to condemn loving oneself is wrong terminology and leads some people into confusion.

Let us think about the idea a person should not love himself. Jesus said, "Love thy neighbour as thyself" (Matthew 22:39). If I am to love my neighbor as myself and am not to love myself, that is a poor standard for loving my neighbor. It is all right for a person to love himself, but it must be done in the context of loving God and his neighbor.

The Bible does not speak of crucifying self nor dying to self. The self is the real you. The only way to crucify self would be to suffer annihilation as a person. Jesus taught self-denial, but that is not crucifixion of self; neither is it self-torture. Self-denial is simply setting aside all plans and all personal interests that interfere with following Jesus.

Self is not some aspect of our being that gives us trouble. Self is the real you—the real person. Selfhood embraces our personhood and personality. A person does not need to crucify "his" self. He needs to surrender "his" self and develop "his" self. He needs self-improvement, not self-crucifixion.

I am sure that many people mean essentially the same thing by the expression crucifixion of self as I suggest by my interpretation of self-denial, but many take it much further. It becomes a hindrance to the development of the personality of the Christian. 11

It will help at this point if we will keep in mind that there are several different aspects or angles of the truth. If we develop our view from just one aspect or angle of a particular subject, we will fail to see it in proper perspective. Our thinking will not be properly balanced by the different angles of the truth.

In 2 Corinthians 4:7 Paul says, "But we have this treasure in earthen vessels, that the excellency of the power may be of God, and not of us." In contrast to God, we see our weakness. We see our utter dependence upon Him. We give Him honor, glory, and praise. We see that without Him we would be nothing and could do nothing (John 15:5). Paul refers to us as "earthen vessels" to stress this side of the picture.

If our total thinking of a Christian as a vessel is taken from 2 Corinthians 4:7, we can see the direction it would take us in our thinking. This is not all that Paul said about us as vessels. In 2 Timothy 2:21 he explains, "If a man therefore purge himself from these, he shall be a vessel unto honour, sanctified, and meet for the master's use, and prepared unto every good work." Here we see Paul talking about the Christian who separates himself from iniquity as being a "vessel unto honour . . . meet [or fit] for the master's use, and prepared unto every good work." This represents true value. We must take 2 Corinthians 4:7 and 2 Timothy 2:21 into account in arriving at a proper estimate of ourselves as Christians.

To have a sense of value carries with it a sense of responsibility. If I have a sense of value, I want to dress and act appropriately to that value. I will dress and act accordingly. Our interest in the whole Christian value system is affected by whether we downgrade ourselves or whether we recognize a value that is given to us by creation and redemption.

True Christian humility is not based on having a low sense of self-worth. It is based on a recognition that the Christian is indebted to God for his self-worth. When he recognizes this dependence upon God, he is thankful. He is not filled with a haughty spirit. He also recognizes a sense of debt and gratitude to other people. Recognition of dependence and the feeling of gratitude leave no room for false pride.

Humility is not a marvel when expressed by a person of poor accomplishments and low self-esteem. It is a marvel when exercised by those who have achieved success and have a sense of self-worth. For such a person to recognize his dependence upon God and upon others and to express his gratitude to God and to others, we call this virtue. It is true humility.

E. The Righteousness of Sanctification

In justification, the righteousness is the righteousness of Christ which becomes ours. It was not acted out or lived out by us. The

187

righteousness of sanctification is our personal righteousness that is worked out in us by the Holy Spirit as we avail ourselves of the grace of God. This righteousness is sometimes called *imparted* righteousness as contrasted with the *imputed* righteousness of justification. The word imparted is misleading. It sounds as if righteousness were a substance that exists outside of us and is imparted to us. It is better to speak of it as a righteousness that is worked out in us or produced in us.

F. The Scope of Sanctification

Sanctification is to extend to all of life's experiences. All of life's experiences involve one or more of the four basic relationships: (1) a person's relationship with God, (2) a person's relationship with other people, (3) a person's relationship with the created order, and (4) a person's relationship with himself. In sanctification, these relationships are to be lived out in subjection to God's authority as revealed in the Bible, the Lordship of Christ, and the leadership of the Holy Spirit.

The four basic values are the foundation for the guiding principles as we function within the framework of the four basic relationships. The four basic values are: (1) holiness, (2) love, (3) wisdom, and (4) ideals. Holiness is concerned with the question: Is it right or is it wrong? Love is concerned with the question: How can I show my concern? Wisdom is concerned with the question: What is the best way to do it? Ideals are concerned with the question: What is good and excellent? Because of holiness, we have convictions. Because of love, we are concerned. Because of wisdom, we have common sense. Because of ideals, we are challenged toward excellence. 12

The influence of sanctification is to manifest itself in our total experience. It embraces our experiences both as a member of the church and a member of society. At this point, it is good to keep in mind that church responsibility is not coextensive with Christian responsibility. The church has a redemptive mission and ministry. Its responsibility is to carry out the Great Commission.

The influence of the church in problems of society, politics, and the broader aspects of life should be indirect rather than direct. The church should teach the Christian values to laymen who in turn should apply them to all of their contacts and experiences. The church should put the broader aspects of life in perspective in the Christian system of life and thought, but the amplification of details and the actual encounters in society should be left up to the laity as they encounter life's experiences in its broader aspects.

To believe in a unified view of knowledge, we must believe that our belief in God and Christian values have implications for the

188

whole of life. To stay within the bounds of the commission that God has given to the church (Matthew 28:19, 20; Mark 16:15; Luke 24:47, 48; Acts 1:8) and to follow the example of the New Testament church which restricted itself to a moral and spiritual ministry, the church cannot afford a direct involvement in the broader aspects of life.

While an ordained minister has a right to speak as a private citizen, his close identification with the church means that he should do so with caution. As a rule, we would do better to train our laymen in Christian values and principles, and let them promote Christian principles in the encounters of life in its broader aspects. Christian responsibility extends to the whole of life's experiences. Church responsibility does not, except in an indirect sense. If there were no other reason for the church to stay out of direct involvement in the affairs of society, the fact that it needs to set its own house in order first would delay such an involvement for a long time.

IV. REGENERATION AND SANCTIFICATION

Regeneration is the first step in sanctification and forms the foundation for all growth and development in the process of sanctification. Without regeneration there could be no sanctification.

A. The Necessity of Regeneration

Paul tells us that " . . . the carnal mind is enmity against God: for it is not subject to the law of God, neither indeed can be. So then they that are in the flesh cannot please God" (Romans 8:7, 8). For a person who is so restricted, there can be no conformity to the image of Christ apart from regeneration.

B. The Means and Agency of Regeneration

Peter says that God " . . . hath begotten us again unto a lively hope by the resurrection of Jesus Christ from the dead" (1 Peter 1:3). Regeneration is involved in partaking of the benefits of Christ's resurrection. By union with Christ, we share the benefits of His resurrection. We are identified with His life as well as His death (Romans 6:4, 5, 8, 11).

The Word of God as a life-giving Word is an instrument in our regeneration. James said, "Of his own will begat he us with the word of truth . . . " (James 1:18). Peter speaks of "being born again, not

189

of corruptible seed, but of incorruptible, by the word of God, which liveth and abideth for ever" (1 Peter 1:23).

The Holy Spirit is the agent who performs the work of regeneration (John 3:5, 6; Titus 3:5; Ephesians 2:10; John 1:13). This means that regeneration is a Divine work.

C. The Nature of Regeneration

In regeneration we are made new creatures or a new creation (2 Corinthians 5:17). We are given a new direction in life (2 Corinthians 5:17 and Ephesians 2:10). We have a different attitude toward sin and Jesus Christ. We have a basic desire in our heart to do right and to be right with God. This change is a *basic* change, not an *absolute* change. It puts a person on the side of God and right, but it does not eradicate all traces of sin.

D. The Results of Regeneration

As a result of the new birth we become children of God. We are restored to fellowship with God and have the ability to function morally and spiritually. To enter into the kingdom of God (John 3:3, 5) does not refer to entering the kingdom of God after death. It refers to entering it now as a functioning citizen of that kingdom. We have to enter the kingdom of God now to be in it after death.

The new birth results in victorious living. John tells us, "For whatsoever is born of God overcometh the world: and this is the victory that overcometh the world, even our faith" (1 John 5:4). Since this will receive further development when I discuss the guaranteed results of sanctification, I will not give further development to it at this time.

V. THE HOLY SPIRIT AND SANCTIFICATION

A. On the Negative Side

On the negative side the Holy Spirit works in us to help us overcome sin. We read in Galatians 5:17, "For the flesh lusteth against the Spirit, and the Spirit against the flesh: and these are contrary the one to the other: so that ye cannot do the things that ye would." The presence of the Holy Spirit is a restrictive relationship that keeps us from doing things we would do without His presence.

The ministry of the Holy Spirit is clearly directed against sin. Jesus said, "And when he is come, he will reprove the world of sin,

190

and of righteousness, and of judgment" (John 16:8). Paul speaks about mortifying the deeds of the body through the Holy Spirit (Romans 8:13). Paul tells us, "This I say then, Walk in the Spirit, and ye shall not fulfil the lust of the flesh" (Galatians 5:16).

B. On the Positive Side

Stated positively, the Holy Spirit works in us to produce virtue that is expressive of Christian values. He works to produce fruit in us. Paul says, "But the fruit of the Spirit is love, joy, peace, longsuffering, gentleness, goodness, faith, meekness, temperance [self-control] " (Galatians 5:22, 23). In Ephesians 5:9 the fruit of the Spirit includes" . . . all goodness and righteousness and truth."

The Holy Spirit is not satisfied by our simply laying aside sins. He wants us to put on Christian virtue. The Christian virtues mentioned as the fruit of the Spirit are involved in the functional likeness of Christ in us.

Christianity is value oriented through and through. This value orientation permeates the whole fabric of the Christian system of life and thought. It is not our right to diminish or tone down this emphasis on values. It is our responsibility to experience and proclaim these values.

C. The Holy Spirit and the Human Personality

The relationship of the Holy Spirit and the Christian is a relationship between persons. This means that we are talking about influence and response, not mechanical cause and effect. When we speak of love as being the fruit of the Holy Spirit, we are not to interpret in terms of mechanical cause and effect but influence and response. When we think in terms of influence and response, we are safeguarding the fact that we are talking about a personal relationship. The response of love is an experience for which we are dependent upon the Holy Spirit, but at the same time we actually love. The action is our own. We are not just talking about action. We are talking about action that is expressive of our inner nature. The Holy Spirit is helping us to become the kind of person who loves.

In speaking about dependence upon the Holy Spirit, some have said, "We are to *trust* not *try*." This would be appropriate if we were talking about mechanical cause and effect relationships. Since we are talking about influence and response, we both try and trust. We set ourselves in action trusting the Holy Spirit to help us. We do not wait for Him to do it for us. Regardless of how much Divine aid we receive, it will be our personality acting when we love and when we practice other Christian virtues.

191

Some have understood Paul to advocate passivity on our part when he said, "By the grace of God I am what I am." He concluded the verse by saying, "Yet not I, but the grace of God which was with me" (1 Corinthians 15:10). In the same verse Paul said, "I laboured more abundantly than they all." "Yet not I, but the grace of God which was with me" is not intended to mean that in no sense were Paul's actions his own. If so, it would cancel out the statement, "I laboured more abundantly than they all." By attributing His efforts to the grace of God, Paul was expressing gratitude and dependence.

The truth is set forth in proper balance in Philippians 4:13 where Paul said, "I can do all things through Christ which strengtheneth me." "I can" denotes personal involvement and capability. "Christ which strengtheneth me" shows dependence. We can depend upon Divine aid, but it is Divine aid to help us be persons functioning in the likeness of Christ. It is not Divine aid that reduces us to puppets.

VI. THE WORD OF GOD AND OUR SANCTIFICATION

In His prayer in John 17, Jesus said, "Sanctify them through thy truth: thy word is truth" (verse 17). In John 8:32 He said, "And ye shall know the truth, and the truth shall make you free."

Knowledge is closely related to truth. Peter says:

Grace and peace be multiplied unto you through the knowledge of God, and of Jesus our Lord.

According as his divine power hath given unto us all things that pertain unto life and godliness, through the knowledge of him that hath called us to glory and virtue (2 Peter 1:2, 3).

A person is one who thinks, feels, and acts. In the mind we receive knowledge as ideas. In the heart ideas take on attitudes. When we truly believe an idea, that idea produces the appropriate attitude in our heart. What we know and feel is what guides our behavior. Our will is influenced by our ideas and attitudes.

In Philippians 4:8, after having called attention to truth, honesty, justice, purity, loveliness, things of good report, virtue, and praise, Paul said, "Think on these things." Why did Paul say, "Think on these things"? It is because thinking transforms behavior. To think on those things was to meditate upon them. There are several references where the Bible speaks about meditation (Joshua 1:8; Psalms 1:2; 19:14; 63:6; 103:4; 119:15; 143:5; and 1 Timothy 4:15).

Why meditate? In meditation, ideas take on depth and become richer, but the main purpose of meditation is for ideas to take on proper attitudes in the heart. In meditation our subconscious mind becomes programmed with ideas and attitudes. This programming of the sub-conscious mind changes our basic inner nature. The actions that arise out of this programming are expressions of the real self. Our sub-conscious mind needs to be programmed with the Word of God. It is then that it will become a sanctifying influence in our life to transform our personality into the likeness of Christ.

VII. THE MINISTRY AND OUR SANCTIFICATION

In Ephesians 4:11, 12 Paul said,

> And he gave some, apostles; and some, prophets; and some, evangelists; and some, pastors and teachers;
> For the perfecting [equipping] of the saints, for the work of the ministry, for the edifying of the body of Christ.

In these verses we see that God has called people and has given them a variety of gifts for ministering to believers. Ministers with a different gift and a different emphasis help in one way while those with another gift and a different emphasis help in another way. It is the plan of God for Christians to benefit from different types of ministries. The work of ministers is designed to help equip the saints for the work of the ministry (verse 12) and to help Christians move toward maturity (verses 13, 14).

The preaching ministry is designed to contribute to our moral sanctification. Paul said to Timothy, "Preach the word; be instant in season, out of season; reprove, rebuke, exhort with all longsuffering and doctrine" (2 Timothy 4:2).

In the New Testament, the sanctification of the members was not only the responsibility of the leadership in the church but the whole body. The writer of Hebrews said:

> Let us consider one another to provoke unto love and to good works:
> Not forsaking the assembling of ourselves together, as the manner of some is; but exhorting one another: and so much the more, as ye see the day approaching (Hebrews 10:24, 25).

VIII. PRAYER, THE MEDIATORIAL WORK OF CHRIST AND SANCTIFICATION

In time of temptation we are invited to come boldly to the

throne of grace. There we will find a compassionate High Priest who can be touched by the feeling of our infirmities. He faced temptation in the real encounters of life. He understands and cares. He is able to help (Hebrews 4:14-16). When we come to Him with a desire to overcome sin and a desire to be holy, we can be sure that that is the kind of prayer He wants to answer.

IX. THE GUARANTEED RESULTS OF SANCTIFICATION

The design of God to make us righteous is not a design that may or may not be effective. A measure of success is guaranteed. First Corinthians 6:9, 10; Galatians 5:19-21; and Ephesians 5:3-5 make it clear that those who are characterized by gross immorality can lay no claim to salvation.

First John makes it abundantly clear that only those who are basically righteous have any right to claim to be a Christian. On the positive side, he says, "And hereby we do know that we know him, if we keep his commandments" (2:3). On the negative side, he says, "He that saith, I know him, and keepeth not his commandments, is a liar, and the truth is not in him" (2:4). In 3:10 he says, "Whosoever doeth not righteousness is not of God."

First John 3:9 is an unusually strong and clear verse on this subject. This verse refers to "whosoever is born of God." This means every Christian because every Christian is born of God. Concerning one who is born of God, John says he "doth not commit sin . . . and he cannot sin." The meaning here based on the Greek tense is: "He does not go on sinning and he cannot go on sinning." It does not mean that he never sins; but it does mean that sin is not the habit of his life, and it cannot be the habit of his life as long as it can be said he is born of God.

It is quite clear that John would have had no hesitancy in saying that those who do not practice righteousness are not saved (1 John 2:3, 4, 15, 16; 3:2-10; 4:5). There can be no doubt about it. The Bible says that salvation changes the life (2 Corinthians 5:17 and Ephesians 2:10). There is an interest in righteousness in the heart of a Christian.

A Christian is one who has recognized his moral guilt and unworthiness. He has come to Jesus Christ desiring to be forgiven of his sin and have his experience with sin changed. He has received a new nature through the new birth. This new nature is interested in righteousness. He has declared war on sin. He may not win every battle, but he is a soldier fighting against sin. When he sins, it is the sin of one who is defeated in battle, not the sin of one who had not declared war on sin. When he does sin there is a process that begins within him to work repentance.

194

The Christian is not and cannot be morally indifferent and unconcerned. There is room for moral growth, but his heart is cultivable soil. Man fell from a state of holiness into a state of sin. Redemption is designed to bring man from the state of sin into a state of holiness. If there is no holiness, there is no redemption.13

I am fully aware that salvation is by grace, and that it is free and thus a gift. To insist that it must have the results that the Bible unquestionably ascribes to it is in no way to confuse or corrupt grace. We need simply to understand what it is that is free. It is salvation which consists of justification and sanctification. Justification guarantees forgiveness to the person who has it. Sanctification guarantees a changed life to the person who has it.

The fact that a thing is free has nothing to do with whether it will work or not. To be free simply means that it does not cost anything. The giver of our free salvation has said that it will work. First John 3:9 says that the presence of the new birth prohibits the practice of sin. Galatians 5:17 says that because we have the Holy Spirit we cannot do the things that we would.

In the chapter on the nature of man, I point out that the freedom of the will is a freedom within the framework of possibilities. The unsaved person and the Christians do not have the same framework of possibilitites. According to 1 John 3:9 and Galatians 5:17, it is not in the frameword of possibilities for the Christian to practice sin. It is within the framework of possibilities for him to please God and to live right.

There is some latitude within this framework of possibilities. There is room for disobedience but not on an unlimited scale. Since there is room for disobedience, Christians must be challenged, exhorted, and admonished. There is also room for variations of growth and progress. Here, there is the need for challenge, exhortation, and encouragement.

X. SANCTIFICATION AND PERFECTION

It is not my purpose here to involve myself in the controversies surrounding the subject of perfection. I will just set forth what I believe the New Testament teaches on the subject and support my case.

In the majority of places in the New Testament where the word *perfect* is found, it is a translation of a Greek word which has as its basic meaning *complete*. This is obvious in 1 Corinthians 13:10. Paul says, "But when that which is prefect is come, then that which is in part shall be done away." In this verse, the "perfect" is contrasted with the "part." It is obvious that the perfect is the whole or the complete.

In most cases the completeness referred to is the completeness that is achieved through growth. Thus, the perfect is the mature. This meaning is obvious in Hebrews 5:14 where the Greek word for perfect is translated by the words "of full age." Paul is telling us that strong meat belongeth to those who through growth and development have reached maturity.

Maturity is obviously the meaning of perfect in Ephesians 4:13. A reading of verses 13 and 14 together shows that the "perfect man" of verse 13 is contrasted with "children" of verse 14. The perfect man has the steadfastness that goes with maturity in contrast to the instability that goes with immaturity.

In 1 Corinthians 14:20 the Greek word for perfect is translated "men." Paul is telling us that in malice we should be like children. We are, in understanding, to be "perfect," or as the King James Version translates it we are to be "men." We are to be mature in our understanding.

The thrust of completeness seems to be a little different in Matthew 5:48. Jesus said, "Be ye therefore perfect, even as your Father which is in heaven is perfect." Let us read the word *complete* in each of the places where the word *perfect* occurs. This will raise the question: In what way are we to be "complete, even as your Father which is in heaven is complete." In the previous context beginning with verse 43, Jesus has been talking about two kinds of love. One was a love that only loves those who love us. This would be an incomplete love. The other was a love which embraced both those who love us and those who do not. This would be a complete love. The Father showed His love to both the just and the unjust by sending the rain and sunshine to both. This illustrates the complete or perfect love of the Father. We, like the Father, are to have a complete or perfect love that loves both those who love us and those who do not.

In Ephesians 4:12 and 2 Timothy 3:17 Greek words with a different connotation are used. In 2 Timothy 3:17 the meaning of the word *perfect* is explained by the last part of the verse. The perfect man is "throughly [thoroughly] furnished unto all good works." He is a prepared person. He is equipped for service.

In Ephesians 4:12 Paul speaks of "perfecting the saints." The Greek word for *perfecting* is closely related to the word for *perfect* in 2 Timothy 3:17. The meaning is "the equipping of the saints for the work of the ministry."

The idea of flawlessness is not the meaning of the Greek word for perfect. The reference in most places is to the complete in contrast with the incomplete, or the finished with the unfinished. An unfinished building would not be perfect even if the workmanship were flawless. The person who is mature physically is perfect even though he is not flawless. The child would not be perfect even if he were flawless in his physical body. It is also obvious that when perfect refers to "equipping," flawlessness is not the point of emphasis.

When we are challenged to be perfect in the New Testament, we are challenged to be mature, complete, and equipped. Certainly, this would call for moral concern and progress, but it does not entangle us with the depressing goal of moral perfection. 14

CHAPTER ELEVEN
NOTES

1. Charles G. Finney, *Finney's Systematic Theology*, edited by J. H. Fairchild, Grand Rapids: William B. Eerdmans Publishing Company, reprint of 1878 revised edition, pp. 391, 392.

2. James Oliver Buswell, Jr., *A Systematic Theology of the Christian Religion*, Grand Rapids: Zondervan Publishing House, c. 1962, p. 146.

3. David Brown, "Romans," *A Commentary Critical, Experimental and Practical on the Old and New Testaments*, Volume VI, 6 volumes, Robert Jamieson, A. R. Fausset, and David Brown, Grand Rapids: William B. Eerdmans Publishing Company, c. 1948, p. 226.

4. Robert Haldane, *Exposition of the Epistle to the Romans*, London: The Banner of Truth Trust, reprinted 1963, pp. 248, 249.

5. William Sanday and Arthur Headlam, *The Epistle to the Romans in the International Critical Commentary*, Edinburgh: T. & T. Clark, first printed 1895, last reprint 1960, p. 218.

6. Richard Chenevix Trench, *Synonyms of the New Testament*, Grand Rapids: Associated Publishers and Authors, Inc., a reprint, n. d., p. 245.

7. *Ibid.*, pp. 243, 244.

8. *Ibid.*, pp. 246, 247.

9. *Ibid.*, p. 247.

10. Joseph Henry Thayer, *Thayer's Greek-English Lexicon of the New Testament*, Grand Rapids: Associated Publishers and Authors, Inc., a reprint, n. d., p. 429.

11. For a more complete discussion of the problem of one's attitude toward himself see Leroy Forlines, *Biblical Ethics*, Nashville: Randall House Publications, c. 1973, pp. 59-67.

12. For a system of ethics based on the application of the four basic values to the four basic relationships, see the before mentioned ethics book.

13. The material under "The Guaranteed Results of Sanctification" up to this point with only slight modification was taken from Leroy Forlines, *Biblical Ethics*, pp. 34-36.

14. Most of the material under "Sanctification and Perfection" was taken from the ethics book mentioned earlier. pp. 138-140.

12

The Condition
of Salvation

I have chosen to discuss the nature of salvation first and then come to a discussion of the condition of salvation. As a rule it is done the other way around. I have chosen to do it this way because I believe we can get a better understanding of the condition of salvation this way.

I. REPENTANCE AND FAITH: ONE CONDITION OR TWO?

A. The Problem Set Forth

As a rule, we say that there is only one condition of salvation. That condition is faith. However, we frequently say that repentance is a condition of salvation. In discussions of repentance and faith, it frequently sounds as if there are two conditions of salvation. How many conditions of salvation are there?

Numerous times in the New Testament, faith is presented as the only condition of salvation (John 1:12; 3:16, 18, 36; Acts 16:31; Romans 3:22, 28; 4:1-25; 5:1; Galatians 2:16; 3:1-18; Ephesians 2:8, 9; and 1 John 5:13).

There are also places where repentance, without the occurence of the word faith, is mentioned as the condition of salvation (Luke 24:47; Acts 2:38; 3:19; 5:31; 11:18; 17:30; 26:20; 2 Timothy 2:25; Hebrews 6:6; and 2 Peter 3:9).

What conclusion do we draw from this? If we draw the conclusion that repentance and faith make up two conditions of salvation, there would be only three places in the New Testament where both conditions would be mentioned in the same passage (Mark 1:15; Acts 20:21; and Hebrews 6:1). Would we conclude that these are the only three places where a person is told how to be saved in one passage? Would we have to pick up one condition in one place and one in another if we did not use one of these verses?

If we want to make repentance and faith two conditions of salvation, what do we do with the fact that the words "repent" and "repentance" do not occur in the Gospel of John nor in 1, 2, and 3 John? Do we conclude that these books do not have the complete requirement for salvation?

I think it would be strange if the Bible only included in three places what is required in terms of response from us. It seems that the preferred conclusion is to believe that there is only one condition of salvation if we can support that conclusion. There is a problem involved in trying to make a choice between repentance and faith for the condition because both are presented in the Scripture as the condition of salvation.

I believe the answer is found in looking at repentance and faith as one condition because both are presented in the Scripture as the condition of salvation. They both speak of the same experience.

B. The Meaning of Repentance

The Greek word *metanoeo* which is translated "repent" means to change one's mind. So far as the Greek word is concerned, in its usage, it could refer to a change of mind whether for good or for bad. R. C. Trench says, "Plutarch *(Sept. Sap. Conv.* 21) tells us of two murderers, who having spared a child, afterward 'repented' *(metenoesan)*, and sought to slay it . . . . "

Trench goes on to say:

It is only after *metanoia* has been taken up into the uses of Scripture, or of writers dependent upon Scripture, that it comes predominantly to mean change of mind, taking a *wiser* view of the past 1

To change the mind in repentance refers to the change of the mind, heart, and will. One viewpoint is exchanged for another viewpoint. There is an appropriate change of attitude and behavior to go along with the exchange of viewpoint. It is a reference to a change of attitude and behavior that Paul has in mind in Acts 26:20. He preached "to the Gentiles, that they should do works meet [fit] for repentance" (see also Matthew 3:8 and Luke 3:8).

In repentance there is a change of mind. There is a change of opinion, viewpoint, or conviction. In the repentance related to salvation, the question is: On what does the change focus? This question will be answered by an examination of the passages where repentance is used in connection with salvation.

The passages where the context clarifies the area of change in repentance are found in Acts. If we read these passages and translate repent "to change one's mind," it will help us to see what areas of thought the speakers had in mind. On the day of Pentecost when Peter said to the Jews, "Repent" (Acts 2:38), in the context they were to repent of their unbelief toward Jesus Christ (Acts 2:23, 36). This would involve not only a change of opinion but of attitude and behavior. The same basic thought is seen in Acts 3:19 and 5:31. In Acts 17:30, on the negative side, they were to change their mind regarding idolatry (verses 22-29). On the positive side, they were to believe in Jesus Christ (verse 31).

C. The Relationship Between Repentance and Faith

In repentance, there is a "from" and a "to." The exact nature of the "from" may vary from one person to another. Some need to change from a simple case of unbelief. Others need to change from false religion or paganism. Whatever the case may be about the nature of what a person may need to change his mind from, the "to" for all is the same. All are to change to a faith in Jesus Christ.

Repentance includes a "from" and a "to," but the stress of repentance is on the "to" instead of the "from." Repentance is a forward moving word. This is not to diminish the importance of the "from." It is to place primary focus on the "to." The "to" of repentance is identical with faith.

Faith and repentance are involved in each other. To exercise faith implies a change from unbelief, whatever the form. Repentance terminates in faith. If we tell a person to repent, or if we tell him to believe, we are telling him to do the same thing. Repent stresses the fact that change is involved. Faith stresses the end to which change is directed.

We can illustrate the difference between repentance and faith this way. If we tell a man in Atlanta to leave Atlanta and go to New York, that would illustrate repentance. If we should tell the man in Atlanta to go to New York, that would illustrate faith. We would be telling the person to do the same no matter which approach we might choose.

Faith is the primary term because it is faith that describes the positive response in which repentance terminates. Repentance speaks of a change from something and to something. Faith explains what the something is to which repentance is directed.

When we speak of repentance and faith in salvation, we are talking about one condition for salvation, not two. To experience repentance and to experience faith is to experience the same thing. Since faith is the primary term, we will now turn our attention to a discussion of saving faith.

II. THE NATURE OF SAVING FAITH

A. The Meaning of Saving Faith

Saving faith is the abandonment of all trust in self or anything else and a complete, confident trust in Christ for salvation.

The problem that plagues us is: How do we avoid leaving the impression that salvation can be a superficial experience if faith is the only condition for salvation? Some try to cope with this problem by the way they explain the nature of faith. They try in some way to explain that faith involves obedience, but at the same time they explain that faith is distinguished from works.

As I see it, we do not avoid the impression that salvation is a superficial experience by the way we define faith. Faith is not complicated. There are two elements: (1) acceptance of redemptive truth, and (2) trust.

In the history of God's people, the content of this faith involved the redemptive truth with which God had confronted His people at a given time in history. They were to accept this revelation to be true. For us, we are to believe the redemptive revelation of God as it is revealed in Jesus Christ. I can see how a person may have saving faith and have some misunderstanding of what the Bible says about Christ. I cannot see how a person can have saving faith and not believe what the Bible says about Jesus Christ. Faith believes what the Bible says about Jesus Christ to be true.

In the trust element of saving faith, there is dependence upon God for salvation. In the New Testament, this is dependence upon Jesus Christ for salvation.

We do not safeguard ourselves from superficial Christianity by the way we define faith. It does not take some special knowledge of Hebrew or Greek to define faith so the safeguards can be built in our definition. What we need is a correct definition of salvation.

We believe "for salvation." Salvation is the goal for faith. There will be no superficial experience for the person who experiences salvation unless salvation is superficial.

Salvation consists of justification and sanctification. The whole study of sanctification, especially the guaranteed results of sanctification, made it clear that sanctification cannot be superficial. We cannot believe for the forgiveness of sins without believing for a change in our experience with God and sin. If we receive salvation, we will receive forgiveness of sin and a change in our experience with God and sin. That will not be superficial.

Where the problem comes is when we tell people they can be forgiven and leave the impression that a change in experience is optional. This opens the way for a lot of professions in which there is no salvation. The tragedy is not that such people receive Jesus as Savior, but not as Lord. The tragedy is that they neither receive Jesus as Lord nor Savior.

There can be no exercise of saving faith without at least some understanding of what salvation is all about. Saving faith is exercised by a person who realizes that salvation is designed to forgive people of sin and restore them to the experience of holiness. Such a person realizes that he is a sinner. He sees sin as serious. He sees himself as unworthy and condemned. He is under conviction. The problem of sin is real in his mind and in his heart. He wants something done about sin in his life. He wants to be forgiven. He wants to be changed. He understands that Jesus Christ has suffered on the Cross and died to save him. He believes what God has said in the Bible about Jesus as Savior. He trusts in Jesus as Savior. In so doing, he trusts in Jesus to forgive his sins and change his life. According to Christian theology, upon this act of faith, based on the atoning work of Christ, the person is justified and sanctified.

There is no saving faith except where a person has become aware of his sins and takes a changed attitude toward sin and Jesus Christ. The termination of that change, we call faith. The process of change including the termination of the process, we call repentance. Both terms need to be used. Faith needs to be used to explain the real nature of the condition of salvation. Repentance needs to be used to make people aware of the fact that a deep change of mind, heart, and will is involved in the exercise of saving faith.

B. Faith and the Personality

The mind, heart, and will are involved in saving faith. With the mind, the truth about sin, Jesus Christ, and salvation is comprehended objectively. The content of the truth is grasped and understood.

With the heart, what is grasped objectively by the mind is grasped subjectively. The truth about sin becomes real. Conviction takes place. The truth about Jesus Christ and salvation becomes real. The reality of the truth conditions the heart for action to follow.

The emotions are definitely involved in the experience of faith and the total Christian experience. We do feel what we believe. We are not emotional blanks. Emotions are a part of the human personality by creation. Emotions need to be based on truth and disciplined by truth, but they must not be downgraded.

With the will there is the commitment of the personality to Jesus Christ. We receive Jesus Christ. The will can act only where there is a prepared mind and a prepared heart. The will, out of the prepared mind and heart, sets in action the response of faith.

C. Faith as a Gift

Jesus said in John 6:44, "No man can come to me, except the

Father which hath sent me draw him . . . . " There must be a move toward man on God's part before there will be any response on man's part. Not only is there a need for a Divine invitation, but there is also a need of a Divine drawing. The Holy Spirit must take the Word of God and work in the human heart and mind to prepare the heart and mind before there can be the response of faith from a sinner.

It does not belong within the framework of possibilities of the unsaved person for him to be able to respond to Jesus Christ apart from the work of the Holy Spirit. The Holy Spirit works as the Word is preached. The human heart can resist this work of the Holy Spirit, but where the Holy Spirit is allowed to work He enlightens the mind concerning sin, Jesus Christ, and salvation. He produces conviction in the heart. The preparation of the mind and heart by the Word of God and the Holy Spirit creates a framework of possibilities in which a person can respond in faith to Jesus Christ. The response of faith is not guaranteed, but it is made possible. The person can say either yes or no.

Faith is called a gift because it cannot be exercised without the work of the Holy Spirit. At the same time, it is a response of the person in such a way that it is a response of his personality. It is in a real sense his own action. If a human being is to be treated as a person, in some real sense the action must be the person's own regardless of how much Divine aid may be given. Otherwise, a human being has been reduced to a sub-personal being.

Some have understood "the faith of the Son of God" in Galatians 2:20 and similar references to mean that saving faith is Christ's faith given to the person. It is a gift in that it is taking Christ's faith and giving it.

In the expression "the faith of the Son of God," the genitive case in the Greek could be considered a subjective genitive and thus be understood as faith belonging to Christ. It can also be considered an objective genitive and would mean faith in Christ. While either interpretation would be possible so far as Greek grammar is concerned, only one is possible in the light of Scripture. The Bible addresses us and tells us to believe. We are nowhere told that Jesus is to believe for us. It is clear that "the faith of the Son of God" is not Jesus' faith but it is our faith in Jesus.

Faith is not some substance that exists outside of us that is to be given to us. It is an experience that must take place within us. That is the only way we can have faith. Faith is a gift in the sense that God gives to us the aid that is necessary, without which, we could not exercise faith. It is not a gift in the sense that it is not an exercise of our own personality.

D. Faith the Condition, Not the Ground of our Salvation

The difference between condition and ground could be illus-

204

trated this way. The condition for a chair supporting me is for me to sit in the chair. When I am sitting in the chair, the chair is the ground of my support.

The ground of our salvation is Jesus Christ and His atoning work. The condition of our salvation is the response of faith.

Sometimes people make the mistake of focusing more on the condition than the ground. In looking for assurance, they examine their faith instead of Christ. If I want to have confidence that a chair will hold me up, I will examine the chair, not my confidence. As I examine the chair, if it is well built, my confidence will be made sure.

If I want my assurance of salvation to be strong, I should examine Christ—the grounds of my salvation. In so doing, I will have a strong faith and confidence. If I turn the spotlight of examination on my faith, I will tend to have doubts. It is not faith in faith that is the condition of salvation. It is faith in Christ.

E. Faith and Doubt

Sometimes, we get caught in the logic that if salvation is by faith, a Christian cannot doubt his salvation because faith rules out doubt. At first thought, the definition of saving faith would make it sound like there is no room for doubt. Saving faith is a complete, confident trust in Christ for salvation. Doubt is not exactly consistent with a complete, confident trust.

How do we harmonize the possibility of doubt with saving faith? Definitions describe a thing in its ideal, healthy state. For example, a definition of a dog would include the fact that a dog is a four legged animal. Yet, I have seen dogs that had only three legs. A dog could be a dog with less than four legs, but it would not be a normal dog in full health. Saving faith in its healthy state does not include doubts. However, saving faith can and does exist where doubts also exist. As a rule, these doubts will clear up with a better understanding of doctrines of salvation.

CHAPTER TWELVE
NOTES

1. Richard Chenevix Trench, *Synonyms of the New Testament*, Grand Rapids: Associated Publishers and Authors, a reprint, n. d., p. 242.

13

Continuance
in Salvation

The main issue in this doctrine is whether the continuance in salvation is conditional or unconditional. Those who believe in conditional continuance speak of the possibility of apostasy. Those who believe in unconditional continuance speak of eternal security and once saved always saved.

The terms preservation and perseverance are also used. Preservation looks at the doctrine from the viewpoint of Divine activity. Perseverance looks at the doctrine from the viewpoint of human involvement.

I have chosen to entitle this chapter "Continuance in Salvation" for three reasons: (1) As a subject it embraces both the Divine and the human side. (2) To speak of continuance in salvation speaks of continuance in both justification and sanctification, not simply continuance in justification. (3) It is a way of speaking of the subject by title that is appropriate whether a person believes in conditional continuance or unconditional continuance.

In earlier chapters, I have indicated that I was not a Calvinist. I am a non-Calvinist because I believe in unlimited atonement, conditional election, resistable grace, and the possibility of losing salvation. These are conclusions of Arminians. Yet, I hesitate to speak without qualification and call myself an Arminian because my interpretation of the way these doctrines are stated in a more complete elaboration differs considerably from many Arminians.

Frequently a weaker view of depravity than I adhere to is advocated by Arminians. Some have an over-simplified view of freedom of the will. There is a hesitancy on the part of some to speak of individual election. They prefer to speak of corporate election. I speak of individual election. Many have adhered to the governmental view of atonement and justification. I believe in the satisfaction view of atonement and justification. To me the governmental view is seriously inadequate. I believe in a stronger view of the sovereignty of God than most Arminians do. The drawing power required and the drawing power supplied by the Holy Spirit would be stronger in my view than many Arminians. I believe that the new birth, union with Christ, and the indwelling Holy Spirit have more guaranteed results than most Arminians do. I do not believe in a second work of grace, usually referred to as sanctification in addition to progressive sanctification that begins with the new birth. Most Arminians do believe in a second work of grace. While I clearly believe that it is possible to lose salvation, my view of continuance offers more assurance and less fear than the view as approached by most Arminians. At the same time, I believe that my view offers more guarantee of holiness.

In the light of the above observations, I would definitely be a non-Calvinist. Since that is negative indentification, I would prefer to go on to some positive identification. Therefore, I would speak of myself as a modified Arminian whenever it is necessary to use a label. In view of the differences stated above, it would be misleading if I were to simply speak of myself as an Arminian.1

Logically, I could begin with either conditional continuance or unconditional continuance. I will begin with my own view. This will make it clear, when I come to unconditional continuance, what the real contrast is in the views. This way I can direct my discussion so the arguments will be pertinent as they relate to the real differences.

I. CONDITIONAL CONTINUANCE IN SALVATION

A. Continuance of Both Justification and Sanctification

To speak about continuing in salvation is to speak about continuing in both justification and sanctification. The package cannot be broken. We cannot have one without the other. The viewpoint that offers continued justification, whether conditional or unconditional, without sanctification has no support whatsoever in the Bible. It is also impossible to reduce sanctification to the point that it is not recognizable.

I have already dealt with this point in the chapter on sanctification. Let me give a summary restatement of the fact that holiness is not optional but is a guaranteed result of salvation. (1) Paul emphatically states that those who live in gross sin will not inherit the kingdom of God (1 Corinthians 6:9-11; Galatians 5:19-21; and Ephesians 5:3-7). (2) The writer of Hebrews says that without holiness no man shall see the Lord (12:14). (3) From both a positive and a negative viewpoint, 1 John makes it clear that for a person to fail to practice righteousness means that he is not saved

(2:3, 4, 9-11; 3:3-10, 14, 15; 4:20; and 5:4, 18).

If the language of the previously mentioned references does not mean that those who practice sin are not saved, one has no hope whatsoever of being able to understand the Bible. These verses do not deal with whether a person has ever been saved. They simply say that such persons are not saved now. They do not measure up to the description of a saved person.

These verses do not say that for a person to practice these sins would cause a person to lose his salvation. That is not the reason given for saying that those practicing sin are not saved. The reason given for denying that people who practice sin are saved is that those who are born of God *cannot* practice sin (1 John 3:9). Practicing righteousness is neither the condition of receiving salvation nor for its continuation. It is a result of salvation, or we might say it is a part of salvation.

The loss of salvation cannot come as a result of practicing sin because a person who is born of God does not have practicing sin in the framework of his possibilities. (See discussion on "The Guaranteed Results of Sanctification" on the chapter on sanctification.) This does not mean that he cannot commit acts of sin. The fact that acts of sin are an open possibility means that it is an open possibility that a person could commit apostasy if that sin is not a process of practicing sin but is an act.

Before Adam and Eve sinned, it was not in the framework of possibilities that they could practice sin, but it was within the framework of possibility for them to commit an act of sin. When they committed that act of sin, their nature was changed. With their change of nature they could practice sin. The sinner does not have it within the framework of possibilities for him to practice righteousness and to be able to please God. By the help of the Holy Spirit, it is within the framework of possibilities for the sinner to respond to the gospel and be saved. If he does respond, this introduces him to a framework of possibilities wherein he can practice righteousness and please God and he cannot practice sin.

It is within the framework of possibilities for a person to lose his salvation if the cause for it can be summed up in an act of departure. There would, of course, be some things that lead up to the act of departure. From the standpoint of reason, it is just as logical that a saved person be able to make this departure, so far as his own will is concerned, under the circumstances, as it was for Adam and Eve to sin and for a sinner to respond to the gospel. I will say more about the following line of thought later, but it is also just as logical to believe that a Christian can depart from his faith, in the light of God's sovereignty, as it is to believe that Adam and Eve sinned in the light of God's sovereignty. The only thing that could make it more logical to believe that Adam and Eve could sin, in the light of sovereignty, and the Christian cannot depart from faith, would be to believe that God wanted Adam and Eve to sin but does not want the Christian to depart from his faith.

B. Possibility of Loss of Salvation Taught in Scripture

In making a systematic study of Christian truth, we are interested in the logical consistency of doctrines one with another. For that reason, I have shown that the possibility of the loss of salvation is consistent with the guaranteed results of sanctification. However, it takes more than logical consistency to prove a doctrine. The real question is: Does the Bible teach that a person can lose his salvation? I believe it does and will proceed to support my case. It will not be my purpose to see how many verses I can set forth to support my position. Rather, I will deal with those that are most helpful and the ones that, so far as I am concerned, cannot be interpreted so as to fit the idea of unconditional continuance in salvation.

One of the basic passages is Hebrews 6:4-6. In this passage, those under consideration have the following characteristics: (1) "once enlightened"; (2) "have tasted of the heavenly gift"; (3) "were made partakers of the Holy Ghost"; (4) "have tasted the good word of God"; (5) have tasted "the powers of the world to come"; (6) It is definitely implied that they had repented in that it is said that it is impossible to renew them again to repentance.

If would certainly seem obvious that the above given characteristics are descriptive of a saved person. Since, however, some say this describes those who had only professed faith in Jesus but had not actually received Him as Savior, we shall make a study of the qualifications.

The word that is translated enlightened in verse 4 is *photidzo*. In Hebrews 10:32, it is translated "illuminated." The writer says, "But call to remembrance the former days, in which, after ye were illuminated, ye endured a great fight of afflictions." It sounds here like he is referring to the conversion experience. Thayer says concerning this word that it means " . . .to enlighten spiritually, imbue with saving knowledge . . . with a saving knowledge of the gospel: hence *photisthentes* of those who have been made Christians, Heb. vi. 4: x. 32."[2]

Many have argued that since the word *taste* is used, they approached the very threshold of salvation, even to the extent of having partial acquaintance with what it is like to be Christian but were not saved. Such an experience is without scriptural support; either a person is saved or he is not.

By comparing the use of the word, *taste*, in other parts of the Scripture, we see that it can mean an experience. Examples are Matthew 16:28; Hebrews 2:9; and 1 Peter 2:3. We shall take

210

particular notice of Hebrews 2:9 where it says, speaking of Jesus, "that he by the grace of God should taste death for every man." Surely this is referring to an actual experience with death.

It is my position that the word, *taste*, is one of the strongest words that could have been used. In tasting, there is always a *consciousness* of the presence of that which is tasted. There is always an *acquaintance* with the distinctive characteristics of that which is tasted. This is evidenced by 1 Peter 2:3. By tasting, the believer learned that one of the distinctive characteristics of the Lord is that He is gracious. There is also a matter of contact in tasting. In other words, tasting may be called *conscious acquaintance by contact.*

When we apply the previous observations to the subject under consideration, we learn that those mentioned here have had an experience in which they become *consciously acquainted by contact* with the heavenly gift. The heavenly gift either means Christ or salvation. In either case, it would mean that the person would be saved, because only a saved person has such an acquaintance with Christ.

Now we go to the third expression: "were made partakers of the Holy Ghost." In Hebrews 3:14, we find a reference in which the same Greek word that is translated *partake* in Hebrews 6:4 is used. It reads: "For we are made partakers of Christ." This would certainly refer to a close relationship. The Greek word for partaker could be translated a *companion or one who goes along with.* When used of being made a partaker of the Holy Ghost, it carries with it the idea of a companion relationship—a going along with. *To go along with* means to *be in agreement.* The person is taught by and led by the Holy Ghost.

The fourth characteristic is: "have tasted the good word of God." These persons had gone further than the original enlightenment of the way of salvation, as mentioned in the first expression. They had an acquaintance with the Word of God. Such an understanding belongs only to Christians.

The fifth expression is that they had tasted "the powers of the world to come," and seems to mean that they had entered into the joys of knowing that they were going to Heaven because of their faith in Christ.

The sixth characteristic is that they had repented. In the discussion on repentance in the chapter on the condition of salvation, I pointed out that repentance and faith are referring to the same experience. The change that is frequently brought in, that they did not have faith, will not stand. They had repented; therefore, they had exercised faith.

Concerning the description of those referred to in the passage under study, Dr. J. D. O'Donnell says,

"If one of such an experience is not saved, it is hard to

imagine what it would take to describe a true believer. Even many securitists admit that a saved person is described but try to diminish the meaning of the passage by interpreting the full passage as a hypothetical situation that will never take place."3

Dr. Robert Picirilli comments:

There is absolutely no doubt those lives refer to genuine Christian experience. If you wanted a better way to describe conversion, you could not find it! Any one of the four expressions cannot fail to represent real salvation. Take the third phrase for example: A 'partaker,' one who partakes of, one who is in fellowship with. Now, only a real Christian is a partaker of the Holy Spirit of God.4

Now we come to the question: What had these people done? In interpreting these verses, we must remember that these Jews were in danger of forsaking Christ and going back into Judaism. These warnings were given to keep them from making this mistake.

In 6:6 it is said "they crucify to themselves the Son of God afresh." Let us note that this is a crucifixion in relationship, that is, to themselves. An example of crucifixion in relationship is found in Galatians 6:14 where Paul says, "By whom the world is crucified unto me, and I unto the world." So far as reality was concerned, both Paul and the world were living and active; but so far as relationship was concerned, they were dead to each other. They had no relationship existing between them.

The relationship of Christ to the unsaved is that of a dead Christ; but to the saved, He is a living Christ. A person could not crucify to himself the Son of God afresh unless he were in a living relationship to Him; therefore, such could be committed only by a saved person.

If we will compare this verse with 10:29, we shall get a more complete picture of what is discussed. In this verse, the person has "counted the blood of the covenant, wherewith he was sanctified, an unholy thing." This would be the case of the Jewish believer who came to the point that he said that Christ's blood was no more than any other man's blood; it was not that blood which was typified by the sacrifices in the Old Testament; it possessed no saving power; Christ was not the Savior.

When the person came to this point, he denounced his faith in Christ; he drove Christ out of his life; in relationship Christ became a dead Christ; thus, he had crucified Christ to himself.

When this person denounced his former faith in Christ, he was saying that there was nothing to the experience he thought he had with Christ. In so doing, he put Him to an open shame.

212

What happens to the person who falls away by unbelief? The writer of Hebrews says that it is impossible to renew them again unto repentance. It is my understanding that this means they cannot be restored to faith. They cannot be saved again.

Let us look now to Hebrews 10:26-29. In Hebrews 10:26-29, the person is qualified as being sanctified (verse 29). The other references in the epistle in which the word *sanctify* is used are: 2:11; 10:10, 14; 13:12. If the reader will examine these verses, he will find that each has reference to sanctification that accompanies salvation. If the writer of the epistle were going to use sanctification in an entirely different sense here, does it not seem reasonable that he would have made it clear when using it in connection with such a drastic warning? Regardless of what the warning is, we must admit that it is to saved people.

I have already called attention above to the fact that the person referred to here had "counted the blood of the covenant, wherewith he was sanctified an unholy thing" (verse 29). This constitutes unbelief.

What is the condition of the person after he has counted the blood of Christ an unholy thing? In verse 26 we see that he is sinning willfully. The Greek indicates that the reference is not to an *act* of willful sin, but a *process* of willful sin. Such willful sinning is not possible as long as a person is born of God. Verse 26 describes the state of the apostate while verse 29, which is past tense, describes the sin that has put the person in this state.

As a further point of clarification, verse 26 says of such a person, "There remaineth no more sacrifice for sins." The word translated "no more" means "no longer." There remaineth no longer a sacrifice for sins. The apostate has sins but no available sacrifice for his sins. This is the reason that it is impossible to renew them again unto repentance.

The same truth that is taught in Hebrews 6:4-6 and 10:26-29 is taught in 2 Peter 2:20-22. In 2 Peter 2:20-22, the ones under consideration are qualified by two expressions: (1) "They have escaped the pollutions of the world." (2) They did it "through the knowledge of the Lord and Saviour Jesus Christ."

In the same epistle, in 1:4, the following expression occurs: "having escaped the corruption that is in the world through lust." It is associated with being made a partaker of the Divine nature which is a privilege only for Christians. The expression in 1:4 is practically the same as in 2:20. Surely they refer to the same thing. It is the only other such expression in the epistle. On what grounds does a person say that one is referring to a Christian and the other only to a professor of Christianity?

Let us examine the second expression: "through the knowledge of the Lord and Saviour Jesus Christ." It will be observed that this knowledge was the basis of their having escaped the pollutions of the world. It will also be noted that, in 1:3, 4, the following things are obtained through the knowledge of Christ:

(1) "All things that pertain unto life and godliness" (verse 3).

(2) "Partakers of the divine nature" (verse 4).

(3) "Escaped the corruption that is in the world through lust" (verse 4).

A careful study of 1:3, 4 and 2:20 will show that, in both instances, the corruption of the world had been escaped through the knowledge of the Lord and Savior Jesus Christ.

When such evidence occurs within the bounds of the same epistle, for considering those in 2:20 as being saved on the same grounds as those in 1:3, 4, on what authority can a person consider one reference to saved and the other to unsaved? Also, not a single expression such as "through the knowledge of our Lord and Saviour Jesus Christ" is found in the epistle to refer to any other than saved. Regardless of what we may interpret the warning to be, we must accept it to refer to people who have been saved.

What is the warning about in this passage? In 2 Peter 2:20-22, it is made plain that the warning here is against forsaking the truth that is in Christ for a false system. This is made clear when we read the entire second chapter. The first part of the chapter makes mention of false teachers, and the last part warns against being led astray by them, telling what the consequences will be.

In this passage it is said, "The latter end is worse with them than the beginning . . . it had been better for them not to have known the way of righteousness." The only way these statements could be true would be that they describe the same condition as the verses in Hebrews; therefore, we conclude that these could not be saved again.

The passages just treated, I think, are the basic passages, but they are by no means all. Let us examine a few more.

In Colossians 1:21-23, Paul is laying down a continuance in the faith as a condition of their being presented holy and unblamable and unreprovable in His sight. Here it is definitely implied that to fail to continue in the faith would mean loss of salvation. It is also worthy of note that Paul is warning his readers not to become entangled with false teachers who were teaching things contrary to the true view of Christ.

Another passage that proves to be very valuable in support of the possibility of a fall is John 15:2 and 6. In verse 2, it is said the branch that bears no fruit is taken away. It has been objected that you cannot press an analogy too far; therefore, this passage cannot be taken to prove that a person can be lost after he is saved because the only thought that is being taught here is that of fruit bearing. I believe in exercising great caution against pressing analogies too far. I believe that much injustice is done to the interpretation of Scripture by overworking analogies and figures. But we must keep in mind that

Jesus Himself is drawing all of the analogies in this allegory; therefore, when He says, "Every branch in me that beareth not fruit he taketh away: and every branch that beareth fruit, he purgeth it," I must make a distinction between being taken away and being purged. Also, "being taken away" requires an interpretation because Jesus draws the analogy Himself and says that there is a work which the Father does of taking away the unfruitful branches.

I think it will be very helpful if we tie this in with Hebrews 6:7, 8. The result of the apostasy that is described in verses 4-6 is seen in the apostate in verse 8 as bearing thorns and briers.

It is a point of interest here to note that verses 7 and 8 are speaking of the same piece of ground. At first it brought forth herbs, and later it brought forth thorns and briers. This is borne out in the American Standard Version and is definitely supported by the Greek (see the Amplified Bible on these verses).

Now comparing our findings to John 15:2, we see the apostate as one who does not bear fruit; instead, he bears thorns and briers. Therefore, he is taken out as one who does not bear fruit.

John 15:6 is referring to the same things as verse 2, only looking at it from a different point of view. Here we see that, if a man abides not in Christ, he is cast forth as a branch.

I think 1 John 2:22-24 is helpful in determining just what is meant by *abiding* and *abiding not*, as is used in John 15. In 1 John 2:22, 23, John warns against those who have false views concerning Christ. In 2:24, he says, "Let that therefore abide in you, which ye have heard from the beginning." In other words, instead of taking the view of Christ as is presented to you by false teachers, continue to believe the correct doctrine of Christ which you have heard from the beginning. Then he goes on to say, "If that which ye have heard from the beginning [the correct doctrine of Christ] shall remain in you [the condition has thus been stated—now follows the promise], ye also shall continue in the Son, and in the Father."

The same Greek word that is translated *abide* in John 15 is translated *continue* in the verse just cited. In 1 John 2:24, the condition for continuing (abiding) in Christ is to abide in the true doctrine concerning Christ. It is definitely implied that, if the reader of 1 John would choose to forsake the true doctrine of Christ, he would not remain in Christ.

Second John 9 gives proof of what we have just said, "Whosoever transgresseth, and abideth not in the doctrine of Christ, hath not God." This verse definitely proves that a person who does not believe in the true doctrine of Christ is not saved. Taken in its context, it seems to be a warning to the saved person not to be led astray by false teachings concerning Christ. To forsake the true doctrine in favor of the false would mean that the person would not have God.

After citing these references, does it not seem to be definite that for a person to abide not in Christ, as in John 15:6, would mean that he forsook the true teachings of Christ? Is it not strongly taught in these other references that to fail in continuing in the true doctrine of Christ would mean rejection by God, which is described in John 15:6 as being cast forth as a branch? The result of being cast forth is to be withered and burned. This is the same thing that happens to the apostate in Hebrews 6 and is set forth in a figure in verse 8.

Up to this point, the following conclusions have been established: (1) The Bible teaches that a saved person can lose his salvation. (2) Salvation continues on the condition of faith and is forfeited by unbelief. (3) As long as a person remains saved, he has both justification and sanctification. (4) When a person does lose his salvation, he cannot be saved again.

There are several questions that are yet to be answered in developing and defending the doctrine. The first problem to deal with is to show the consistency of this doctrine with other doctrines.

C. Possibility of Loss of Salvation Compatible with Atonement and Justification

I have already dealt with this problem in the chapter on atonement and justification when discussing the objections raised against the satisfaction view of atonement. The reader may refer there for a reconciliation of the possibility of loss of salvation with the satisfaction view of atonement and justification.

I might explain that while the satisfaction view of atonement and justification are consistent with the possibility of the loss of salvation, it is not consistent with some patterns of thought in connection with the possibility of losing salvation. If we believe in the imputation of Christ's death and righteousness as the ground of our justification, we do not have room for a half-way state between being saved and being lost. If we are in union with Christ, we have His death and righteousness and are justified. If we are not in union with Christ, we are not justified. We can be in danger of losing our salvation, but we have lost it only when the union is broken and we no longer have the death and righteousness of Christ.

A lot of the reasoning that goes with some views on the possibility of losing salvation is more logically related to the governmental theory of atonement and justification. The governmental theory lends itself to vagueness and flexibility concerning what saving faith is. Since faith is considered as righteousness or takes the place of righteousness, there can always be the question of whether there is enough faith. It may not require such a conclusion, but it admits of the possibility of being in a somewhat half-way state that would not be settled by God until such a person dies. When God

216

acts as judge, as in the satisfaction view, He must be precise. When He acts as ruler, as in the governmental view, He can be general and flexible.

D. Possibility of Loss of Salvation
Consistent with God's Sovereignty

If God says that every Christian is eternally secure and can under no circumstance ever lose his salvation, we would certainly judge God to be less than Sovereign if anyone did lose his salvation. However, there is nothing in the nature of God's sovereignty to forbid Him to be able to work in a plan whereby He used the approach of conditional continuance in salvation rather than unconditional continuance. As Dr. Picirilli explains, "We believe in a Sovereign; but a Sovereign God is just as free to make salvation conditional as any other way. And our God is big enough to handle a real contingency in His universe."5

E. Possibility of Loss of Salvation Consistent
with Salvation by Grace Through Faith

Salvation by grace means that it is an unmerited favor. It is a gift bestowed upon us that we do not deserve. It is something for which we in no way pay. Our justification is a gift from God. We participated in no way in the ground of our justification. It is the death and righteousness of Christ that form the grounds of our justification, not our obedience. This fact always remains unchanged. The act of baptizing us into Christ, regenerating us, and the indwelling of the Holy Spirit are all gifts of God grounded in the atoning work of Christ which has been applied to our account. Every loving move of God toward us is based on His grace which is grounded in atonement. Nothing that I have said about conditional continuance in salvation has at any point contradicted these observations.

There is nothing whatsoever about the nature of a gift that either keeps it from being rejected when offered or keeps it from being returned if received. It is inherent in the nature of a gift that as long as it remains a gift the recipient of the gift can in no way participate in the payment of the gift. The very nature of the requirement of justification and the qualifications of a human being who has sinned means that a human being can never participate in the payment for his own justification. He can neither provide absolute righteousness nor infinite sufferings.

The Bible plainly conditions salvation on faith. There is no more contradiction of the fact that salvation is free by insisting that it is kept on the condition of faith than that it is received on the condition of faith. It is surprising that anyone would think so. It is folly to charge that to require the continuation of faith for the continuation of salvation makes faith a work and thus puts salvation on the basis of works. The Bible, itself, clearly removes faith from the category of works (Romans 4:3-5).

Dr. Picirilli comments:

> Any time the Bible talks about *believing* for salvation, the verb 'believing' is always in the tense in the Greek that means *continuing* belief . . . . Verses like John 5:24, 'he that . . . believeth' always have the verb in the tense that denotes the action in process. In other words, we could well interpret John 5:24: "He that goes on believing in me shall not come into condemnation." So in this way too, the *conditional* nature of such promises is made clear.6

It would be helpful at this point to elaborate on what it means to say that a person has saving faith in Jesus Christ. It means more than saying that he maintains his orthodoxy, although it certainly involves these basic concepts. When a person exercises faith in Jesus, he is recognizing Jesus as a Redeemer from sin. This includes both justification and sanctification. Faith in Jesus as Redeemer always implies that the person who is exercising this faith also wants redemption. He is trusting in Jesus both to forgive him and make him the kind of person he should be. There is the desire and the expectation that God will be working to make the person into the likeness of Christ. We are not to suppose that people have saving faith who are basically indifferent to moral and spiritual concerns. This would contradict both the nature of saving faith and the nature of salvation.

F. Roads to Apostasy

One of the main roads to apostasy is through false doctrine. This is one of the reasons why the New Testament takes such a strong stand against heresy (Galatians 1:8, 9; 1 John 4:1-3; 2 John 7-11; Jude 3-19; and others) and gives so much attention to grounding Christians in the faith.

The danger may be presented to the Christian by cults and various forms of liberal doctrine within many denominations. One of the tragedies of born again Christians attending liberal seminaries is that many have lost their faith.

Another area of danger is in the educational world where secularism is predominant. Some are unable to maintain their faith against the onslaught of naturalism. The problem here centers to a

218

large extent around the fact that they confront naturalism from proponents that are superior to them academically. In many instances, they do not know of anyone to whom they can turn to explain the difficulties they are facing. They are overcome by naturalism when they are unable to defend themselves. This is one of the reasons that Christian young people should attend Christian colleges where their faith will be strengthened rather than undermined.

A third road that leads to apostasy is tampering with sin. This can lead to a spirit of defeat and place one under the chastizing hand of God (Hebrews 12:7-11). In the determination that God has, that His people will be holy, He places His people under chastisement. God's determination to make His people holy will bring a Christian to a point that he will either have to repent or forsake God altogether. If he should turn from God this will mean turning from faith. He will make shipwreck of faith (1 Timothy 1:18, 19).

G. Assurance of Salvation

No writing on perseverance is complete unless it is also discussed from the standpoint of assurance. Certainly the grounds of assurance are strong enough in the Scriptures that a child of God can enter into the blessings of assurance and not be constantly worried by the fear of falling.

When we stop and think what the new birth does for a person, surely we have strong grounds to believe that he will continue in the faith. By the new birth a person is made a new creature (2 Corinthians 5:17) and possesses a new nature. This new nature within him is thirsting and hungering for the things of God. There is also a distaste for the things of sin. With this change wrought in his heart, the person who is born again will never be satisfied apart from a close walk with God.

The relationship the indwelling Spirit has with the believer is another ground of assurance that the believer will continue in the faith. The Holy Spirit has a vital interest in us and works patiently and untiringly with the believer to get him to be an obedient child. He does this by producing a consciousness and conviction of sin in the heart of the Christian. He chastises the believer (Hebrews 12:7, 8, 11), making it so that he cannot enjoy life except when living in harmony with God. He teaches the Christian many wonderful truths about Christ that encourage him to live for Christ. Along with all else He does, He gives strength to the believer in his warfare against the flesh (Galatians 5:16, 17). Thus, we see that the Holy Spirit seeks to lead the believer away from that which would ensnare him; He enables him to walk in this way and keeps him from enjoying walking any other way.

John 10:28, 29 gives the Christian strong grounds to stand on.

In Christ he has eternal life and will never perish. When a person is saved, he is baptized into Christ's body; and as long as he is in Christ, he has eternal life and will never perish. This is what we have in Christ, and we are also promised that no one can take us out of Christ. Salvation is a personal matter between the believer and Christ. No outsider can, in any way, take the believer out of Christ. If he is ever taken out, it will be an act of the Father as husbandman, as is set forth in John 15:2, and that only on the grounds of not abiding in Christ (John 15:6). To be in Christ means to have eternal life, and no outside force nor combined forces can take us out of Christ.

Another ground of security is that God will not cast us out at the least little thing we do. We are saved by faith and kept by faith. We are lost, after we are once saved, only by shipwreck of faith.

The view, as we have given it, gives a person all the assurance he needs to have joy. It does not keep him in constant fear of failing; yet, at the same time, he is aware of the fact that it is possible to fall. It also keeps salvation on a faith basis instead of mixing it with works. It is not just a line of reasoning, but has the support of the Scriptures.

Some people work on the assumption that since there is some response required of the human being himself, there can be no assurance. This is to misunderstand the case. We move with assurance in life in areas where not only our own will but others' wills are involved. People who are happily married have assurance that their marriage will not end in divorce. Yet, they would have to admit that the possibility is there that it could be otherwise. The possibility could arise on the part of either one, but they do not move with fear because of the possibility. The same principle could be applied to any number of personal relationships.

Some who hold to unconditional continuance in salvation seem to think that conditional continuance makes the continuation of salvation a matter that is so totally of man that God is out of the picture. This is not the case. God is working with the person to help him continue in faith and to grow in grace. The continued response of faith is not in context where the Christian is totally independent. It is in a context where he is dependent upon God. God is working in and through him. Yet, there is a sense in which his decisions are his own. It is possible for him to go contrary to God's leadings. Those who love God and understand the positive grounds for assurance do not live with fear that they will go contrary to God's leadings and depart from the faith.

H. Some Practical Problems

There are some people that are hard for us to identify in the

220

light of our theology. It seems as if they have definitely been saved at some time in the past. It seems that they have not committed apostasy or turned from their faith. Yet, it seems that they are living in sin or practicing sin. I would say that obviously one of our judgments is wrong. Either, the person never was saved, has lost his faith, or is not living in sin. I may not be able to decide what his real case is. I would certainly not offer assurances to such a person. I would not propose to give an official diagnosis of his case. I am sympathetic with those who may feel obligated to consider such people as neither exactly in nor exactly out, but I think the position that I have set forth which says that a person must be either in or out is more tenable.

I believe a person is either saved or unsaved, but I cannot pass judgment on all cases. It is my opinion that a similar position will have to be adopted in some cases regardless of what a person's view may be.

Some people prefer to limit their use of the word apostasy to a departure from the faith on theological grounds, i.e., trading the truth for heresy. I use the term apostasy to refer to shipwreck of faith in the broad sense. It is what a person leaves, not what he goes to that counts. Some may go to a clearly defined system of unbelief. Others may simply turn to unbelief.

There is a problem about the use of the word backslider. The question is often asked: Is the backslider saved? It depends on how the word backslider is used. The word does not appear in the New Testament. In the Old Testament, it is a very strong word. In almost every instance, except one, the Hebrew word means to turn away or to turn back. The exception is Hosea 4:16 where it means stubborn or rebellious. If by backsliding, we mean a person has turned away from God, such a person is not saved. He has made shipwreck of faith.

In the common use of the word backslide, it has a variety of meanings. Some use it only of serious cases. Others use it to refer to lesser degrees of drifting. I prefer not to use the word backslide because of the various interpretations that people give to it. They understand me according to their meaning of the word, not mine. To say that a backslider is not lost means to some people that a person could be saved and then fall into the worst conceivable state of sin and still be saved. This simply is not true whether a person believes in conditional or unconditional continuance in salvation.

A lot of careless words are spoken on the subject of security—sometimes in stating our own view and at other times stating the view of other people. A well formulated doctrine of security requires a lot of careful thought and study. The same is true if we are going to understand the other person. The subject of continuance in salvation is an important subject and should receive some of our most careful thought.

221

II. UNCONDITIONAL CONTINUANCE IN SALVATION

A. A Statement of the View

The historic position of Calvinism has been the perseverance of the saints, not a guarantee of their future salvation whether they persevere or not. As Dr. John H. Gerstner explains concerning the Calvinistic view: "Perseverance not only does not, but cannot, lead to antinomianism because, by definition, it means persevering in holiness and not unholiness."7 Berkhof explains concerning the doctrine, "It is maintained that the life of regeneration and the habits that develop out of it in the way of sanctification can never entirely disappear."8

In speaking of extreme views on the doctrine of continuance in salvation, William Wilson Stevens explains:

> One is held by those who say they believe in the doctrine (eternal security of the believer) but who have really perverted it, maintaining that one is justified and is eternally safe regardless of what he may become in his person and character. He is saved eternally because the justifying, sanctifying, and regenerating power of God so completely changes him that he will never revert to his old way of life. Nor does the New Testament say that one will be saved whether or not he persists in faith, but that he will persist in faith and therefore be eternally saved.9

Dr. Buswell comments:

> In a young people's conference I once heard a Christian layman speak as follows: 'I was once a member of a young people's gospel team. *We were all saved*, and we had some success in preaching the gospel. But one member of the team got into worldly company. He married a very worldly girl. He denied his Christian profession of faith, and he died a drunkard. Now you see, young people, he was a Christian; he went to heaven; but he was a 'carnal Christian' and he did not have the reward of a 'spiritual Christian.'
>
> No wonder the Arminians are scandalized by what is falsely called Calvinism. 10

Much of the popular preaching is more like the perversion of Calvinism that it is historic Calvinism. Such preaching has done great harm to the church. Since I have already dealt with the fact that in salvation justification cannot exist without sanctification, I will not give further attention to the corruption of Calvinism. I will simply

222

show the fallacy of denying the possibility of the loss of salvation. We will now turn our attention to the arguments used to support unconditional continuance in salvation.

B. The Argument Based on the Sovereignty of God

The basic foundation of the Calvinistic view of continuance in salvation is based on their interpretation of God's sovereignty. Dr. Lewis Sperry Chafer says:

> The failure of one soul to be saved and to reach glory whom God has ordained to that end means the disruption of the whole actuality of divine sovereignty. If God could fail in one feature, be it ever so small, He could fail in all. If He could fail in anything, He ceases to be God and the universe is drifting to a destiny about which God himself could know nothing. 11

An interpretation of Divine sovereignty is the foundation principle and the guiding principle in the thought of thorough going Calvinism. There can be no question that God must accomplish what He sets out to do if He is to be Sovereign. The question is what has God set out to do. Has He set out to include all Divine activity in a cause and effect relationship as distinguished from an influence and response relationship? Does God have the same cause and effect relationship with persons that He does the material universe?

If God works within the same cause and effect relationships in His relationship with persons that exists in mechanical relationships, the Calvanistic system has much to commend itself. By applying the cause and effect relationships to persons, I do not mean to infer that the nature of the object in personal relationships may not be taken into account, but it is cause and effect because the cause guarantees the effect. It cannot be otherwise. This must be true in both redemptive and non-redemptive matters. If not, God is not Sovereign.

The ultimate question in all of this is: What has God revealed to us about His sovereignty in His Word? The problem is that if a person goes to the Bible with the preconceived notion that the only way for God to be Sovereign is for Him to perform all of His activity in the framework of cause and effect relationships, he will force that interpretation on all Scripture passages regardless of what they say. Therefore, we need to give some attention to whether this is the only way an absolute Sovereign can act.

Is it impossible, in principle, for God to direct His sovereignty within the framework of influence and response as it relates to His relationship to persons? Is He incapable of working within this framework? Does He have to restrict Himself to cause and effect relationships to keep from losing His sovereignty? My answer to all these questions is no. I would think any person would think long and hard before he gave a yes answer to any of these questions. Yet, if the answer to these questions is no, there is no logical necessity for a person to believe that all of God's activity toward persons must be with the intent of a guaranteed effect. We do not have to study the Word of God with the predisposition that it cannot but teach a view of sovereignty in which Divine activity must always have a guaranteed effect.

I believe that God accomplishes all of His purposes. He achieves all of His goals. The choice to create man a person was His own choice. That choice meant that He would deal with man as a person. He would work with him within the framework of influence and response. This meant that man's responses could include both obedience and disobedience. God does not lose His sovereignty when man disobeys. We are not to assume that God desires man's disobedience. We are to assume that God desires that disobedience would be an open option for man. In the cause and effect relationship approach to sovereignty, it is rather difficult to see how disobedience ever entered the universe without either destroying God's sovereignty, if He disapproves of sin, or corrupting His holiness if He does not. It does not help very much to say that God's ways are inscrutable to us.

In the influence and response approach, God does not depend upon omnipotence alone to execute His sovereignty. He depends upon wisdom. It takes far more wisdom for God to be Sovereign within the framework of influence and response than it does within the framework of cause and effect. I think the influence response approach exalts the sovereignty of God more than the cause and effect approach. As Dr. Picirilli said in a quotation given earlier in this chapter, "Our God is big enough to handle real contingency in His universe."

The Calvinistic view of unconditional election is the logical outgrowth of the doctrine of sovereignty as perceived by them. The doctrine of unconditional continuance in salvation is the logical follow through of unconditional election. As Dr. Buswell explains:

> If God has unconditionally elected to save people, and if He has provided atonement which makes their salvation certain, it follows by inevitable logic that those whom God has elected to eternal salvation will go on to eternal salvation. In other words, a denial of the doctrine of the perseverance of the saints is a denial of the sovereign grace of God in unconditional election. 12

If we grant that God's sovereignty must work within the

framework of cause and effect, unconditional election, irresistable grace or effectual call, and unconditional continuance in salvation all follow through with absolute precision of thought and logical necessity. It is a very simple system. It may be hard to believe, but it is not hard to understand. If we grant that God's sovereignty could work within the framework of influence and response whether it does or not, the Calvinistic system does not follow through as a logical necessity. We would be dependent upon revelation to tell us how God chose to operate.

If we grant that God's sovereignty works within the framework of influence and response, Calvinism is either ruled out or one would be using influence and response simply as a disguised form of cause and effect. It requires more thought to comprehend personal relationships than it does mechanical relationships. The simplicity of cause and effect relationships is not found in influence response relationships. The operation of God's sovereignty within the framework of influence and response requires more thought to be appreciated and understood. This should not be surprising since we are dealing with personal relationships.

A more thorough treatment of the various points of Calvinism would require a separate treatment. My purpose in these observations has been to show that there is no logical necessity which requires that the Calvinistic system be true. I am quite certain that it is within the framework of logical possiblities for God to choose to use the approach of conditional continuance in salvation in dealing with man. There is no logical necessity for God to lose His sovereignty and the universe either fall apart or run on an uncertain course if a person should lose his salvation. This would be true only if God chose to operate within the framework of unconditional continuance in salvation but failed to achieve His purpose.

I believe the Scriptures reveal that God has chosen to operate within the framework of conditional continuance in salvation. I have already stated my own case for believing that the Scriptures teach this view. In a later discussion, I will show that the Scriptures which are used in support of unconditional continuance do not require one to believe that view.

C. The Argument Based on the Nature of Atonement and Justification

Berkhof comments:

> In His atoning work Christ paid the price to purchase the sinners' pardon and acceptance. His righteousness constitutes the perfect ground for the justification of the sinner, and it is impossible that one who is justified by the payment of such a perfect and efficacious price should again fall under condemnation.[13]

225

It is true that as long as a person has the death and righteousness of Christ he is justified. He cannot be lost and at the same time have the death of Christ. However, since he has the death and righteousness of Christ only by identification conditioned on faith, on the condition of unbelief the identification can be broken and the person would no longer have the death and righteousness of Christ. (For a more thorough explanation of this point, see the discussion under objections to the satisfaction view of atonement in the chapter on atonement and justification.)

The Calvinist, to be logical, must decide between basing his view of unconditional continuance on atonement or the power of God. If atonement seals the security of the believer so that it cannot be undone, there is no place for being kept by the power of God, at least so far as justification is concerned. By the nature of the case, it could not be forfeited. The only place for the keeping power of God for those who base unconditional continuance in salvation on the nature of atonement and justification would be in the area of sanctification. The keeping power of God would have no bearing on continuance in justification.

Either choice that the Calvinist makes is not without consequences for him. To ground unconditional continuance on atonement and justification means that it cannot be grounded in the power of God that is related to His sovereignty. To take the grounds for unconditional continuance away from the power of God creates a real problem for those who say the passages used to support conditional continuance are, instead, warnings that God uses as a means of helping those who are saved to persevere. Berkhof explains concerning the warnings:

> There are warnings against apostasy which would seem to be quite uncalled for if the believer could not fall away, Matthew 24:12; Col. 1:23; Heb. 2:1; 3:14; 6:11; 1 John 2:6. But these warnings regard the whole matter from the side of man and are seriously meant. They prompt self-examination, and are instrumental in keeping believers in the way of perseverance. They do not prove that any of those addressed will apostatize, but simply that the use of means is necessary to prevent them from committing this sin. 14

To interpret these warnings, as Berkhof and many other Calvinists do, to be real warnings used to prevent apostasy on the part of believers means that, in principle, a person could lose his salvation were it not for the power of God. For this to be true, the loss of salvation would have to be consistent with every other doctrine except the promised power of God. Yet, Berkhof, as quoted above, grounds unconditional continuance also in atonement and justification. It cannot be both ways. If the Calvinist chooses to ground unconditional continuance in atonement and justification rather than the power of God, he cannot interpret the passages referred to as warnings used by God to help the believer persevere. This would be true because, in principle, there would be no possibility of losing his salvation. There must at least be the possibility in principle, if not in fact, of a person losing salvation before warnings can be said to be used in helping a person to keep from losing his salvation. The warning is not a warning if it does not say to the person that he would lose his salvation if a certain thing were to take place.

Those who ground unconditional continuance in salvation on atonement and justification must come up with some other interpretation of the "warning verses." The other interpretation that is given for these passages is that they are warnings to professing Christians. Herman Hoeksema explains concerning the warning in Hebrews 6:4-6 as it relates to the impossibility of renewing them to repentance:

> But the author has in mind their former state, as they appeared, as they were known by men, as they used to be members of the church visible in the world. They were baptized. And they went through the outward show of repentance, and for a time walked in that repentance. But now they have definitely fallen away even from the outward show. They have become unbelievers. They have become wicked. They have become a part of the Antichrist. And the text says that it is impossible that those who so fall can ever again be renewed unto repentance. The case of these people is therefore hopeless. Their falling away is final. They can never return. 15

My own treatment, and why I believe the people referred to in this passage had been saved, appears earlier in this chapter. I will not restate my case here. I will simply say that I fail to see the logic in warning those who profess to be Christians but are not, that if they fall from that profession, they can never be renewed to that profession again. What those who merely profess need to know is that they are not saved. They need to be told how they can tell that their profession is empty. They need to examine themselves in the light of the guaranteed results of salvation.

If a person chooses to ground unconditional continuance in salvation in the power of God rather than atonement and justification, by so doing, he admits that in principle a person could lose his salvation but not in fact. This means that unconditional continuance must either relate: (1) to logical necessity growing out of a cause and

227

effect relationship view of sovereignty, or (2) God's promise of unconditional continuance. Either way, we expect to find a scriptural basis for unconditional continuance that would take the form of a promise. I have already given my reasons for believing the Scripture teaches the contrary. I will deal in a later point with the verses thought by some to make such a promise.

D. The Argument Based on the Mystical Union with Christ

Berkhof explains:

They who are united to Christ by faith become partakers of His Spirit, and thus become one body with Him, pulsating with the life of the Spirit. They share in the life of Christ, and because He lives they live also. It is impossible that they should again be removed from the body, thus frustrating the divine ideal. The union is permanent, since it originates in a permanent and un-changeable cause, the free eternal love of God. 16

There can be no question that as long as a person is in union with Christ he is saved. To be in union with Christ is to be saved. For one not to be in union with Christ is not to be saved. The question of whether this union can be broken is for God to decide and let us know in His revelation. It is not for us to decide on the basis of what we think is logical necessity or what we think is unthinkable. Jesus has answered the question for us in clear terms, "Every branch in me that beareth not fruit he taketh away" (John 15:2). I should also point out that those who are basing their view on unconditional continuance on the keeping power of God are admitting, in principle, that they see no problem so far as union with Christ is concerned and believing that a person could lose his salvation.

E. The Argument Which Says
That Conditional Continuance Makes
Salvation Dependent On Man's Will

Berkhof comments:

The denial of the doctrine of perseverance virtually makes the salvation of man dependent on the human will rather than on the grace of God . . . . The idea is that, after man is brought to a state of grace by the operation of the Holy Spirit alone, or by the joint operation of the Holy Spirit and the will of man, it rests solely with man to

228

continue in faith or to forsake the faith, just as he sees
fit. 17

The truth of the above statement depends upon how one
interprets "it rests solely with man." If we interpret it to mean that
God saved the person and forsook him and left the matter of
continuing in faith in his hands, that is untrue. The statement sounds
a great deal like that. The believer has a close and intimate
relationship with God. In this relationship the believer experiences
both dependence and independence. To put the believer in either a
totally dependent role or totally independent role is to misunderstand human personality and personal relationships. His continuance
in faith is certainly dependent upon Divine aid. Should he depart
from faith, it would certainly mean that he had failed to respond to
Divine influence. There is certainly no contradiction betwen these
observations and being saved by grace.

F. Arguments Based on Scripture

The one most frequently used is John 10:28, 29. There are
three arguments found in these verses: the first, the words "eternal
life"; the second, the words "they shall never perish"; the third,
"neither shall any man pluck them out of my hand."

Let us consider the first one. It must be admitted that eternal
life can be possessed only in the sense of potential. The believer
certainly does not possess eternity. Some have taught that there is no
past and future with God, but no one has ever said that of the
believer.

The eternal life of the believer is in the Son as is taught in 1
John 5:11, " . . . God hath given to us eternal life, and this life is in
his Son." This life is the believer's by identification with Christ.
Should that identification be broken, he would be severed from this
life, yet it would not alter the fact that he had possessed it.

It should also be pointed out that Adam possessed the potential
for eternal life before he fell, but he lost it with the fall.

It is seen then that the loss of salvation is not inconsistent with
the words, "eternal life."

The second argument is based on "they shall never perish."
John 3:36 teaches that the reverse is true of unbelievers when it says,
" . . . He that believeth not the Son shall not see life . . . . " No one
says that, since it is said of the unbeliever that he shall not see life, he
is permanently bound without hope in that condition. It is a fact
that, as an unbeliever, he shall not see life; but if he becomes a
believer, he will see life.

Now, if the words, "shall not see life," are not contradicted
when the unbeliever becomes a believer and sees life, where is the

contradiction when it is said that a believer "shall not perish," but if he becomes an unbeliever he will perish? The fact is that a believer, as long as he remains a believer, "shall not perish."

The remaining argument is based on the statement, " . . . Neither shall any man pluck them out of my hand." The next verse adds a similar thought concerning the Father's hand. The teaching is simply this: The believer's relationship with God is a personal one between him and God. Though the whole universe were to combine its powers against the believer, they could not take the believer away from God. Some would add, "Neither can the believer take himself out of the body of Christ." Yes, that is true. But, it is also true that he could not have placed himself into the body of Christ. However, upon his faith in Christ, the Holy Spirit placed the believer into the body of Christ. If the believer renounces his faith, God will take him out.

The next passage to be considered is Romans 8:35-39. It is my opinion that this passage does not deal with the question of security but teaches that a person is never a child of God and, at the same time, separated from God's love. In other words, the believer is never to interpret hardship as meaning that God does not love him. Instead, he should recognize that God's love is still with him and say with Paul, "Nay, in all these things we are more than conquerors through him that loved us" (Romans 8:37).

Suppose, however, that the passage does deal with the matter of security. It would be explained the same way that the statement of Jesus would when He said, "Neither shall any man pluck them out of my hand" (John 10:28).

Another verse that is frequently used is Romans 11:29, "For the gifts and calling of God are without repentance." This means that if God has made an unconditional promise, it will forever remain an unconditional promise. On the other hand, if He has made a conditional promise, He will never change the condition of that promise. This is the line of reasoning used by Paul in Galatians 3:15-18. The Abrahamic Covenant that had already promised justification on the condition of faith could neither be set aside nor have the condition changed when the law came.

Philippians 1:6 is frequently used. Paul says, "Being confident of this very thing, that he which hath begun a good work in you will perform it until the day of Jesus Christ." This is a confidence that we can have as believers. God will perform the work of salvation until the day of Jesus Christ in those who continue in faith. This is not a promise made to unbelievers. There is no contradiction if one who is a believer becomes an unbeliever and the promise no longer applies. 18

I have not exhausted every argument for or against either view. I believe that the basic principles have been brought out and that the major verses have been given attention.

230

CHAPTER THIRTEEN
NOTES

1. I believe this identification of my theological position, which may help the reader place my position in the context of theological schools of thought, will be appreciated. Frequently, in reading, I wish I knew the school of thought to which the author belongs. I like to see a person's thoughts in their systematic context.

2. John Henry Thayer, *Thayer's Greek-English Lexicon of the New Testament*, Associated Publishers and Authors, Inc., a reprint of the 1889 edition, n. d., p. 663.

3. J. D. O'Donnell, *Free Will Baptist Doctrines*, Nashville: Randall House Publications, c. 1974, p. 78.

4. Robert Picirilli, *Perseverance* (a booklet), Nashville: Randall House Publications, c. 1973, p. 20.

5. *Ibid.*, p. 22.

6. *Ibid.*, pp. 25, 26.

7. John H. Gerstner, "Perseverance," *Baker's Dictionary of Theology*, Grand Rapids: Baker Book House, c. 1960, p. 404.

8. L. Berkhof, *Systematic Theology*, Grand Rapids: William B. Eerdmans Publishing Company, c. 1941, p. 546.

9. William Wilson Stevens, *Doctrines of The Christian Religion*, Grand Rapids: William B. Eerdmans Publishing Company, c. 1967, p. 258.

10. James Oliver Buswell, Jr., *A Systematic Theology of the Christian Religion*, Volume II, 2 volumes, Grand Rapids: Zondervan Publishing House, c. 1962, p. 146.

11. Lewis Sperry Chafer, *Systematic Theology*, Volume III, 8 volumes, Dallas: Dallas Seminary Press, c. 1948, p. 316.

12. Buswell, *op. cit.*, p. 145.

13. Berkhof, *op. cit.*, p. 547.

14. *Ibid.*, p. 548.

15. Herman Hoeksema, *Reformed Dogmatics*, Grand Rapids: Reformed Free Publishing Association, c. 1966, p. 558.

16. Berkhof, *loc. cit.*

17. *Ibid.*, p. 549.

18. Some of the material used in this chapter was taken from *The Doctrine of Perseverance* (a booklet) by Leroy Forlines, first published in 1959, republished by Evangelist Van Dale Hudson, Amory, Mississippi, n. d.

Index

234